Voices of Resistance

DAKSHINAYAN

INDIAN THOUGHT

Voices of Resistance

TELUGU PROGRESSIVE-POLITICAL LITERATURE

Edited by

Volga

Kalpana Kannabiran

Translated by

Vasanth Kannabiran

Series editor

G.N. Devy

Orient BlackSwan

The **Dakshinayan Indian Thought** series has received funding from the Rajiv Gandhi Foundation, New Delhi.

VOICES OF RESISTANCE: TELUGU PROGRESSIVE-POLITICAL LITERATURE

ORIENT BLACKSWAN PRIVATE LIMITED

Registered office
3-6-752 Himayatnagar, Hyderabad 500 029, Telangana, India
E-mail: centraloffice@orientblackswan.com

Other offices
Bengaluru, Chennai, Guwahati, Hyderabad, Kolkata,
Mumbai, New Delhi, Noida, Patna, Visakhapatnam

First published 2023

ISBN 978 93 5442 377 2

Typeset in Minion Pro 11/13.5 *by*
LiteBook Prepress Services, Chennai 600 069

037528

Printed at
B.B. Press, Noida 201 301

Published by
Orient Blackswan Private Limited
3-6-752, Himayatnagar, Hyderabad 500 029, Telangana, India
E-mail: info@orientblackswan.com

Contents

Acknowledgements

This project is one that we would never have dreamt of embarking on, were it not for Professor G.N. Devy's persuasion, patience, insistence and encouragement. The larger dream of which this is but a small part is one that we share, individually, and in our shared politics over three decades as part of a feminist collective that was born from and strengthened through a love of literature, importantly translation. We are grateful to Professor G.N. Devy, Series Editor, Dakshinayan Indian Thought Series, for this rare opportunity.

Needless to say, we were able to work through this and complete the task at hand because of unwavering support and help from co-travellers, friends and colleagues. We are particularly indebted to Singamaneni Narayana and Akkineni Kutumba Rao for shouldering much of the responsibility of providing us access to the materials we required, and for helping us obtain permissions to include works in this collection.

This volume was the last project housed in the Asmita Resource Centre for Women, coming after the completion of twenty-five years of feminist organising, publishing and immersion in creative writing. We take this opportunity to thank everyone at Asmita who had been part of its amazing journey over this entire period. *Voices of Resistance* owes its existence to our longstanding collective effort to imagine an intellectual history for a better, humane, just world. Stanley Thangaraj has been a pillar of support through the duration of this project. We are grateful to T. Anuradha for research assistance and to V.U.V.S. Subbalakshmi for secretarial support.

We are grateful beyond measure to Vasanth Kannabiran for undertaking the task of translation and completing it with unimaginable speed and skill.

We are grateful to Bhasha Research and Publication Centre and to the Rajiv Gandhi Foundation for supporting this publication.

Finally, our sincere thanks to the Dakshinayan team at Orient BlackSwan, especially to James Kanjamala, for the extremely valuable editorial support we received at all stages of this project.

Volga
Kalpana Kannabiran
April 2023

A Note on the Literary Habitations of Progressive Politics

Volga, Kalpana Kannabiran

I

This collection attempts to explore the resonances and shades of articulations of the 'progressive-political' in Telugu literatures across historical periods. Ideas of the 'progressive' and the 'political' are embedded in individual and collective endeavours. In the late colonial period and post 1947, for instance, the 'progressive' *as* political was the rallying ground for writers and performers shaping a different *programschrift* for creative writing and performance. We have taken an encompassing view that enables us to garner insights on writers' ruminations on humaneness, the meanings of shared humanity, justice and social transformation from unlikely locations in time and genre. We had earlier traced the intellectual history of social reform and protest/resistance in the Telugu areas of Madras Presidency and the Nizam's dominions (and Andhra Pradesh post-1947) that was crafted by women over the course of a century, starting with the late-nineteenth and early-twentieth centuries (Volga et al. 2001). This was a period thick with movements for social reform, the assertion of women's rights, and the emergence of a strong and autonomous leadership of women in different fields. We build on this early work and broaden it considerably even while working through a very different track, examining the articulation of progressive politics in Telugu literatures—going back to early writing starting with Tikkana and threading our account through to the present moment. We also acknowledge the collective contribution of the various anthologies of Telugu writing in translation that have appeared in the recent years—too many to list, but that have together certainly influenced our reading of the literatures, our selections and our insights, as also our translations and our awareness of the perils that lie therein.[1]

1 Among the selections in this collection are several that have been translated before—we present new translations of the entire collection by a single translator, for the most part translated for this volume.

We look at an eclectic assembling of the written word (for the most part)—poetry, song, novel, short story—across this period, that speaks to the idea of politics and the publics in specific, insurgent ways. It is indeed an insurgent mode that sets up counterpublics that we identify as 'progressive-political'. The literatures and their grammar and protocols are far from homogenous. Neither is the interrogation of authority/dominance all-encompassing in the work of each writer—there is a specific overarching experience that each writer focuses on, which holds valuable lessons for us. There is, for instance, especially on the gender question, a patriarchal echo (subterranean where this is not explicit) in most writing that is not self-consciously feminist across locations. Social locations of the writers are widely varied. Working through this internally diverse and plural domain of writing, we present one selection. In the presentation of these literary fragments, although we have for purposes of organising the material followed a chronological sequence (which is undoubtedly valuable), rupturing this seamless progression is a counter-narrative that interrogates the dominant voices in the progressive stream. The polyglot repertoires of Telugu present a challenge to translation and offer a possibility for animated dialogue and 'interillumination' (Bakhtin 1990). This raises critical questions that have to do with the incessant insurgencies in intersecting circles of literary production.[1]

The vantage point for any fresh insights from history (intellectual history in this case) is of course the present, which itself is intensely mobile (was future, will be past); nevertheless, the account that takes shape does so around the concerns of *this* present—immediate, urgent and forward-looking. A search for the literary habitations of progressive politics is at the centre of this endeavour, at the precise moment when progressive politics of all shades is in peril. In an important sense therefore, this is a re-telling of intellectual history as it emerges from Telugu literatures. There is by now a recognition of the ways in which history may be 'recast', reinvented, retold—of how the telling of history may

[1] We draw on Ranajit Guha's insights on insurgency in deploying the term here (Guha 1983).

be interrogated from new and emerging subject-positions and/or vantage points. The speaking subaltern and speaking for/of/with the subaltern, both important streams in intellectual history, even while they contest each other in important ways, together and in dialogue build new vocabularies of political speech through the literary. The figure of the subaltern shifts depending on time, larger political contexts, and ideological and ideational concerns—under pre-colonial states, colonialism, neo-colonialist depredations, the deployment of violence and technologies of power, now the 'low caste', now the colonised native, now the 'high-caste woman', now the worker, now dalit, now bahujan, Muslim, transperson, wife, courtesan, 'prostitute', woman…

The concern with egalitarianism expresses itself in opposition to specific forms of inequality, unequal treatment and domination—different forms within the same moment and different forms across different periods. This concern courses through four centuries of writings around caste; state authority; colonisation; intimacy and relationship; gendered oppressions; the effects of domination and inequality on political, economic, and social status, on cultures and proselytisation (religious faith and social reform); and most importantly, resistance.

Feminist historiographies in India have been torchbearers in the recovery of lost voices and lost practices of politics, as Marxist historiography and nationalist historiography had been before it. Dalit perspectives on intellectual history and literary criticism have opened up the debates even further, with trenchant critiques of the left, the right, the liberal and the feminist, tracing different trajectories and pathways of politics that place the experience of caste oppressions at the centre of human social experience on the Indian subcontinent. Importantly, this writing goes beyond the immediacy of suffering to offer radical philosophical ruminations on what it is that ails the human condition, and where indeed the seeds of liberation lie ripening to sprout. In the present moment, the infinite registers in which Muslim voices challenge homogenising mainstream narratives and illuminate diversities and polyglot cultures hold rich possibilities for challenging virulent Hindu majoritarianism.

The influence of Ambedkarite reasoning and philosophy is pervasive and evident in the progressive-political literatures of the late colonial period and the seven decades since 1947, irrespective of the specific location of the writer. The idea of the 'progressive', especially in this period, draws from reasonings of justice and dignity that finds its clearest and most definitive articulation in the Constitution of India. Whether the writing specifically focuses on caste, gender, religion, minorities, state, justice, class, domination, oppression, resistance, freedom of association/speech, or dignity, it draws on a broad framework of 'constitutional morality' that was crafted under the leadership of Dr Ambedkar within the Constituent Assembly and in the contexts of social movements. Whether or not writers expressly locate themselves within organised collectivities like progressive writers' movements, feminist collectives, or dalit/Ambedkarite political formations/movements, the connection between political and social movements for change in the direction of equality and dignity and progressive literatures has been an enduring one through this entire period, well into the present—contentious, contestatory, and dialogic at the same time, as it should be. There is, in our view, a shared ground.

This is by no means an exhaustive account. We have attempted to open just one window into the literary imaginations around questions that preoccupy us today: egalitarianism, dignity, oppression, violence and resistance. The strategies—literary, political, spiritual—to define counterpublics in ways that upstage, interrogate, question and uproot the habits of dominance of the publics are illuminating. Dissent is constitutive of these strategies.

We see through this writing claims to a new, truly plural, dialogic, non-hegemonic and egalitarian public and specific contestations of these claims, through a retrospective construction of the history of ideas. Muddupalani, the celebrated courtesan, swings into view through her condemnation by Veeresalingam Pantulu for immorality, triggering her resurrection three centuries after her time by noted musician-dancer from the devadasi tradition, Bangalore Nagaratnamma. There are complex echoes of this contestation in debates on the spiritual, moral and literary that signify the place of the courtesan/prostitute, of the wife, and of the woman in a heterosexist, brahmanical patriarchal caste order.

The contestations proliferate and grow to match the voice and visibility of the practice of politics in other sites. Through the prism of dalit literary imaginations, which is the public and which the counterpublic? The dalit counterpublic is constituted through a contestation of the hegemonic publics along multiple axes in a stratified society. When untouchability forces people apart, the configurations of the publics and indeed their locations constantly shift and threaten in their intractability. The 'velivada' constitutes a counterpublic that calls out and challenges the segregationist, dominant brahmanical public in powerful and enduring ways.

Languages of command and of affection, of oppression, of resistance and of ethical anger, of negation of unjust tongues, and of dissemination; tongues of songs and ballads, of epics, counter-epics and languages of millennial awakening; and of course, speech of lifeworlds as lived, through words and the feelings embedded therein, imaginings of justice and love for humanity—these show us the power of the written word in all its hues.

Cutting right through it all is the importance of the collective memory of autochthonous traditions of radicalism in politics as a wayfinder for our shared present and our futures.

II

> 'The many great souls before us: our salutations to all'
>
> —Tyagaraja

Left out of this account is the large corpus of oral literatures and enduring traditions of orality incessantly (re)produced over this time by adivasi, artisanal, agricultural, fishing and itinerant performing communities—nomadic and settled—that speak to the idea of the politics of insurgent lives, the insurgent spiritualities of wandering minstrels, and lived experience outside the borders of the textual community. In looking at a textual corpus (despite its diversity), we are acutely aware of its exclusion of these largely bahujan lifeworlds.

In classical literature, among the sringara and bhakti poets, there are many who have asserted creative freedom and struck an insurgent note; there are many who opposed the oppressions of caste and religious orthodoxy. From Srinadha to Potuluri Veerabrahmam, there are so many more writers. Likewise, from the early modern writers, alongside Veeresalingam and Gurajada, there are important voices like that of Panuganti Lakshmi Narasimha Rao and Chilakamarti Lakshmi Narasimham. We recall them as having an important bearing on the purpose of this volume, although we have not included their writing here. Despite the fact that his critique of colonial rule was staunch, uncompromising, and invaluable, Viswanatha Satyanarayana's equivocation on questions related to varnasrama dharma and women's place in society (questions of immeasurable significance today) made him an outlier for this volume.

There are several fine romantic poets—Rayaprolu Subba Rao, Nayuni Subba Rao, Vedula Satyanarayana, Mallavarapu Visweswara Rao, Chavali Bangaramma, Tallapragada Viswasundaramma—whom we remember but have not been able to include. Writing with a progressive pen on a range of contemporary issues was Tapi Dharma Rao (his writing for instance on the history of marriage and obscenity in temple art were widely read and discussed); among the progressive writers, Anisetti Subba Rao, Srirangam Narayana Babu; in the folk tradition, Konakalla Venkatratnam—we recall the significance of their work. From the Digambara poets, we have included Cherabandaraju. Among revolutionary writers, we have gathered a small but critical representation here. Writing on literary criticism, history, and social critique, revolutionary writers opened new pathways, but many could not be included in this selection owing to the limited scope of this project. We recognise this limitation.

Among dalit, minority and feminist poets, and contemporary writers likewise we have selected a few. Gogu Syamala, Satish Chander, Sky Baba, Vempalli Shariff, Ba Rahimatulla, Attada Appalanayudu, Anwar, Chandralatha, K.N. Malliswari, Kaluva Mallaiah, Boya Jangaiah, Peddinti Ashok Kumar, and Mudiganti Sujatha Reddy are among those we would have liked to include.

However, since contemporary poets and writers in Telugu are being translated into English, Hindi and other Indian languages, the availability of this writing to the non-Telugu reader is a reassurance to us.

From the hundreds of writers who have made a difference to the worlds they lived in and who, through their writing, have signalled change, we have put together a small selection in English to open a window into this world of ideas in all its different hues. We hope that this effort will trigger more work in this direction and make the rich world of Telugu progressive writing available for translation into other Indian languages, even as we look forward to similar work from other languages being translated into Telugu—enabling thereby the sharing of histories of ideas around the progressive-political, and a shared vision of a new political firmament in our troubled times.

References

Bakhtin, M.M. 1990. 'Epic and Novel'. In Bakhtin, M.M. *The Dialogic Imagination: Four Essays*. Ed. Michael Holquist. Trans. Caryl Emerson and Michael Holquist. Austin: University of Texas Press, pp. 4–40.

Guha, Ranajit. 1983. *Elementary Aspects of Peasant Insurgency in Colonial India*. New Delhi: Oxford University Press.

Volga, Vasanth Kannabiran, Kalpana Kannabiran. 2001. *Mahilavaranam / Womanscape*. Secunderabad: Asmita.

Editors' Note

The date of composition or first publication of a text, where possible to trace, has been included at the end of the text.

Where necessary, untranslated words have been glossed as footnotes for easy reference. Certain terms that appear multiple times have been glossed the first time they appear when there is no change in meaning in subsequent occurrences.

TIKKANA

Tikkana (1205–88) was a minister in the court of Manumasiddaraja, a vassal of the Kakatiya empire, in Nellore during the thirteenth century. He was known for his translation of the Mahabharata, from the 'Virata Parvam' to the end, into Telugu. He was also the author of the *Nirvachanottara Ramayanamu*. His beautiful rendition of the epics makes use of common metres and a simple style. Tikkana is celebrated as a 'kavibrahma' who questioned the authority and arrogance of kings.

Mahabharatamu

Whatever others may do
O king, to perturb your heart
Not to do unto others likewise
Is the noblest of all dharmas.

Source: Extract from *Srimadandhra Mahabharatamu*, 'Santhi Parvam', Panchamasvasam, verse 220 by Tikkana (edited by G.V. Subrahmanyam, Tirupati: Tirumala Tirupati Devasthanam Publications, 2003, p. 749)

Manchena

The fourteenth-century Telugu and Sanskrit scholar Manchena was the author of *Keyura Bahu Charitramu*. A disciple of the great Tikkana and a celebrated social poet, Manchena was known for his refusal to dedicate his writings to kings in return for gifts.

Keyura Bahu Charitramu

Rather than sell the maiden of poetry
  tender as the new leaves of a young mango plant
  and eat that prostituted food,
What if true poets
  farm or dig tubers in the forest
  to feed themselves, their wives and children.

Source: Extract from *Keyura Bahu Charitramu* by Manchena (Madras: Vedam Venkataraya Sastri and Brothers Publishers, 1970, p. 3)

Annamacharya

Tallapaka Annamacharya (1408–1503) was an oral poet in the bhakti tradition who composed over 30,000 sankirtanas. His compositions, engraved on copper plates, were discovered in the early twentieth century, hidden in a cell in Tirumala.

A devotee of Sri Venkateswara, his compositions reject social divisions and speak powerfully to the value of equality and oneness of the soul.

Creation

Tandanana[1] *ahi, tandanana pure*
Tandanana bhala, tandanana

The creator is one! The creation is one!
The creator is one! The creation is one!

There is none great or humble
For all, Srihari is the inner soul.
All living creatures the same
For all, Srihari is the living soul.

The deep slumber of the king
The sleep of his servant beside is the same.
The noble brahmin ends in the same earth
The humble chandala[2] in the same earth.

The sun that shines on the majestic elephant
Is the same that shines on the village dog.
He who protects equally the virtuous man and the poor sinner
The name of Lord Venkateswara is the same.

Source: Extract from *Annamacharyula Amrita Varshini* by Annamacharya (edited by I.V. Sitapati Rao, Hyderabad: Annamacharya Trust, 1987, p. 124)

---

1 rhythmic musical syllables
2 an 'untouchable' caste; a person from this caste

Atukuri Molla

Molla (1440–1530), the author of *Molla Ramayanamu*, was born in Gopavaram in Nellore into the kummari (potter) caste. She wrote in a style that was marked by simplicity and brevity, and was known for her opposition to the practice of dedicating literary work to kings and rulers.

Molla Ramayanamu

The gracious valorous ocean of virtue shining forth
The tongue singing the praise of the mightiest king on earth, Rama
Can it ever desire to praise these paltry worldly kings
And seek to satisfy ephemeral desires?

***

By chance the touch of the dust of Rama's feet
A stone turned to a woman, they say;
If the dust of his foot touch my boat, what then?
Wondered timorous Guha laving Rama's lotus feet.

Source: Extracts from *Molla Ramayanamu* by Atukuri Molla (edited by Bommakanti Venkata Singaracharya and Balantrapu Nalinikanta Rao, Vijayawada: Emesco Books, 1997, pp. 6, 36)

POTANA

Potana, a fifteenth-century Telugu and Sanskrit scholar, was the author of *Mahabhagavatamu* in Telugu. A celebrated social poet from Bammera in Warangal, he is known for the ease and elegance of his writing, and for his refusal to dedicate his work to the ruler.

Mahabhagavatamu

Were there not kings, O Bhargava?
Were there not kingdoms?
Did they not swell with pride?
Where are they now?
Could they bundle and carry their wealth?
Is even their name remembered on earth?
Great ones like Sibi craved but virtue
With all their hearts;
Can they be forgotten even today?

Source: Extract from *Sri Bammera Pothanamathya Praneetam Sri Mahabhagavatamu*, Volume 2, Chapter 8 by Potana (edited by Rayaprolu Subba Rao, Hyderabad: Potti Sreeramulu Telugu University, 2000, p. 591)

DHURJATI

Dhurjati (1480–1545), an acclaimed poet in the court of Srikrishnadevaraya, was a native of Srikalahasti. He is known for two works *Srikalahastisvara Mahatyamu* and *Srikalahastisvara Satakam*.[1] His work has been celebrated for its unparalleled poetic style.

Srikalahastisvara Satakam

Kings drunk with power, their service hell
The damsels and steeds in four directions
Ornaments, seeds of the soul's suffering
Sufficient unto the day, I am content
Awaken in me the wealth of wisdom
Sri Kalahastisvara!

Source: Extract from *Srikalahastisvara Satakam*, Suvarnamukhi Vyakhya by Dhurjati (edited by Madugula Nagaphani Sarma, Hyderabad: Sveeya Prachurana, 1984, p. 39)

---

1 *satakam* = hundred poems (usually a compilation of 108 poems)

VEMANA

The philosopher-poet Vemana (1652–1730) wrote a thousand poems in the ataveladi metre. Drawing from the artefacts of everyday life, his poetry is sharp in its critique of caste, religion, superstition, guile and kingship.

Satakam

A single plate for all on this earth
Mingling bonds, intermixing castes
Placing your hand on his head, tell him so he can believe you
Visvadabhirama vinura Vema[1]

Little realising good, creating religions galore
Men on earth grieve at the sight of one another
Like dogs panicking in a house of mirrors
Visvadabhirama vinura Vema

Truth and falsehood the dark-throated god knows
Only the water truly the shallows knows
The son's birth only the mother truly knows
Visvadabhirama vinura Vema

Why abuse the mala[2] time and again?
Is not bodily flesh the same?
Where is the caste that flows in him?
Visvadabhirama vinura Vema

---

1 Hear O Vema, beloved of the universe

2 a dalit caste

Religious rogues ten thousand on earth
Hover to harvest ignorant people
If cranes gather, will they not crowd to break the bunds?
Visvadabhirama vinura Vema

Thousands and thousands gather
Like mad dogs chanting meaningless Vedas
But for the hoarse throat, what gain?
Visvadabhirama vinura Vema

Gazing on stones man perceives Siva
Stones are but stones, not Siva
What dwells in stones, that dwells not in living creatures?
Visvadabhirama vinura Vema

Wherefore temple towns for stone idols?
Temples, gopurams,[1] pots of sacred food?
Does God crave clothes and food?
Visvadabhirama vinura Vema

Countless those who count faults
All the people in the world have faults
Those who count faults know not their own
Visvadabhirama vinura Vema

Source: Extracts from *Sataka Samputam*, 'Vemana Satakam' by Vemana (edited by Nidadavolu Venkat Rao, Hyderabad: Andhra Pradesh Sahitya Akademi, 1966, pp. 36, 42, 76)

[1] tall, intricately sculpted pyramidal stone structures that crown temples in South India

MUDDUPALANI

Muddupalani (1739–90), a poet, musician and dancer in the court of the Maratha king of Tanjavur, is best known for her masterpiece in sringara rasa, *Radhika Santvanamu.* This work was condemned for its eroticism by the noted reformer Veeresalingam Pantulu, resurrected by the dancer-poet Bangalore Nagaratnamma, and banned by the British government.

Radhika Santvanamu

Suffice it to weave poetry extempore
Should one not create epics profound.
Suffice it to strum the strings of the veena
Should one not melt stones with fluid ease.
Suffice it to trill notes and ragas
Should one not render varnams[1] that uplift.
Suffice it to dance many dances
Should not one draw out the navarasas.[2]
Suffice it to make love in marvellous ways
Should not one grasp the heart of the beloved.
This raw shoot born yesterday
Asking him to desert me, my little parrot!

Source: Extract from *Radhika Santvanamu: Muddupalani Praneetamu* by Muddupalani (Machilipatnam: Sringara Kavya Mandali, 1936, p. 81)

---

1 short musical compositions in Carnatic music

2 the nine emotions

Kandukuri Veeresalingam

Kandukuri Veeresalingam Pantulu (1848–1919), a pioneering social reformer, advocate of widow remarriage and educationist, set up schools to promote women's education and shelters for young widowed women. A prolific writer, he introduced the Telugu reader to varied literary forms—the novel, play, essay and autobiography. Through his work and writing, he laid the foundations for rationalism and radicalism in Telugu society.

Autobiography

Virupaksha Sankaracharya Swami started from Vizianagaram. Accepting bikshas and padapujas[1] along the way, he proceeded to our Godavari mandalam.[2] These acharyas keep acquiring wealth in the name of bikshas and padapujas, but never suffer from the anxiety of imparting religious education to their pupils. Some of them knew the names of sweets and delicacies better than the names of religious texts. There is an old story about this. One swamulavaru[3] went to a householder's home for biksha. After the meal, thinking that he may recite from a Vedanta grandha, the housewife came to this famous hermit and asked him, 'Swami! Shall I bring the Bhagavad Gita?' Never having heard the name before, that swami thought for a while and, assuming it must be a delicacy, said, 'Amma! My stomach is full now; wait for a couple of hours and then bring it.' Among learned sanyasis, many have only this kind of knowledge about religious matters. When he was near Tuni, hearing about the widow marriages happening in

---

1 *biksha* = alms; *padapuja* = ritual worship of feet
2 region/area
3 honorific for swami

Rajamahendravaram, our swami said that when he arrived here he would excommunicate all those who had taken part in that work. Our *Viveka Vardhini* has carried many articles regarding the qualifications of religious heads, the unethical deeds that they undertake for wealth, and the true responsibilities of pupils to bring them to the correct path, opening the eyes of the public to these facts.

[…]

After Lakshminarasimham garu's[1] accusation, Sri Sankaracharya and his followers in my town were highly excited, and in the pride of victory could not see the earth or sky. The day after the accusation passed, they took Sankaracharyavaru in a procession over our street before my door. They lit a thousand lamps and paraded him across the streets of Rajamahendravaram. But they passed our house without any nuisance very quietly. I sent that information to Kakinada via telegram, and the townspeople placed that letter in a palanquin and took it in a procession that very same night. They had a big celebration and, standing in front of Pydah Ramakrishnayya[2] garu's house and without caring about his wealth or influence, they clapped and shouted in front of his doorstep, creating as much of a disturbance as possible. This ruckus affected Ramakrishna garu's courage and made him repent and change his stand. In these happy days, the swami did not leave Rajamahendravaram and tried to insult our side by holding processions with music through the streets. Accepting bikshas, he stayed there for a few months. In those days, though the swamulavaru kept prohibiting widow marriages, his disciples, who were brahmacharis, were maintaining secret relationships with whores. Some students in the school who discovered this secret, waited one night and caught a brahmachari sishya who was living with a brahmin widow, and dragged that couple into the streets, exposed them in public and shamed them. So the sishyas were all very angry with the students, and were

1 the suffix *garu* is an honorific
2 the suffix *ayya* is an honorific

waiting to take revenge on them in some manner. As they waited, they found an opportunity soon. After two days, when the sishyas were bathing in the Godavari around noon, two students went there to bathe after the school closed. When the sishyas began to abuse the students of the school, one student told them that they should abuse the one who had made the mistake and not the students. The arguments grew hotter and the sishyas, who had fattened on good food and sweets every day, caught the young fellow and beat him up mercilessly and brutally. The other student ran away and reported the matter in the town. All the students in the school gathered and because their fellow student had been beaten they vowed to punish those brutal sishyas. They collected in groups before the house they were staying in, and began to roam about the street. Frightened by the rage of the students, the sishyas did not venture out into the street, and also brought two policemen to guard their door.

[...]

The swamulavaru had given up his hair and sacred thread, but not given up love and hatred; he grieved for the state of his sishyas and cursed the students. Thinking that the townsfolk would come and plead with him and calm him down, he sent messages that he would leave his peetam[1] and depart. That night, there was a rumour in town that the students had beaten and killed the swamulavaru's sishyas. So the opponents who were opposed to widow marriages were not able to show their faces in the street out of fear. I came to know this news only when I was returning home after enjoying the cool breeze on a boat on the Godavari. Another man, who had passed the law exam and was practising as a lawyer—a well-known householder who had joined us earlier but was now the leader of the anti–widow marriage group—was also sitting a little distance from me. Someone came and told him this news about the sishyas in a whisper. He was frightened and quickly put out the lamp in his servant's hand; covering his head and clutching his life in his palm, he reached home through bylanes, without walking on the main

[1] religious institution

streets. In that situation, not a single supporter came to reassure him; they advised him through a message to leave town quickly. Accordingly, the next morning before the students could leave school, the swamulavaru transported his peetam from that town and set off in a steamboat along with his sishyas, and he relieved my townspeople from the difficulty of providing his bikshas. If the swamulavaru had remained in our town, then the students would have taken his peetam and thrown it into the Godavari. The student who was first injured filed a complaint against the sishyas, and the sishyas filed against the students in court. But the judge fined the sishyas five rupees each, and released the students because there was no proof. Because of this swamulavaru's difficulties, our opponents' pride suffered and so for some time they did not trouble us much.

Written 1915

Source: Extracts from 'Sveeya Charitra' by Kandukuri Veeresalingam (*Veeresalingam Rachanalu*, Volume 1, edited by Akkiraju Ramapati Rao, Hyderabad: Visalandhra Publishing House, 1986, pp. 121, 155–58)

Gurajada Appa Rao

Gurajada Venkata Appa Rao (1862–1915), a playwright, writer and poet from Vizianagaram, was a pioneer in Telugu theatre. He was a leader of the movement for the promotion of spoken language, and, along with friends, founded the Andhra Sahitya Parishat in 1911. His legendary play *Kanyasulkam*, a literary masterpiece in *mandalika* (non-sanskritised Telugu dialect), was a powerful social critique on a range of intersecting evils—caste, the subordination of women, the importance of education, and the dangers of obscurantism and superstition.

Pearl Strings

If the whole world becomes a single home
And all caste differences vanish away
Bonds of love freed of wealth
Let festivals rain

Written 1910

Religions all will fade away
Wisdom alone will stand and shine
And heavenly joy
Will illuminate the earth

Written 1910

Calling mala toil foul
The mighty creating castes
Cast out some in a country
Alas, the mala outcast

Calling soiled bodies malas
Building upper castes of soiled minds
Varna dharma is an unjust dharma

Good and evil in people
If counted make but two castes
If good is mala, then I must be mala

Written 1911

Desa Bhakti

I tell thee, love thy country
Foster what is good
Cast aside empty words
Set to work on lasting good

Do not pursue only your own gain
Be of help to another man
A country is not just mud
A country is its people

All countrymen should walk together
Merrily arm in arm
Castes and religions should move
Like brothers

What if faiths differ?
As long as hearts are one
Love will rise and grow
And will shine forth in the world

This country, a majestic tree
Shall burst forth with flowers of love
Soaked in the sweat of men
Its roots shall thrust forth rich harvests

Hidden among the leaves
The kokila trills
Her song
Rousing passion for the land

Written 1910

Man

Ignorant one!
Bowing before man-made stones
Investing them with power
You treat men worse than stones.
Why?
Searching forests and hills
For a god hidden there
Why, oh, why?
Will he not appear
If you but open your eyes?

Is he not present in every man?
Grasping this truth, if you ask
Will he not melt and grant
Salvation?

Written 1912

Source: Extracts from 'Mutyala Saramulu', 'Desa Bhakti', and 'Manishi' by Gurajada Appa Rao (*Gurajada Rachanalu: Kavitala Samputi*, edited by Setti Iswara Rao, Hyderabad: Visalandhra Publishing House, 1991, pp. 5, 6, 25, 61–63, 67)

Bhandaru Acchamamba

Bhandaru Acchamamba (1874–1905) is the first short-story writer in Telugu and the first women's historian in Telugu. Born in Nandigama in Krishna district, she studied Sanskrit poetry, the sastras and the Veda-Puranas on her own. She also learnt Marathi and English. Committed to promoting women's education and progress, she travelled all over Andhra, writing in journals, speaking, and setting up mahila sanghams. The first mahila sangham she established was in Bandar in 1902, Brindavana Stree Samajam. Her history of women, *Abala Sacharitra Ratnamala*, tells the stories of different women who achieved distinction in various periods of history.

Dhanatrayodasi

It was about seven in the evening on Dhanatrayodasi[1] in Bombay, and every side was filled with celebrations and happiness. Although

[1] two days before Deepavali (also known as Dhanteras), during which Lakshmi (the goddess of wealth) is worshipped

it was not as illuminated as during Deepavali, every house was lit well enough with strings of lights to display its appearance and beauty. There was the sound of crackers from every side. Every house had platters of golden ornaments to worship Goddess Lakshmi. But one house showed no signs of festivity. One could call this a modest home. It was stuck between two huge sowcars' bungalows, and looked as if the goddess of misfortune Jyestha Devi had come to see her younger sister Lakshmi's festivity. Though it did not match the grandeur of the street, this house was a pleasure to the beholder because of its cleanliness and order. My dear friends will perhaps be angry with me for narrating the story of a poor family at a time of festivities in this great town instead of recounting the lore of the rich. Sisters! If you listen to me without turning away, you will realise the importance of this family tale I want to tell.

I already told you that the family I am talking about had big houses on either side. They were well lit. But in the house in the middle there was a single lamp burning. Beside the lamp, Vijayalakshmamma was sitting, sewing blouses for a fee for others. Beside her sat a six-year-old girl and a sweet three-year-old boy, asking innocent questions that gladdened their mother's heart. Vijayalakshmamma had cooked the evening meal and was waiting for her husband to return. He worked as a clerk for a rich sowcar[1] called Venkata Setti. Since it was Dhanatrayodasi, she knew her husband wouldn't come back till the Lakshmi puja was over. So she had fed the children and sat sewing while waiting for him to return. Unaffected by the festivity around her, this woman, waiting for her husband, had a very beautiful face. Though her eyes were on the blouse she was stitching, her mind was completely on her husband's return. Aha! Unmoved by the festivities in the village, awaiting her husband's return, this lady's face was so radiant! This sight can only be appreciated by those who behold such women. While her hands were busy sewing the blouse, her mind was preoccupied with her husband's arrival. All of a sudden, the sweet little boy, her son, hugged her drawing her attention towards him.

---

[1] trader

She had till then been answering his questions with 'hun', deeply engrossed in her work. But the minute the little boy put his arms around her neck, she pushed her sewing away and drew him to her, saying, 'My little one, what do you want? You were playing with your sister till now, why don't you play a little while longer? I am stitching blouses for people, I need to finish this fast.' The boy got up and as he stretched himself, the light of the sparklers next door caught his eye. Excited at the firecrackers, he lisped, 'Amma, it looks so nice. I want to go there with akka and watch the lights.' Since it was close by, Vijayalakshmamma called out to her daughter, 'Rukmini, take this little Ramudu to the neighbour's house to watch the celebrations. Be careful, don't take him too close to the lamps, and don't get into any quarrel with anyone.' The children went to the neighbour's compound. As she watched them go, the mother was filled with sadness, and tears welled up in her eyes. Poor thing. She was remembering her past. Earlier when they asked for crackers, she quietened them somehow. Now the children no longer asked the mother. Instead of saying that people are bursting crackers in the next house, they simply said they would watch the fireworks and return. She was very sad that she could not fulfil the desires of such lovely and understanding children. It never bothered her that they did not have a good house to live in, or nice clothes to wear or the means to make snacks for the festival. Although she faced troubles every day, she was happy to carry on with a husband who was a good man. But thinking of the troubles her children bore saddened her in untold ways. She regretted the fact that she, who came from a family of wealth and comfort, had fallen on such difficult times.

The boy asked if he could go and watch the celebrations. She sent him with his sister and asked her to mind him while they went next door to watch the festivities.

Vijayalakshmamma and Venkataratnam had been quite rich when they were young. Kalakaluru Mallayya, who lived in an agraharam,[1] had only one son, Venkataratnam. He was married with grand celebrations when he was just ten. Because he had only

[1] brahmin quarter

one son and desired to show that he was the richest man in the village, he borrowed and spent a sum of fifteen thousand rupees on the wedding. The couple on whose wedding fifteen thousand rupees was spent, now found it difficult to even see fifteen rupees. However, in these times, it is not surprising to see the ruination of agraharas. Mallayyagaru's agraharam had already been pledged by then. The expenses in his house even before the celebration had led to the mounting of debts day by day. In this situation, he decided to celebrate the marriage of his only son before it was too late, and incurred more debts to conduct the marriage.

These loans had made it difficult for Venkataratnam to even eat comfortably. They sorrowed at the hardships of their young children. None of the lenders bothered Mallayyagaru during his lifetime. But immediately after he died, they came all at once and recovered their loans charging half a rupee interest for every rupee. Poor Venkataratnam. Even before he came of age, he had to bear the consequences of the shrewdness or stupidity of his elders. Venkataratnam was an honourable man. Although he had spent his growing years in a prosperous agraharam, he was unaffected by it. He was not an arrogant, orthodox or lazy man. His wife was, like him, a virtuous woman. At times he felt sad that she had reconciled herself to their life of poverty. At the time of his father's death, he had just appeared for his college entrance examination. Although he was young enough to study further, not having the means to study he took up a job. It is very difficult to find a job these days. Somehow, he found a job as a clerk with the rich sowcar Venkata Setti for a salary of ten rupees a month. They made ends meet with those ten rupees. It is but natural that they were concerned about their children. She knew that their affluence in the past and the ruin it brought on them was responsible for the difficulties her children were facing. She struggled to control the sorrow that overtook her when she recollected her past. As she was deep in thought, she suddenly heard Ramudu crying and ran to the neighbour's house. As she entered, she saw a woman hitting Ramudu. When she asked what the little boy had done, she was told that he had picked up a cracker and held it near a lamp. A child of that house hit Ramudu, and, scared that his mother might hit him hearing Ramudu crying, started crying himself that Ramudu had hit him. Hearing him cry, his mother came running and started raining blows on Ramudu. Even mothers who beat their children cannot bear to see others beat them. Only mothers like Vijayalakshmamma, who never hit their children, can understand how they feel when they see their children being beaten by others. She was very angry, but being a sensible person, she swallowed her anger and left the house with Rukmini and Ramudu. Although she comforted her children once they reached home, she did not have the strength to stop her tears. Wasn't it the god of poverty who was responsible for the ill treatment of her helpless children? She soothed her son, stroked his body and wiped the tears from his eyes. There was nobody there to comfort her. Had Venkataratnamgaru been there he would have comforted her. He was the only person who could soothe her. As soon as she heard her husband's footsteps, she pushed back her tears and went out smiling. Aha Vijayalakshmi, how can I describe your virtues? You swallow your sorrow knowing that if your husband, returning from a hard day's work, hears what happened he will be distressed—and you come out to greet him smiling, with the child in your arms. Indeed, if all the women follow her virtuous example, how much our country will progress.

Venkataratnam came home, but unlike every day when he looked happy and greeted his wife and children cheerfully, his face was full of sorrow. He was sweating profusely. Every day, when he returned, he would first cheerfully greet his wife and kiss his son before going in. Today he just looked at his wife and son and went in silently. When she saw her husband like this, Vijayalakshmi thought, 'Maybe he had too much work today and is tired. Look at him sweating', and wiped his sweat with the end of her sari. She put her sleepy son to bed and helped her husband change his clothes. He sat leaning against the mattress deep in thought. Vijayalakshmi put his clothes away and sat down beside him. When he didn't speak for some time, Vijayalakshmi moved close to him and asked, 'What is this? Why don't you speak? Do you have a headache?', touching his head. 'I don't have a headache', said Venkataratnam. But she was not satisfied with his answer. 'Then why are you so sad? Why is your face so dejected? What is the reason?'

Hearing his wife's words, Venkataratnamgaru asked with concern, 'Don't you feel unhappy when you think of our ill fortune?' No sooner she heard him, Vijayalakshmi remembered her own sadness a little while ago, and realised that there was some reason for her husband's melancholy. With great effort she pushed her own feelings aside and said cheerfully, 'Is that what you are worried about? I am not in the least bothered about this.' 'Ahaa! You are like this now, but when we compare our earlier affluence with our present condition, I feel very distressed. We who lived with status and wealth are now having to live in grinding poverty! On this day, when everyone puts out their best finery for worship, you, who have worn the most precious jewels, have not even a gold bead on your body to offer. Does this not bother you?'

Vijayalakshmi: 'I never feel worried. You are worried that we have no wealth. But when I see the arrogance and thoughtlessness of rich people, I feel that our condition is much better. The happiness we find in this condition because we walk the path of truth, we would not be able to find as rich people. If your love is mine, then no other wealth matters to me.'

Venkataratnam was startled at his wife's words. His heart was troubled, and it showed in his face. There was a trace of fear on his honest face. At a loss of words, he collected himself and said, 'Dear one, of what use is this love?' Vijayalakshmi could not see the difference in his face, but she was not happy with the way he spoke, and said, 'You sadden me with your words.'

Venkataratnam: 'If that is the case I will not speak. Are you not worried about the dire straits are children are in? Does it not upset you to see other children dressed in new clothes, eating festival food, and bursting crackers on Deepavali while our children are forlorn having none of this?'

Vijayalakshmi: 'What is there to be sad about? It does not bother me, but why are you talking like this today? Did our children ever ask us to buy them these things and toys?'

Venkataratnam: 'This is why I get more upset'—with this paused and said grimly—'If I tell you something, will you… No, nothing', and he bit his tongue as if to stop himself from saying something terrible. Poor Vijayalakshmi could not understand what he was trying to say. Finally, she asked, 'What did you want to say to me?'

Venkataratnam pulled himself together and said, 'Let it be, what you say is right. Why should we worry about unnecessary things?' His expression did not change. It was not clear what he was hiding. She trusted her husband's words. Now he said, 'I am hungry. I am irritable because of heavy work today. Let us eat and go to bed!' Vijayalakshmi immediately readied herself to serve her husband dinner, ate after he had eaten, and finished her housework before going to bed. Venkataratnam was asleep by then. After sewing the whole day, Vijayalakshmi also lay down.

She fell asleep innocently the minute she lay in bed. But the worried Venkataratnam, though he pretended to be asleep, did not sleep a wink that whole night. The incident at Venkata Setti's house disturbed his sleep that night.

That evening, because there was Lakshmi puja in Setti garu's house, Venkataratnam was there making all the arrangements for the puja. Then the pedda gumasta[1] there took Venkataratnam aside and said secretly, 'Venkataratnam! Because you are a very sensible man, I am requesting your help. Promise me that you will not reveal what I tell you to anyone else.' Since the old clerk was a good man and trustworthy, Venkataratnam promised not to tell anyone.

'Venkataratnam, the precious ornaments taken out for the Lakshmi puja today don't count. There are ornaments worth a thousand times this in the shop that you probably know of. You must also know that all this wealth is in my control.'

Not understanding the drift of these words, Venkataratnam said, 'Yes, I know.'

At these words of the old clerk, Venkataratnam grew suspicious, but kept quiet because he wanted to hear what the old clerk had to say.

The old gumasta: 'If we take some wealth from there, it is no wrong. Nor will the Setti suffer any great loss. Our misery and poverty will vanish. My salary is fifty rupees. Ten rupees more than yours. Isn't it difficult to maintain our families on these meagre wages?

---

1 *pedda* = chief/senior; *gumasta* = clerk

Don't be afraid that this will come out. I can guarantee that it won't. This matter that I mentioned must be completed before the annual accounts are done. There are only two days left. What do you say?' Venkataratnam's eyes reddened with anger. He wanted to make him shut up, but the clerk was his superior, so he swallowed his anger quietly.

As soon as the old man finished, Venkataratnam said, 'Ayya![1] Krishnamurtigaru? It doesn't matter if you mock me like this; but if this is true, then your decision is not acceptable to me. Because I have promised you, I will not reveal this matter to anyone.'

Hearing these strong words, the old clerk Krishnamurti's enthusiasm was waning. But without giving up, he tried to win over Venkataratnam with sweet words. Although he had seen all the wealth that Setti possessed, he was not tempted. Then the old clerk with his cunning began to describe Venkataratnam's poverty and the suffering of his wife and children. When that expert in trade began to describe his poverty in such heartrending words, Venkataratnam's eyes began to fill with tears. Seeing those tears, the old clerk asked, 'What, Venkataratnam, isn't your family condition as I have described it?'

Venkataratnam, wiping his eyes, said, 'Yes, it is like that.'

The old clerk said, 'Then it's up to you. Won't you accept my words?'

Venkataratnam: 'Tchi! Krishnamurtigaru, don't speak to me. Your words may corrupt my mind.'

That old man, who understood human nature perfectly, knew that people need time to think about turning towards the wrong path from righteousness, and waiting might make his task easier. He said, 'Okay, as you wish. You can think it over tonight and come to my house tomorrow morning and tell me what you have decided. These are the days of the Deepavali festival, there is probably nothing for the festival in your house. So take this hundred rupee note. Don't refuse it', and put the note in Venkataratnam's pocket.

On the way home from the shop that householder's mind was beset with all kinds of thoughts. 'Should I do what the old clerk

---

[1] sir

wanted me to do, or shouldn't I?' There were so many questions that disturbed his peace of mind. His conscience was telling him that if he did what he was asked to do, the glory of his lineage would be destroyed. The cunning Krishnamurti appeared before him and urged him to do as he says. He was confused. He fumbled when he tried to tell his wife about this. Intelligent readers will have grasped this.

Although he was lying with eyes closed, pretending to sleep, all the earlier thoughts kept haunting him. But since he could not decide, he could not sleep. When his wife was asleep, he began to pace up and down that room. He remembered the note the clerk had given him and, taking it out, he examined it in the lamplight and fell into thought. Then his face lit up as if he had taken a firm decision, and he thought, 'Yes, this is what I should do. After all, Krishnamurtigaru was saying this for our benefit', and he gazed at his sleeping wife. Immediately, he remembered what she said a short while ago, and his determination deserted him: 'If I commit this wrong, how will I show my face to this virtuous woman? Tchi! I cannot do this.' Then he saw his two children sleeping on either side of their mother, and his good sense left him—'I cannot see these children suffering, so I must do what I can without the knowledge of others.' And he took the note out again and sat looking at it. At this point, for some reason, Vijayalakshmi woke up, and he leaned against the wall dropping the note.

When Vijayalakshmi saw this, she was surprised and worried. She asked her husband, 'What is this? What are you doing at midnight? Why don't you tell me what has been bothering you since evening?'

Then she saw the note. Her heart sank in fear. In a grievous voice she said, 'Ayya, can't you tell me where the note is from? Today is full of bad omens. I pray you, please tell me about this matter.'

Venkataratnam, who was a little tempted by the old clerk's words, tried to change his wife's mind. But it was of no use. After she heard his words, her anxiety grew and her body began to tremble. Her anger grew, her eyes reddened, and the tears began to flow. Although she was very angry, she did not lose sight of the fact that he was her husband and that she should not scold him. But she knew that to delay at a moment like this would allow him to fall into bad conduct. Knowing that it was her duty to set him right, she said, 'I doubted that you had earned this note honestly. What is the reason for you to do this? Have I ever troubled you for clothes or jewels? Have the children ever worried you for anything? Is that the reason for your misconduct? If that is why you have thought of this, I swear by your sacred feet, I will never ask you or let the children ask for anything. Understand us, and desist from this behaviour. You said that nobody knows of this. But can you commit this act and deceive the almighty Parameshwara? After you do this, will your conscience remain clear like before? Will we be able to feed ourselves in peace with stolen wealth like we have been with the ten rupees that we have earned through our hard work? Will we be able to escape the guilt each time we touch this wealth that it is wealth earned through treachery? O Parameshwara! Father, I do not have the power to stop this act. I will no longer have the satisfaction that I have living in poverty!' Unable to control her grief she wept bitterly.

Seeing her weeping, Venkataratnam returned to his senses and, drawing his weeping wife to him, he embraced her.

'Jewel of a wife! Your good advice has dispelled the ignorance and darkness in my mind. I will never again do any bad deed. Although we live in poverty, we can enjoy the fruits of a virtuous life. Aha! It is only because of your truthfulness that I have been released from a grave sin. It is like a rebirth. The name Vijayalakshmi is so apt for you. You have been victorious today. When all the people in the world worship Goddess Lakshmi, I was lamenting that I could not worship the goddess. But when I have the goddess incarnate in you, of what use is a worldly Lakshmi.' And Venkataratnam drew Vijayalakshmi, unadorned by gold but clothed in virtue, into his embrace. Vijayalakshmi, bursting with happiness, leaned on her husband's shoulder. She regretted that she was unnecessarily harsh with her husband. After a few moments, she asked, 'You will not do that, will you?' Venkataratnam said he would not do it and embraced her again reassuringly. She then got up and held his feet. She felt her husband had been released from a great difficulty, and had returned to her. Venkataratnam raised her and the couple slept peacefully that night.

The second day, because it was Narakachaturdasi, the family rose early in the morning. Then Vijayalakshmi asked her daughter to perform a mangala arati for her husband and son, and asked them to have a ritual bath. It was now dawn. Venkataratnam ate the lump of jaggery that his wife gave him with affection, wore his clothes, and went to Krishnamurti's house.

As soon as he reached there, he threw the note before the clerk and said, 'I cannot agree with your suggestion. Have mercy.'

And he set off to work. But Krishnamurti did not let him go. He made him sit and said, 'Wait till I come back from inside', and he went in.

Venkataratnam, not understanding the reason, sat thinking. Besides Krishnamurti seemed happy, and not dispirited as he had looked the previous day. Venkataratnam was thinking about this and waiting for the clerk when he saw Krishnamurti and his employer Venkata Setti coming towards him.

As Venkataratnam rose to greet his employer, Setti garu came to him, patted him on his back and said, 'Venkataratnam, shabash! You are intelligent and hardworking. I wanted to test your honesty, and so I asked Krishnamurti to do this. You have passed my test and overcome your poverty. Yesterday your mind seems to have been tempted. But that was not your fault, but your poverty's. Rather than one who has never done a bad deed, one who has been tempted and has overcome it is a virtuous man. The first can make a mistake. But the second will never commit a mistake. The hundred rupees you were given yesterday is yours. You earned it with your character. Secondly, from today, I will give you twenty rupees and make you the assistant to Krishnamurti.'

Venkataratnam could not remain silent listening to this praise, and he narrated the night's happenings to them. Venkata Setti was overjoyed; he told his wife, summoned Vijayalakshmi and praised her saying she was truly Vijayalakshmi. 'Henceforth you are like my daughter.'

From that day, Venkata Setti treated Vijayalakshmi like his daughter. Venkataratnam worshipped his wife as a goddess.

And the couple enjoyed the wealth that they had acquired through their courage.

Written 1902

Source: 'Dhanatrayodasi' by Bhandaru Acchamamba (*Tolikathalu*, edited by Sa. Vem. Ramesh and R.M. Umamaheswara Rao, Tondanadu Telugu Rachayitala Sangham, 2014, pp. 81–93)

UNNAVA LAKSHMINARAYANA

Unnava Lakshminarayana (1877–1958), born in Vemulurpadu in Guntur, studied law in England and returned in 1916 to practise as a barrister in Madras. Active in movements for women's emancipation, he founded Sarada Niketan in 1922, an educational institute for women which became a hub for the anti-colonial struggle. A Gandhian social reformer and nationalist, he courted arrest for participation in the Quit India movement. While in jail, he wrote *Malapalli* in 1920, a novel that offered a powerful critique of caste society in his time. The book was banned twice by the British government in Madras—first, on publication in 1922 (lifted in 1928), and again, in 1936 (lifted in 1937).

Malapalli

'Yesterday the malas and madigas[1] held a meeting in Bezawada, and raised a commotion asking for higher salaries and wages. If we try to lower it now, there will be more trouble. Let us see how far this sabha goes, and then decide…'

1 a dalit caste

While this discussion was going on, Choudarayya stepped out onto the street. Seeing Sangha Das's door unlocked, he called out to Venganna, who hearing this, came out chewing tobacco, 'Ayya'.

Choudarayya: 'I asked you to tell me when the malavadu[1] returned. Why didn't you?'

Venganna: 'I was about to do that. He has started a school in the cowshed and is taking a class for the farmhands.'

Choudarayya said, 'This fellow is not going to let me rest', and, putting a heavy staff on his shoulder, he set out. Seeing him come, the farmhands closed the doors of the cowshed, bolted it, and ran out of the eastern courtyard into the barren lands. Choudarayya kicked the door and shouted, 'Open the door!' Das opened the door slowly and, looking like a frightened deer, stood to a side.

Choudarayya was grinding his teeth. His body was not in his control. His body was stiff. His face was all screwed up. His eyes were bulging out. He tightened his lips and couldn't breathe. His body was sweating profusely. His mind was filled with anger. Clutching the staff tightly, he struck Das on the head.

Sangha Das collapsed like a creeper torn off, and lay on the floor. His head was smashed like a pomegranate.

A blood that was angered by the injustice in the world.

A blood inspired by noble thoughts.

A blood exhausted in the service of others.

A blood purified by sacred thoughts.

It was flowing out as if through pipes.

The earth grew pure.

Choudarayya's eyes grew dim at the sight of that blood. He threw the staff on the rubbish heap, bolted the door, and rushed into the house. He felt as if someone was chasing him. Lakshmamma came to the threshold and asked him what happened. He didn't answer, but ran into the house and rushed to the western room and climbed on to the cotton bales heaped there.

Lakshmamma came running in and asked, 'Something terrible has happened. You won't tell me what it is?'

---

1 mala man

Choudarayya said, 'I hit the malavadu in the cowshed with a stick and he died. Go fast and get him buried in the wasteland.'

'What do you mean you hit him and he died' said Lakshmamma, going pale at the thought of the gravity of the situation as she stepped out of the entrance.

One of the malas who had run into the barren land saw Choudarayya raising the stick. He heard the sound of the blow.

'Aiyyo! He has killed him!' he shouted.

All the farmhands came running. When they saw the flow of blood, they grew furious.

'Aiyyo! Our jewel is gone', they said.

The door was bolted. It fell after three kicks. In that heat, they ran out shouting, 'Where is he?! Where is he?!' Seeing Lakshmamma, they asked, 'Where is he? Where is that fellow?'

Adam: 'Where is he? I want to see his blood flow.'

Satti: 'Where is he? I will tear out his gut and wear it like a sacred thread.'

Lakshmamma retorted quickly, 'He did not come home. He went into the shed.' The people rushed towards the shed shouting, 'Thrash him! Thrash him!' Lakshmamma shut the door and bolted it. Choudarayya was not to be found in the stable. They ran out onto the street. The door was bolted. They were shouting and getting ready to kick the door open. Even after ten kicks the door did not open. The fury subsided a bit. They looked at the old compound wall and stood still—like hunters after the beast had escaped. Things cooled down a bit.

Satti: 'Adamsahebu! I will go to the Malapalli[1] and bring his people. You go and register a complaint with the munsiff.'

Sattigadu[2] ran to the Malapalli. Some people went to the cowshed. Adamsahebu went to the munsiff and reported the incident.

First published 1922

Source: Extract from *Malapalli* by Unnava Lakshminarayana (Vijayawada: Jayanti Publications, 1992, pp. 191–92)

---

1 mala hamlet

2 *gadu* = a disrespectful suffix, usually used for men of lower caste

Tripuraneni Ramaswamy

Tripuraneni Ramaswamy (1887–1943), from Angaluru in Krishna district, studied law and English literature in England. Setting up a legal practice in Tenali, he channeled his literary energies into combatting casteism and social injustice. His most acclaimed works are *Shambhukavadha* and *Sutapuranam*. His translation of Vedic mantras from Sanskrit to Telugu and his opposition to traditional Hindu marriage ceremonies freed non-brahmin communities from their dependence on brahmin priesthood. *Sutapuranam* written in classical Telugu was adapted to colloquial Telugu by B. Ramakrishna.

The Dialogue between Manu and Brihaspati

Two great lawgivers had a heated debate with arguments and counterarguments in Indra's sabha at that time. I didn't know who they were. I was very curious to know more about them. Unable to stop myself, 'I wonder who they were', I asked those present there. (*Here again, he is visible to all*).

They told me that one of the two was the guru of the gods, Brihaspati, and the second person, the custodian of Hindu society, that is the Hindu lawgiver Manu.

On hearing those two names my curiosity knew no bounds. I was impatient to know what that debate was about and how it ended.

The guru of the gods, Brihaspati, on seeing Manu, burst forth:

Emayya Manu…! You have written the smriti haven't you! Why did you write it? You seem to have written it because you had nothing better to do. Or did you write it because it would earn you name and fame? Your smriti has caused chaos in the lives of the poor. So many have had to bow their heads. Are you aware of what a piteous state the people of Bharatadesam have been pushed into…? Did you observe it?

Look at the heavens… We have not scripted smritis that divide us like you did. We don't prescribe higher and lower punishments for wrongs based on caste. We don't have laws based on caste.

All are equal here. We don't conduct ourselves in partisan ways. You have committed a serious wrong. Your compassion towards living beings is obvious from your dharmasastra!

Is it just to prescribe different punishments to different persons for the same crime? Harsh punishment for those who are not twice-born, the shudras; and for the twice-born who commit the same crime, a different punishment—do you feel this is reasonable? Even among dvijas, the kshatriya is given a lesser punishment than a vaisya. The brahmin is given an even lesser punishment than a kshatriya. How just is this? The brahmin who lives by his caste alone is given only a nominal punishment even for a grave crime. Is this reasonable?

What kind of justice is it to prescribe that the organ with which the offence was committed will be cut for non-twice-born shudras? This means that in this land there is no equality before law, doesn't it!

And you have condemned everyone as mlecchas. What is the reason behind ranking the Andhras with mlecchajatis? Do you know anything about who they are? With such extreme writing you are just accumulating eternal damnation. Who asked you to write this useless smriti?

What is the system you have built for the shudras, their wives and children who have borne their suffering and troubles, labouring without respite, their blood turning to sweat to create wealth for your enjoyment?

Why shouldn't a shudra earn wealth for himself? Why should a shudra only eat your leftovers and nothing else? If he sets aside some grain for himself after having laboured hard, why should you pounce on him and grab his grain? Why should he not be allowed to wear clean clothes? Why should they only wear the rags you throw away?

Should a shudra not study? Will you pluck out his tongue if he does? Will you pour molten lead in his ear if he listens? If despite this, shudras persist, you kill them in broad daylight without the slightest hesitation?

Manu…! Is this your justice? Is this the greatness of your dharmasastra? If anyone says anything… you say 'I wrote the smriti for the good of the people'? Looking at your writing, is it not clear what good it can do, and is its deceit not revealed?

You say that if a shudra collects wealth, the rest of the world will be steeped in misery. Is the shudra not human? Is the shudra a lowly being? Are you, who has uttered such profanities a hero? If you have any courage, come and speak in Indra's presence.

Emayya…! Custodian of the dharmasastras…! Answer my question—'The shudra must be a slave', you write firmly. How did you write this? How did your conscience allow you to write like this and to condemn them like this? Do you have no humanity or compassion?

Oye! Great man! You don't have one-tenth the compassion a butcher has. How did you become a sage? How did you write the smriti? How did you decide what the law will be?

We too have many castes—kinneras, kimpurushas, garudas, gandharvas, yakshas. We have lived together here for a few hundred years. There has never been any conflict. This country, which creates the high and low, with kings encouraging these divisions and treacherous pandits proclaiming this as law, can only be a mleccha country for all time to come.

It is the duty of the king to treat all people as equals, to ensure that they are without troubles, and rule according to just law. A biased king is no king. Hearing the guru of the gods, Brihaspati speaking like this, Manu was startled. Collecting himself in a minute, he addressed Brihaspati thus:

'Guruvarya! What you say is true. Some brahmins tried to outsmart everyone by turning the smritis upside down. They are the ones who forced me to write these smritis. I was misled by their words. This was a very hasty act. Forgive me my ignorance.'

Brihaspati listened to Manu's words. He grasped the essence of what he said. To make him aware of reality, he said, 'O Manu! Keep your useless stories to yourself. I will grant you a divine revelation.

Here! Take a slow look at Bharatadesam. Also listen to what the non-twice-born people are saying about you.'

As I am well acquainted with the social reality of Bharatadesam, and know the troubles and suffering of people there, I was not surprised by the dialogue between Manu and Brihaspati. Seeing Manu freeze into silence and seeing his stunned looks when he heard Brihaspati, I came away from there.

Source: Extract from *Kaviraju Suta Purananiki Vyavaharika Bhasharupam* by B. Ramakrishna (Hyderabad: Peacock Classics, 2011, pp. 100–02)

Bhagya Reddy Varma

Bhagya Reddy Varma (1888–1950) was born Madari Bhagaiah to mala parents in Hyderabad State. The founder of the Adi-Hindu movement in Andhra, he started the Jagan Mitra Mandali in 1906 and the Manya Sangham in 1911 to raise consciousness among 'untouchable' communities through folklore and literature. He is known for his work in the cause of empowering dalits, setting up schools for dalit children and dalit panchayat courts for settling disputes. He chaired the All-India Conference of Scheduled Castes in Lucknow in December 1930 and was a supporter of Dr Ambedkar. His writings inaugurate the dalit standpoint in modern Telugu literature.

Vettimadiga

Police patel Rami Reddy was sitting on the village platform. He looked as if he was very troubled and had some urgent work. Rami Reddy came from an influential family in the village. He owned nearly two hundred acres of land. So, he had an income of about five or six hundred rupees a year. Our Reddy garu had some knowledge of Urdu and Telugu. There were few police patels who were as fluent as him. He had a reputation for causing fights between the villagers. It would be right to say that there was no one in the village who did not hate him wholeheartedly. Yet, either out of fear or because they might have some work with him, people would treat him with great respect. If anyone developed an enmity with Reddy garu, he had to leave the village and find another to live in. Otherwise he would be accused, dragged to court, and convicted of some crime, or he would be set on by ruffians and end up having to chant, 'Food! Oh, my Ramachandra!' That was the reason why the villain Rami Reddy was feared by the whole village.

Rami Reddy's urgent work was that he had to send a letter to a relative who lived in a village three amadas[1] away. He sent the talari[2] to fetch the madiga who was allotted to the village. But the talari came back empty-handed and said that the village madiga had urgent work today and was unable to come.

Hearing this, the landlord was like a venomous black serpent whose tail was trampled. 'The allotted madiga has urgent work, is it? Who will do my work? Am I your grandfather or your great-grandfather? Don't you have any sense? Instead of bringing the madiga here, you tell me this shamelessly? You are not capable of even this?' Taking off his slipper, he began to thrash the talari until his anger subsided, and then asked him to bring the madiga in five minutes or he would kill him. Since the talari knew the temper of the patel, he set off without a squeak to find the madiga.

The patel, still boiling, began to abuse thus: 'What is this madiga's urgent work? Who does he think will do the government work? Times have changed. Even the madigas have developed eyes on their heads and they can't see above or below. I will teach them a lesson tomorrow. If I don't seize their grain, I am not Rami Reddy. I don't know what strange times these are, but no one respects the government nowadays. When they are shown pity because they are poor and shown mercy, they take advantage and climb on our heads.

---

[1] an *amada* is a distance of twelve miles

[2] watchman; constable

That is why the elders said that they should be slippered regularly. They say vetti[1] is hardship. Why were they allowed to stay in the village? Maybe it was so that they could sit at home and eat like doras![2] I will now show my character. I will destroy their homes. Let me see who will oppose me.'

The month of kartika. After toiling for six months and harvesting grain, with the desire that one could cook some gruel or kanji for the next five months, it was time to thresh the grain that was harvested and bind the sheaves. Fixing buckets and pipes to draw water, providing all the implements to work, after labouring night and day for the landlord, the fruit of that labour could now be realised. That day, it was Malladu's turn to do the vetti work. But the landlord for whom he had worked was heaping the harvested grain. So Malladu was caught in a bind. If he went on vetti duty, then he would not get even a bit of grain, and even the share of grain he was entitled to would go down. If he didn't go for vetti work, he would only add fuel to the fury of that stone-hearted patel. He was nervous.

Thinking of all this, he set out to plead with the patel to ask for a substitute for today. By then the talari came red-eyed with anger and dragged Mallaiah, beating and abusing him, to the patel. What could the ignorant Malladu, who was a coward and knew no law, do? He had no support.

The minute the patel set eyes on him, he pulled out his stick and began to beat him mercilessly. Could Malladu hit back with any courage? He beat him until his hands began to ache. In spite of all that beating, poor Malladu did not open his mouth. Finally, unable to bear the blows, he fell unconscious. He had a severe blow on his head. Blood began to flow out like a flood. Only after he saw the blood, did the anger of the patel garu subside. Then he sent the talari for a couple of his servants, and ordered them to carry him back to his house. They carried Malladu like a corpse back to his house.

He did not recover for nearly five or six months. He was an invalid, lying on the floor, unable to move. His wife and children suffered greatly because there was no food to eat or clothes to wear.

---

1 bonded labour

2 dominant caste landlords

The patel, who could see this with his own eyes, never offered a paisa to help. The readers should understand what a cruel-hearted man Rami Reddy was. Imagine how many patels like this there are throughout the country.

Written 1932

Source: 'Vettimadiga' by Bhagya Reddy Varma (*Telangana Kathalu*, edited by Kaluva Mallayya, Sadanand Sarada and Chandra, Hyderabad: Visalandhra Publishing House, 2005, pp. 22–25)

Sripada Subramania Sastri

Sripada Subramania Sastri (1891–1961) was born in East Godavari in an orthodox family. A master of short stories, his critical energies were focused on brahmin society, its customs, and the condition of widows. Using social realism in his stories, he was, by his own account, influenced by the manner of speech of women. 'Gulabi Attaru' and 'Vadla Ginjalu' are well known among his stories, and his novel *Atmabali* addresses the sexuality of widows.

Barefoot on Burning Embers

'Instead of sitting like a log of wood, can't you make some sandal paste?'

'But elder brother-in-law left yesterday.'

'Can't you see anyone else who can use sandalwood here?'

'Why don't you just tell me?'

'Your mother and father? Do I have to spell it out?

'How would I know? A person like me?'

'Really, didn't it strike you at all? Are they old or limping? What is wrong with them? They can apply sandal luxuriously!'

'…'

'Anyway you don't have that possibility in your life! If you want to prosper in your next life, you should prepare sandal paste for married women and thread flowers for them. And for your parents too! What more pious deed can you perform?'

'I saw. I experienced! What joy it is to prepare sandal paste for others! What pleasure does sandal bring! If I create such comfort for others, how much merit I will earn! And so many to serve in this life, and yet the fear that I may not enjoy comfort in my next life. I am alive only because I am unable to end this life! Even then, what is the guarantee that I will be born a human in the next life?'

'True! How can a stupid girl like you deserve a human life again?'

'What comfort will it bring me? Better to be born an animal or a bird, this grinding sandal paste and this grumbling!'

'Who knows how many you troubled and whose happiness you destroyed? How many bonds you destroyed? Otherwise, why would you suffer this fate? So when I say be mindful for your next birth, it is for your sake not mine.'

'Who said it is for you? Does it matter whose sake? Will I escape my fate? You are an affectionate person, so you want me to make sandal paste for your daughter. Who said it is wrong? It didn't even strike me. Did I refuse or will I not do it? Since you have said it so clearly and sternly, see if I fail to do it every day now. Can I just eat and simply sit here? After all, I have strength left in my hands.'

'Oh, you! Slap your face! One small word and you give me such a lecture!'

'…'

'You who hesitate to serve your mother and father, what will you do for others!'

'…'

[…]

'Stitch it by tomorrow morning. I want to wear a new sari and go to daughter Sodamma's mother-in-law's house. It will look good with it, won't it, Chelli?'

'Oiling and washing Chelli's hair, combing Tammudu's hair, Akka's baby's bedclothes—'

'How long will all that take?'

'Then the cowshed?'

'You will do that.'

'Milking?'

'You will milk her and throw it there. Buttermilk too. You will wash father's dhoti and dry it. That's all! What other work do you have?'

'How does that concern you? I will see what I can do.'

'Don't say you will see. Say you will do it.'

'Does that mean the job won't be done if I don't say I will?'

'How hard you are, my mother!'

'…'

'You are saying "no" although I am begging you. Will you stitch it by the evening?'

'I will stitch it.'

'Don't forget, girl! I will come and sleep next to you after lunch. This terrible heat… unless I sleep for a while after lunch… You will have made it by the time I wake up?'

'…'

'Your brother-in-law praises you a lot. After we get a job, you can come and stay with us. Will you?'

'…'

'Why don't you say something?'

'Why should I talk? How will I pass my days if I don't stay with someone?'

'What a thing to say, you wretched creature! Am I so wearisome to you? Do you think that I can't manage if you don't come? We will engage a cook. We don't need anyone.'

'…'

'Oh! Say one word, and the tears come. No fear.'

'…'

'I can't be a hypocrite like Chinnakka. I am so fond of you—why say it? If you come with me to my house, I will chase my sister-in-law out in a minute. Won't I hand over the management of my house over to you?'

'…'

'Look at the way you slave here. If you come to my house and mind my children, will I ask you to do any work?'

'…'

'And the Madhavaswami temple is near our house. Every day, you can go and listen to the Purana. What more do you want? A handful of rice, a length of cloth—will I let you down? Your brother-in-law will give you the keys of the house. In a month, you will have a handful of rupees, rituals, fasts, pilgrimages to Kasi and Rameswaram—no obstacles in my house!'

'…'

'Maybe you are full of desire to go with Chinnakka. She won't take you. She is so stingy! Will she even feed you? Anyway, she has nothing to give you. They can only chatter "paas pees" in English, but they have no land. Just two acres. And that too dry land. We have ten acres of wet land by the lake. And her husband… You should never go to a place like that.'

'What are you doing, Rukku?'

'I just put the sandal in the house and came and sat down. I wanted to sew Peddakka's daughter's dress.'

'What is the hurry for that?'

'Everyone thinks their work urgent. "You still haven't finished it", she said, irritated, a minute ago.'

'If you find someone to work free that's it! Why can't she do it herself?'

'I didn't ask.'

'Don't ask. Just throw it there and come here.'

'Why?'

'I will tell you. Just throw it and come.'

'I will throw it. Tell me.'

'By the time she finished frying the lentils, ammamma turned sore.'

'Hmmm'

'Your father wants me to massage his head. No one else is good enough.'

'Hmmm.'

'Ammamma wants to make some uppupindi.'[1]

'...'

'You must cook.'

'...'

'Why do you turn pale?'

'...'

'Only today! Tomorrow, I will observe madi.'[2]

'After cleaning the lentils and making sandal paste twice over, my arms ache, amma!'

'"Twice over, thrice over", why are you making such a big thing of it?'

'...'

'Cook the raw plantain in the lentil, then take the dried brinjal, drumsticks, jackfruit and ladies fingers, and make a pulusu.'[3]

'Why don't you ask Peddakka or Chinnakka to cook?'

'Why will they do it for us? If I tell them, then their husbands may get angry! Their mothers-in-law will say something.'

'...'

'They have their place, we have ours. We should feed them if we have the patience, or send them home. We should not give them any work.'

'...'

'It's already six. Get up, don't sit. Your father is saying that we should cook before sunset! Throw that cloth away. Why are you still looking?'

'...'

'Remember! We need mango pickle for the leftover rice in the morning. Ask ammamma how many mangoes you should make.'

'...'

'There is not even a twig to light the fire. Before it gets dark, climb the small attic and get enough for four times and place them on the sill. Don't forget.'

'...'

---

1 porridge made from rice flour

2 state of ritual purity (of a brahmin)

3 sour gravy

'If ammamma wants to make crisp rotte,[1] then break a coconut and give her the pieces for the chutney as well. Do you hear anything?'

'...'

'Get up. You must get up. It won't get done if you sit like this.'

'—Tccha! Rammayya, my father! Is my life going to pass like this, great lord...?'

'Ey! Who is in the kitchen?'

'It's me, Tammudu!'

'You must serve my food in a minute.'

'...'

'Why don't you answer? It's getting late for the cinema. Serve quickly.'

'If you are in such a hurry—'

'I am in a hurry. Shall I take a plate or will you give me a leaf?'

'What were you doing all this while, ra?'

'Don't I have to get the money?'

'Is this the time to get money?'

'I have been asking since morning. Amma agreed at three o'clock. But wretched ammamma...'

'Aa... aaa...'

'Will I keep quiet if my money for a cinema ticket is snatched from me?'

'...'

'Why are you standing like that? Why don't you serve me?'

'I haven't put the rice to boil yet, ra.'

'What were you doing till now, you wretch! If I go for the second show, it will spoil my studies. Have you put in the rice at least now?'

'Before the water boils?'

'You stupid face. What the hell should I do now?'

'There is old rice. Will you eat that?'

'Your words disgust me. Okay, at least that, then.'

'Ask Chinnakka or Peddakka to serve you.'

'They are refusing to come. They are busy.'

'What are they doing?'

---

[1] unleavened bread; roti

'Chinnakka is tying jasmine flowers, Peddakka is playing shells with Syamalamba, the neighbour. You serve me.'

'I shouldn't touch the food, ra.'

'It won't hurt me. This wretched custom be damned.'

'…'

'Or else you stay awake till 10.30.'

'Since she has bathed already, ask ammamma if she will serve you.'

'I don't want her to.'

'Why?'

'If her eyes fall on me, I can't digest my food.'

'…'

'Jackfruit pieces, drumstick pieces—keep many aside for me. If you don't, I will bite you… You know that?'

'Why don't you understand even this, son-in-law?'

'So, what do you want me to do?'

'Do you want me to spell it out?'

'…'

'Did it really not occur to you?'

'No.'

'Ayyo?'

'…'

'You have studied FA, after all.'

'Why can't you just tell me?'

'Listen then. Her life is finished. Nothing will make a difference.'

'So?'

'It is inevitable. Days will pass, but nothing will change.'

'So… what is it?'

'To have an oil bath? Comb her hair? Plait it? Why does she need that godforsaken hair?'

'—What are you doing, amma? You're spilling the pulusu.'

'The ladle is hot, I'm not able to hold it, father.'

'Just now Ramadeekshitulu said that day after is Dasami. A good day. If we go to Koti Lingam, it's a minute's work, son-in-law.'

'…'

'You are not looking at the long-term effects. These are not good days for young girls whose husbands die. Only day before yesterday, a widow was married in Veeresalingam's orchards. It seems they are looking for four more widows' sons to marry these widows. They don't look for a proper time. They just marry them off when they get somebody. It's no use regretting later.'

'But she is not even seventeen', said her father.

'So? What difference does her age make? Precisely because she is seventeen we should take measures before evil thoughts come to her.'

'…'

'Maybe you are soft because she has your mother's name. But it is like scratching your head with burning firewood.'

'What does your daughter say?'

'Why bother about her?'

'Even then—'

'When the need arises, the mother will say yes.'

'What about me?'

'What do you care? A male king? I am there to take her and get her shaved before sunrise before even the three-eyed one sees.'

'—What are you doing amma, why are you emptying the water like that!'

'The jug is greasy with oil, it slipped from my hands, father.'

'Did you see that…? Did you hear that? She is incapable of a single task. Even with what little she does, she lacks propriety and patience. Do you think cooking and serving is as simple as having your meal served to you?'

'…'

'Why don't you answer me?'

'What do you want me to say?'

'Do you think I will fall silent if you don't speak?'

'…'

'The elders come to gouge my eyes out the minute I step onto the street. Are you aware of anything?'

'…'

'Since you don't speak up for anything, stay quiet even for this. Nothing you do is going to stop anything.'

'…'

'The day after tomorrow, Wednesday, is Dasami. This is the last time I will ask you what you think.'

'…'

'Did you hear what I said?'

'How can I not hear if you shout into my ears?'

By the time Rukkamma stretched out on her cot it was eleven in the night. All the others in the household were fast asleep all over the house. The old woman, lying on the charpoy in the kitchen, was snoring loudly like a clutter of cats fighting. Rukkamma's cot was in the courtyard. She did not remember how she reached there.

Once there, she felt utterly helpless, in a house so big and so full of people.

The lamp shone bright like a marigold, and yet the house felt like a dark prison. She was at a total loss. If a thought occurred to her it was fleeting. If she called out, she would be in the middle of a dense forest full of thorns.

Unable to bear her loneliness, she shut her eyes tight. That only made her feel worse.

She saw Chinnakka holding a blouse-piece on one side, Peddakka, shirt-piece in hand, grinding her teeth, following the barber who entered sharpening his knife on another, her toothless ammamma, cavernous mouth wide open like a demon, scissors in hand on another, and her mother and father, exuding the fragrance of the sandal paste she wore down her arms making, on another side—

Rukkamma was shaking all over. Unable to lie down, she got up with a start and sat on her mat. Unable to sit, suffocated, she stood up. No sooner she stood up, she walked to the door, opened it and stumbled onto the street. She felt like she had escaped from jail.

Her feet were aflame and restless, her eyes aglow with an inner fire.

In a minute, the streets of Innispeta spun into view like a scene in a film.

When she slowed down, she found herself behind Nalamvaari Rest House. In front of her was Varadarao's hotel where she saw some people.

'Oh my god!' She froze standing.

A jatka[1] driver resting under his jatka parked against the wall was looking on.

'Do you need a carriage?'

'...'

'You need to pay me only if you ride on the clouds.'

'...'

'It is the middle of the night. Scorpions, snakes—give me a rupee or half or a quarter.'

When he did not get a reply to any of his questions the jatka driver grew suspicious and approached her. Looking at her he asked, 'Where would you like to go, ammayigaru?'[2]

'V peta—', she said softly.

'Danavayigunta', he whispered.

'What will you take?' she asked soundlessly, moving her lips.

'To Pantulugaru's orchard?' he asked trying to recollect something.

Relieved, she shook her head.

'I will take you there in minutes. Please climb into the carriage ammayigaru', he said and started the carriage.

'But I don't even have a copper coin', she said taking two quick steps forward.

'If you are going to Pantulugaru's orchard, you don't need to pay me ammayigaru', he said, tying the horses to the carriage and bringing it to her. Swiftly, without uttering another word, she jumped into the carriage and sat down crouching.

The crack of the whip.

He ran along till the horses picked up speed and then jumped in.

'I know joys and sorrows, ammayigaru. I have one daughter. Her husband died ten days ago, barely a month after she matured. She

---

1 two-wheeled horse-drawn carriage

2 *ammayi* = young lady (here, respectful reference to a younger lady of higher caste)

had not even been with him. Each time I see her or think of her, my stomach churns, ammayigaru. I do this work, but what can I say about my wife? She has stopped eating even gruel and has taken to bed. I can neither console my daughter nor care for my wife. If I stay at home, how will we live? Even God does not see my troubles.

'There were two marriages in Pantulugaru's orchard the night before last. Yesterday there was a third. There would have been a fourth but my carriage got stuck on the way, and her father and brothers dragged the girl back with them. My heart aches for her. She stepped out with so many dreams, so many desires. What is she going through now? What will be her fate? I am tormented by thoughts about her, ammayigaru.

'They are looking for another girl...

'He looks like a prince, that boy...

'A monthly salary of 60 rupees...

'Although it is his second marriage, he would not be older than twenty years.

'The father is determined.

'You will be married to him as soon as you reach there.

'You have only earned punyam. Do not be frightened, ammayigaru. You only have joys in store, not troubles.

'After ten days—once some time has passed, my daughter too...'

Worried that someone might catch up with them and stop the carriage like the other day, the jatka driver cracked the whip again.

The jatka rode on the clouds and turned the corner.

Written 1934

Source: Extract from 'Arikaalla Kinda Mantalu' by Sripada Subramania Sastri (*Sripada Subramania Sastri Uttama Kathalu*, edited by Vedagiri Rambabu, New Delhi: National Book Trust, 2012, pp. 65–88)

Garimella Satyanarayana

Garimella Satyanarayana (1893–1952), born in Gonepadu in Srikakulam district, was a poet and freedom fighter whose songs became songs of the freedom struggle, sung by lakhs of people across Andhra, especially the song 'Maakoddee tella doratanamu' ('We don't want this rule of white lords'). Jailed several times for his participation in the Non-cooperation Movement, he lost his family while in jail and lived in dire circumstances after his release.

Unjust Times

Unjust times are upon us
We must all rise from slumber
Wealth and enjoyment should reach the people
Come, let us find ways to reach them
Unjust times are upon us

Ploughing along the length of the stream
To manure, plough, reap and harvest is our lot
The other's fortune it appears is
Boasting, abusing and carrying away the yield
Unjust times are upon us

Toiling and producing amid factories and machines, our lot
Enjoying the fruit of our labour
Swaggering with beautiful girls
On their arms, another's
Unjust times are upon us

Working wage-less, hungry,
Crouching in crumbling huts, our lot
Living proudly in palaces,
Enjoying sweet pastures, another's
Unjust times are upon us

Written 1938

Source: 'Anyaya Kalamu' by Garimella Satyanarayana (*Raitu Kavita*, edited by Papineni Sivasankar, Bandla Madhava Rao and M.V. Rami Reddy, Guntur: Muvva Chinnabapi Reddy Memorial Trust Prachuranalu, 2004, p. 191)

Chalam

Gudipati Venkata Chalam (1894–1979), popularly known as Chalam, was a prolific and influential writer and philosopher. Challenging brahmin orthodoxy in his personal life, he was the first writer to write from the standpoint of women on questions ranging from sexuality to division of labour and childcare, and on that basis, develop a cogent critique of the traditional family. His large corpus of novels, plays, stories and essays shook the foundations of the literary world in his time.

Stree

Foreword

A woman has a body: that needs exercise. She has a brain: she must be given knowledge. She has a heart: that must be given experience. Will a country that does not recognise this understand the matters I write of? They will think that I have fallen to the attraction of western culture, and, unconscious of my identity, I am crowing whatever words come to my mouth. I know that. But if I had read a book like this when I was young, then I would have been able to make my life many times more virtuous and meaningful. Perhaps there are people like me in this new age.

***

Again today

At the end of the first edition, I said, 'Today it seems that these paths and these practices are good. I may be mistaken.' I thought that, as time passed, my opinions may change. Many people have been waiting for many years to rejoice if my intentions and practices changed. Not out of any interest in me, but so that the youth who are following my path and getting ruined (developing well) would be disheartened and turn into lifeless junk and rot like them. That youth are the hope of the future is just a myth. When youth are doing better than their elders, there is so much envy. That is why those who have been of use to the world and who speak of people's truth are those who have revolted against their elders! The youth who obeys his parents has no future. Those who listen to their gurus are worse!

I observe those who rebelled in those days against their elders, growing old and preaching morals to younger people, exercising authority and oppressing them. I watch parents who, after abusing their parents for getting them married early, are now forcing their own children to marry at an early age. I also know people who joined me, praised my stories and opinions, showed much interest in their own freedom, raised their voices, later got married, got jobs, built houses, and disappeared without a trace. The goddess of freedom is more frightening than the Kolkata Kali. She eternally demands our happiness a daily offering and demands to be bathed in tears. There are few who can worship her till the end with their human truths. Many people want to escape their personal troubles through freedom, but cannot bear that goddess in their lives.

I wrote this in the first edition on 2-12-1930. Today, that is, 2-12-40, ten years later, I re-read *Stree* to see if my views had changed. I have travelled far in these fifteen years (I wrote *Stree* in 1925)—inside, not outside. These exhausting journeys are unavoidable for persons who advance not in age, but in thinking.

My responsibilities are greater now than they were then. I have feared for years that we would be faced with times like this. Mine is a life that is free—without the affections of others, cast away and left alone. I have no doubts about what I write and what I do.

In earlier times, I felt it was important to assert myself to people I did not like. The more angry they got, the happier I was. I only had vain thoughts of demolishing people who opposed me through my words and my strengths. You will find my writings of that time full of extreme views, one-sided statements, vengeful curses, and unnecessary eroticism. Today, when I see that there are people who—although they cannot approach me in person, nor through their views, voices, letters, and sounds of silence—still come to me because they value my words, I feel shackled. My carefree journey has ended. I worry that I may mislead people with what I write and what I don't, what I speak and what I don't.

To those who complain sincerely that I am arrogant and I don't talk (this does not include those dear friends who spread scandals about me to prevent people from coming to me)—I want to say that the reason why I don't speak is that I fear I may not speak the truth (the fear is not that my untruths will cause me harm, but that they will cause harm to others). My silence and economy of speech, I believe, will be more useful to people who are free thinkers; I do not believe I have the authority to assert that my path is the only correct one; I respect people, their views, and their independence; I have the firm conviction that each person's is the path of truth. I only provide illustrations, not to claim that my path is eternal and no other person can measure up. There is a vast difference between writing about what may be generally good for the people, and telling someone in particular what is good for them. The trouble is that I am angry with society and I love people. Society (including me) is more senseless than me and many others. But there is nobody who is better than me, and no one who is worse than me.

I read *Stree* carefully. There was nothing I needed to correct except printing errors. I do not have any new, creative ways of writing about desire between women and men. But I do want to warn you never to trust those who speak of religion, religious prescriptions and Vedanta, as they do not have faith nor principles.

There is no doubt that all those who do not accept people and books that speak of freedom are rogues, slaves and robbers.

Many have suggested that people have been corrupted by reading my books (mainly *Stree*). What does 'corrupted' mean? I have not come across a single person who has been thus corrupted. No matter how hard I try, I am unable to understand how anyone can get more corrupted than these householders who neither have appearance nor desire, and go about their nishkama karma[1] by force of habit. It is possible that I am the only sinner in this world of saints. Similarly, if there are actually people who have been corrupted by reading my books, they are so fortunate! When the world is changing before one's eyes beyond anything one imagined, when entire countries are getting swept away, there are still people decorating the feet of brides with turmeric, others picking leftovers from used vessels, and old mothers-in-law quarrelling over the lack of modesty on the part of their daughters-in-law. And Telugu storywriters, school teachers, and newspaper critics, searching for decency and indecency—is one to be amused by or is it cause for alarm?

Every person who buys a newspaper only buys it to read the stories that these people consider immoral. It seems as if all literate Telugu persons are immoral. These critics however have not stopped reading each story six times over and proclaiming in the papers that they are immoral. What can we do? These museum objects will become rarer in another ten years. I worry that there may not be anyone left to laugh at them, so let us bless them that they may live on for another ten years for our amusement.

Sex is a law of life—from children to old people, it stimulates and nurtures them whether or not they are aware. It is futile to delude oneself that one is not aroused or that one does not need it. There is no life without it. Saying that sex does not stimulate is like saying we are not alive, or life is not important. Those who sincerely accept that they have sexual desires, and that they derive enjoyment from it, are blessed. There is no higher accomplishment, nor an equal joy. Sex does not leave you even if you try to deceive yourself in your

---

[1] selfless action (a reference to the Bhagavad Gita)

pursuit of false morals and fame. It will reduce you to misfortune, helplessness and meaninglessness before it lets go of you.

Bezawada, 2 December 1940

***

A third word

I wrote *Stree* for those who value woman–man relations, who believe in the values of *sringara* and enrich their own lives and the lives of others around them. For those people who do not understand my pedagogy of freedom, or misunderstand it, the institution of marriage is necessary. Instead of being ridden by guilt, apologetic and self-centred in their conformity to social rules and moral restrictions, we need people of courage who, because of their respect for society and their love for the heart, resist these norms. My anger in my writing is against the ignorance of society, and the love is for people who are crushed by this cruelty. In films and stories, we hear in the youth's proclamations of valour, words like 'this wretched society', or 'why should we care about society!' or 'This society is hypocritical'. These are not only meaningless, they are dangerous. That society is merciless. It is only people who cannot remain firm/steadfast even for a minute who resort to this talk.

In any era, there are always a few people who have the determination and capacity to resist existing norms. If they want their struggle to bring good to themselves and to others, they must consent to freedom for all. They must give up their power over their own. They must confront the troubles that result from their revolt with dignity. This crusade will inevitably result in some change in people's hearts; they will begin to see things in new light; they will hopefully understand that silence, hypocrisy and ignorance, will only lead them to weaken others, render them helpless, and perpetrate injustice. In this process, it is my conviction that the people will be able to open their eyes to new light.

As civilisation progresses, as work, awareness and desires grow, the humanity towards people decreases. The feeling that 'she is my woman', and the thinking about her as a body that gives pleasure, gives way to the attitude that a woman is an object, an idea, a creature who has no other place to go. Similarly, the man for the woman—the medium that supplies her with food, jewellery, respectability—nothing more.

The husband is not able to treat his wife as a woman. Similarly, the woman is unable to treat the husband as a man. They have even lost interest in each other's bodies. Only modesty and shame, if one thinks of it that way! It is primarily education and religion that have brought us to this unfortunate state. As long as we believe that wealth and property are the source of happiness and comfort, there will be no place for any other values. Man is moving further away from the heart, from the earth that birthed him, and from the light that opened his eyes. People see one without wealth as useless, and one who is happy is a sinner.

Elders respond to any talk of new ways, especially in worldly matters, with 'How will the world go on?' 'If nobody wants to bear children, what will happen to the world?' It is as if there cannot be responses to these questions, and as if they are carrying the burdens of the world on their shoulders. If asked 'What if there are no people in the world?' they take no account of the question and cast it aside without the slightest hesitation. We have arrived here one way or another. We could not avoid coming. And so let us think of ways of being happy. If we cannot be happy, let us at least try to ensure that those in front of us are free of troubles and help them. We ask, bringing the power of birthing within our control, 'These are issues if we are born. What if we are not born?'

If the socialist says 'We will see that nobody suffers from poverty', the votaries of religion say, 'Did we come into the world to be happy!'

Bertrand Russell says, 'Men would rather die than think.'

This world, family, property, morality, they see all this as permanent. Not as something that is in practice now. I am writing so much, but until a huge movement like communism comes and, like a flood, sweeps all this rubbish away, these people won't budge. Even if I write many essays like this, these solidified societies can only be swept away by mighty wars or movements or communism.

These writings are only steps for those great changes.

Unless communism comes and destroys these cave-like homes, these pickle shelters, these rooms for the gods, these kitchens, and builds in their place common messes and huge playgrounds for children, and schools, will people stop picking at each other, and drinking each other's blood—this husband, wife, child, mother-in-law, old hag or widow—will they stop torturing each other?

As the sun rises, lentils, cow dung cakes, states of purity, aversions, sprinkling courtyards, authority, grumbling and snacks take over. When will people ever learn to leave all this, and look at the sunrise and smile with happiness and pleasure?

In these dull deadened lives in the family, each wields authority on another—in the home, one simply takes the others' things, they hide things from each other, weeping, abusing, scolding. They have not yet begun to grasp the suffering and lowliness of this life they lead.

Bezawada, 27 July 1945

Source: Extracts from *Stree* by Chalam (Vijayawada: Arunodaya Publishing House, 1976, pp. 1, 4, 6, 10)

Basavaraju Apparao

Basavaraju Apparao (1894–1934), a poet in the romantic tradition, also wrote *Andhra Kavitva Charitramu* in 1921.

The Philosophy of Love

Grieve so your heart lightens
And your pride-filled mind is free
Better far to love and fail and grieve
Without your beloved's love
Than preen and shine

Your wealth is but ashes! Harken!
Only the creeper of love
Will bear the fruit of life!
What is larger than love?
Love is greater far than the greatest title

For the comfort of loving
For the salvation of loving
For the love of loving
What more do you desire
Grieve so your heart lightens
And your pride-filled mind is free

Source: Extract from 'Prema Tatvam' by Basavaraju Apparao (*Vaitalikulu*, edited by Muddu Krishna, Hyderabad: Visalandhra Publishing House, 1994, pp. 21–22)

Gurram Jashuva

Born in Vinukonda in Guntur to an intercaste dalit couple, Gurram Jashuva (1895–1971) and his brother were raised as Christians. He graduated as a scholar of Sanskrit and Telugu. A literary colossus who confronted the caste system in his writings, he was awarded the Padma Bhushan in 1970 in recognition of his contribution to Indian literature.

His iconic literary masterpiece *Gabbilam* ('The Bat') is a treatise on justice that tells the story of the sufferings of a dalit man using a bat as a messenger to God. In this epic poem, Jashuva speaks of discrimination based on caste and faith, and of the obscurantism and social injustice that prey on the most vulnerable people in society.

The Bat

Unable to feed stony village gods, day in and day out
Unable to pay the fee of priests claiming 'Tradition! Inevitability'
Reduced to cowardice, trapped by mantras and tantras of idle godmen
Quaking before the vicious roar of a hundred thousand cruel religious lions

Unable to bear the wealth of beloved brothers
Incapable of shedding the desire for meaningless rituals
The progress of our land, praised by the gods
Hangs clawing between heaven and earth

[...]

The one who salutes the poet
Says in an aside that it is the art he salutes
He who melts and praises the poetry
Keeps a distance from the poet
Unable to find a flaw in his learning
He clucks a tongue at his caste
The patron pouring plenty to his own caste
Sends others away with sweet words

Rejecting the sculptor who sculpts life
While worshipping the sculpture
Where such crooked hearts dwell
Art is but dead art

Written 1946

Source: Extract from *Gabbilam* by Gurram Jashuva (*Jashuva Sarvalabhya Rachanala Sankalanam*, edited by M.V. Rayudu and T. Syama Narayana, Bengaluru: Manasu Foundation, 2015, pp. 895–96)

Nanduri Venkata Subbarao

Nanduri Venkata Subbarao (1895–1957), born in Vasantavada in West Godavari, graduated as a lawyer and practiced law in Eluru. He created *Yenki Paatalu*—an anthology of songs using folklore and local dialects, and featuring folk protagonists Yenki and Nayudu—which shook the established literary conventions of his time. Bringing raw emotion into poetry and song, *Yenki* has enjoyed an unparalleled place in the Telugu literary imaginary.

The Yenki Who Chewed and Swallowed Me

There is no lass like Yenki! Oh no! Oh no!
Yenki will not come to me! No more! No more!

Strings of beads wrap her throat,
A measure of blossoms in her hair
Lifting her eyes
She showers gold

There is no lass like Yenki! Oh no! Oh no!
Yenki will not come to me! No more! No more!

The birthmark on her cheek
To describe, a lakh words will not do;
A single smile is a thousand
Flashing diamonds and gems

There is no lass like Yenki! Oh no! Oh no!
Yenki will not come to me! No more! No more!

If she but sings
Your sins will vanish
If she tells a tale
She holds you forever!

There is no lass like Yenki! Oh no! Oh no!
Yenki will not come to me! No more! No more!

The whole garden is dark,
The backyard lies pitch dark,
Going to eat, my heart throbs
Full of fear!

There is no lass like Yenki! Oh no! Oh no!
Yenki will not come to me! No more! No more!

A girl who would bring
Colour to a palace!
A girl who chewed and swallowed
My wealth and my heart!

There is no lass like Yenki! Oh no! Oh no!
Yenki will not come to me! No more! No more!

Source: 'Namili Mingina Naa Yenki' by Nanduri Venkata Subbarao (*Vaitalikulu*, edited by Muddu Krishna, Hyderabad: Visalandhra Publishing House, 1994, 66–67)

Kanuparti Varalakshmamma

Kanuparti Varalakshmamma (1896–1960), born in Bapatla, Guntur, and married at the age of thirteen, had little formal education. She was self-taught, developing her literary skills through reading and writing. She authored 'Sarada Lekhalu', the first political column written by a woman in Telugu. Varalakshmamma's writings stirred women to action and resistance in the early part of the twentieth century. She was an uncompromising critic of male domination and set up the Stree Hitaishini Mandali in 1931. She was one of the few writers whose style was considered as elevating and bringing a new dignity to Telugu prose.

You Have the Majority in Parliament

1

It was nine in the morning and Rajeswari was busy with some work. Raghava Rao, who was sitting in the hall on an easy chair and looking at his letters, called out.

'Rajeswari!'

'Ooy', said Rajeswari and, coming to him, asked, 'Why did you call?'

'You have a journey. Pack your boxes', said Raghava Rao.

'Where?' asked Rajeswari.

'Guntur', he said.

'What? Has my niece come of age? Did my uncle write?' asked Rajeswari quickly.

'No, your niece hasn't matured. Nor has your brother. There are women's sabhas in Guntur. Some big men's wives have invited you to come.'

'What is this "big men's wives"? Don't they have a name or place?'

'I don't know what they have or don't. I am only telling you what is in the letter.'

'Aren't their names in the letter?'

'Won't I read it if they are there?'

'Will there be invitations without names?'

'See for yourself if they are there or not, wife of Raghava Rao.'

And he gave her an invitation letter.

Rajeswari took the letter and read it.

'They are all wives of people with high positions, and so they write "so-and-so's wife" with pride. What is wrong with that? Now everyone writes like that, don't they?' she said, smiling.

'Oho! You don't see anything wrong with this? Thank god. We can relax for short while then.'

'When have you not been relaxed? Why don't you tell me what you see wrong in this?'

'Why are you so curious? I won't tell you.'

'We could not understand it because we lack the intelligence. Why is it you who know everything cannot tell us?'

'You want individual freedom, don't you?'

'Aaa.'

'You want equal rights with men, don't you?'

'Certainly.'

'I think this is empty rhetoric. You do not have a deep desire for it. It is only sharp words. It is certainly not a deep ambition.'

'That is not correct. If you listen to your inner voice, you will know how agitated we women are for freedom.'

'I don't need to work that hard. It is evident from your invitation.'

'What is evident?'

'That you still desire to be sheltered by men.'

'Why?'

'In spite of having their own name, they ignore that and describe themselves as so-and-so's wife.'

'Oho! What a good conclusion you have reached. Will our dreams crumble just because we use our husbands' names? All the white women follow this practice. Haven't their rights remained unharmed? Are they not enjoying equal rights along with their men?'

'They do, but even for them, this destruction of the self is not good. Each white woman marries one man after another—when relations go bad with one, she simply divorces him and marries another. With each man she marries, she changes her name to his name. Whatever equal rights she may have, in the matter of the name, they are not equal. Although you have no equal rights in anything, you follow them in this and lose even that right. From time immemorial, in our country, we have no tradition of using the husband's name. Vaidehi, Vaidarbhi, Panchali, Shaibya, Janaki, Draupadi—all these names point to this. All these names—short and sweet—refer to women's land, their lineage, their fathers. Today's names—Sarada Ramanarao, Parvati Narayanamurthy, Satyavati Sitapati, or else, Mrs Sharma, Mrs Shastri, Mrs Nayudu. When translated into Telugu, this sounds unbearable—Pillaiwife, Guptawife, Chowdarywife. There is no father's name. No mother's name. You demolish what you already have and yet you speak of equality, personal freedom and all kinds of rights. I feel like laughing. Rajeswari! You women are so enamoured by these names, but we men, however educated or rich our wives, or earning well, will commit murder if we are called "so-and-so's husband" and will never accept it. Why, if someone calls me "Rajeswari's husband", see whether I don't slap the fellow's cheeks!' said Raghava Rao.

'Well, we don't go to such extremes,' said Rajeswari, gurgling with laughter.

'Born and brought up in a slave culture, what do you understand of individual respect?' said Raghava Rao.

'Yes, and you who have grown in a race that has denied for generations the rights of women, will you agree to be called "so-and-so's husband"?'

'Bearing it will…'

'Anyway, when is the journey?'

'So you will go for the women's sabha, is it?'

'I will go. For some time now, I have wanted to go and see. Last time, I missed it. But this time, I will go. If it had been in some far-off district, I couldn't have gone. Since it is in our own district, I will go and see.'

'Okay then, pack for the journey.'

'When?'

'The three o'clock train today.'

'The three o'clock train?! Won't it be really dark by the time we reach Guntur?'

'Ayy! You who cannot get off a train in the dark want equal rights with us?'

'After confining us in kitchens over the ages and stamping down our capabilities, what can we say if you now badger us for not travelling alone? It is only if we were allowed to be independent from childhood that we could have developed courage and confidence.'

'Don't worry. There will be many women waiting to receive the wives at the railway station and reach them to their place of stay.'

'I won't go to the place where delegates are staying. I will go to mamayya's place. Where will I be able to get milk and other things for the children?'

'In that case, I will send a wire to your mamayya right now. He will send someone to receive you at the station.'

'Why don't you also come? After all, it is Saturday and Sunday; there will be no court.'

'So in a meeting called to deprive us of our rights, not only do you want to go as delegate, but you want me to accompany you?'

'Who is passing resolutions against you men? We are only asking for certain conveniences. How can they be called resolutions against you?'

'If we give you the conveniences you ask for, it means inconvenience for us, doesn't it?'

'Selfishness is a synonym for men.'

'We are not the kind who want to violate others' interests.'

'So are you coming to Guntur or not?'

'Please, no.'

'Then please send mamayya a telegram. He will send someone to the station', said Rajeswari going inside the house.

'I better send the telegram immediately', said Raghava Rao, getting up from the easy chair, going inside, putting his money purse into his pocket and wearing the uttariyam[1] on his shoulder before leaving the house.

Rajeswari called out from the kitchen, 'Are you going to send the telegram?'

'Yes.'

'Will you go to the bazaar after sending the telegram?'

'If you ask me to go, I will. What do you want?'

'Get a packet of biscuits for the children in case they cry at the meeting. And for mamayya's children, two pounds of peppermints.'

'Alright; I will get it.'

'Why are you going without listening?'

'What now?'

'Eight yards of threaded fine flowers, to wear in the hair…'

'Abbaba! You women's travel is frightening.'

'Since even a small needle has to come from you, even if we ask for an important thing, you fuss "abbaba". How many suits did you make to go to Bombay last time? How many shoes you bought! Did you think even in passing why so much? You earn plenty and you spend freely.'

'Why don't you also earn then? Our job will be lighter.'

'If only that were there. Our dependence as women would end and shatter into pieces.'

'Oh, see. How many feelings are arising in your mind!'

'What is the use? Mere bubbles! Rising out of water just to disappear in the water. They don't have anything special.'

'This is really the age of women', said Raghava Rao with a smile, and coming in he took some money and left for the bazaar. Rajeswari was engrossed in preparing for the journey.

2

The horse carriage stopped in front of the house exactly at two o'clock. Rajeswari had packed everything she needed, bathed the children and combed their hair, made them wear good clothes, dressed herself, and was locking the doors of the house.

---

1 a long scarf worn on the shoulder

Raghava Rao, sitting in the veranda, called out to the servant on seeing the carriage and, asking him to take the luggage, came in and asked Rajeswari if he should buy tickets in first class. 'But in first class there are no special compartments for women', she said. 'It is possible that there won't be in this train', said Raghava Rao. 'In that case take third-class tickets. We can chit chat', she said.

'Why can't you talk in first class?'

'With whom?'

'With those who are there.'

'What can I talk to men who are strangers? If you were with me, I could have sat in any train.'

'Okay, you want me to follow you like a bodyguard wherever you go.'

'Forget all that. If you take a third-class ticket, there will surely be a ladies' compartment, so I can sit there.'

The servant and the driver put the luggage in the carriage. Rajeswari and the children climbed on. Raghava Rao went ahead on the cycle to get the train tickets.

The jatka with Rajeswari and the children reached the station. Raghava Rao asked a licensed porter to carry the luggage to the train, paid the jatka fare, and escorted his wife and children to the platform. Raghava Rao was concerned. 'I don't know how you will manage the children—they will go too close to the windows, they will play with the doors, they will bend over, be careful.' 'You take care of the house. I am leaving it to the servants. Subamma is nimble fingered', said Rajeswari. As they were talking, the train came whistling to the platform. Raghava Rao helped his wife and children board the train and bid goodbye. 'Ayyo, you are leaving? There doesn't seem to be anyone I know in this train. I don't know how I will manage the children', said Rajeswari looking at her husband downcast. He saw her jittery looks and thought to himself, 'I wish I had also gone along.' But the train pulled out with a whistle, mercilessly separating husband and wife.

Raghava Rao waited till the train was out of sight before returning home.

When Raghava Rao returned from the court, he used to follow his wife, telling her stories and making jokes. So when he saw a house without wife or children, he was depressed. He didn't feel like staying at home even for a minute. Although it was not time, he took his bat and went to the club. He stayed there till eight, and fixing the next day's programme, he asked his friends to come over to play cards and then went home.

3

On Monday, when Rajeswari got off the five o'clock train and came home, the children waited for their father who hadn't yet come home. Soon thereafter Raghava Rao came home. 'Father, we came by this train', said his son; 'Mamayya also came with us, father', said Leela. 'Who? Sreenivasulu?' Raghava Rao asked. As he spoke, Sreenivasulu came into the veranda from the backyard. 'What, Sreenivasulu! Have you decided to punish your in-laws for their thoughtlessness in marrying their daughter to an unemployed BA by staying in their house?' Raghava Rao asked.

'No, bava!'[1] said Sreenivasulu grinning.

'Oh okay. Look at how you have spun this! He returned the day before the mahila sabha, that is the day I reached there. And already you are talking as if he has spent years in his mother-in-law's house', said Rajeswari.

'Oho! Why don't you tell me, did he come as delegate to your sabha?'

'How can he come as delegate to a women's meeting?' asked Rajeswari innocently.

'He is a storyteller. So he weaves tales!' said Sreenivasulu.

'Don't talk about my stories. Your sister will be furious.'

'And so, why should you be scared?' asked Sreenivasulu.

'Ever since your sister has had the first place in the meeting and has had three resolutions passed in the sabha I am terribly scared. I don't know what new resolutions she will bring. These are days when you should fear women. I don't know whether you realise it.'

'Abbo! What are you afraid of? The way you men are writing about women these days, no men would have written at any time.

---

1 brother-in-law

Take any story, any essay, any song, or any poem: they are full of accusations, observations, and undignified descriptions.'

'There! She has started the angry lectures.'

'Yes, when I see these obscene writings, I feel angry. Women are described as objects of enjoyment, belonging to men as passive objects. Philosophers calling us inferior creatures. Everyone writes as they like according to their mood. One is reminded of the story about four blind men and an elephant. Trying to understand what an elephant is, one of them held the legs and said it was like a pillar, another held the ear and said it is like a winnowing tray, the third held the trunk and said it is like a pestle. Woman is also described by different people according to their understanding. But there is no one who knows the depths of a woman's heart completely. God has created women from the same material with which he created men. So women are like men with the same body and character as men, not an object unfit for companionship and without any feelings.'

'Abbo! Abbo! Sreenivasulu, this human creature equal to men, who could not go to Guntur alone, has turned topsy-turvy. Do you see these arrogant postures now?' said Raghava Rao laughing helplessly.

'If you keep a bird in a cage forever, won't it be crippled and lose its capacity to fly? Anyway, whose fault is that?' said Rajeswari.

Without answering her, Raghava Rao said, 'Oho! The longer we stay here the more the wrongs we seem to commit! Come along, let's go out Sreenivasulu!' The brothers-in-law went out. Rajeswari settled her travel things.

4

He asked Rajeswari to sit for the meal with them. When she said she would eat later, Raghava Rao did not agree. Everyone sat down to eat. 'What ra, Sreenivasulu, it doesn't seem like you are thinking about a job', said Raghava Rao.

'These are no longer the days when it is possible to get jobs through recommendations by friends.'

'In that case, stay on in your father-in-law's house. These days, several educated, unemployed men are settling for this. Coffee, snacks, meals, et cetera are all served on time and with care. The wife is also around. It is a comfortable life.'

'A son-in-law who stays in his mother-in-law's house is not respected.'

'Orey, if you are so easy-going nobody will give you a job, and your parents-in-law will not treat you well. You wife will stop listening to you. In the end you will not even be good enough to act in a film studio or record for a gramophone.'

Raghava Rao and Sreenivasulu were sitting on chairs and chewing betel leaves.

The child was moving in the cradle, and Rajeswari went and patted the child to sleep.

'Rajeswari! You went to Guntur and came, but you never told me what happened in the sabha. How did the divorce resolution go? You haven't told us anything.'

Rajeswari saw that the child was asleep and, coming out, said, 'What divorce? It did not figure in the mahila sabha.'

'Didn't the divorce resolution come up in the mahila sabha at all? We are saved! Our life as a couple is now stable.'

'If the divorce resolution is passed, why should it affect our marriage?'

'It is a problem. If your friends like it and take a divorce, and if that attracts you, what will I do? These three…'

'You are talking like Rangamma's husband.'

'What did he say?'

'"Osey, you are the mother of six children. They are passing the divorce resolution in the mahila sabha. According to that, we have to separate. Then who will look after you and your children? Who will marry a woman with so many children? You will be ruined for no reason. That is what that mahila sabha is. Don't go to that sabha and don't give any subscription", he said. She was frightened and said, "Sister-in-law, I won't come to the mahila sabha. My husband said this." Whatever it is, these men are scared of this divorce as if it were a beast. So they will create false stories and frighten women.'

'I am not scared. You can easily get a divorce, and another…'

'Abba! What are these words! You don't know good and bad. You catch whatever you want.'

'Abbo! You are so critical of divorce—but equal rights, independence, and so on, you get so enthusiastic.'

'Those are natural human rights. Every woman should have them. But not divorce; we have passed something concerning men.'

'What is that?'

'No man can marry again in his wife's lifetime.'

'Make a lakh of resolutions—what do we care?'

'What do you lose? After all, the majority in the parliament is yours.'

Gruhalakshmi, January 1936

Source: 'Chatta Sabhalo Majority Meedegaa' by Kanuparti Varalakshmamma (*Streela Kathalu*, Volume 4: 1901–1980, edited by K. Lakshminarayana, Anantapur: Rama Publications, 2007, pp. 36–46)

Suravaram Pratapa Reddy

Suravaram Pratapa Reddy (1896–1953) belonged to Mahbubnagar, and was known for his active role in the Telangana struggle against the oppression of the Nizam's rule in Hyderabad State. A social historian, he wrote the first history of the Telugu people, *Andhrula Sanghika Charitra*. A poet and short-story writer, he was a leader of the cultural renaissance in Telangana, compiling a list of over three hundred Telangana poets under the banner 'Golconda Kavulu'.

Eleven Gourds and Twelve Kotwals

(During Moghalai rule, the buffalo belonged to the man with the stick! This was the principle on which work was carried out. This story illustrates how a poor, naive peasant became a rich man.)

One day, a village farmer took eleven bottle gourds in his blanket and went to a village to sell them. Twelve housewives gathered in a place bargaining. By then, the mali patel[1] arrived. He said, 'Orey! Who gave you permission to sit here? Give me a gourd like a good fellow and leave.' And he took a really big gourd and left.

The farmer sat grumbling. Just then, like a hammer blow on a swollen nail, the police patel arrived. 'Bring that fellow here. I have to enter his name in the list of musafirs!' he roared. The talari came and grabbed one gourd as his share and one gourd as the patel's share and left.

After some time, the pedda talari came. He said, 'Hey! A couple of days ago, a fellow like you was here. He was selling vegetables in the day, and in the night he broke into the komati's[2] house. Come on! I will tie you up in the square.' He caught his hand, and picked up a gourd.

'Ayya! Maharaja! I am not a thief. I am not a lord. I am from another village. I keep coming often. I have already lost three gourds now. Where have you dropped down from now?' The farmer pleaded. But the talari hit him on the head with the gourd and went away with it.

In this manner, eleven people like the priest, the potter, the carpenter, and others came and grabbed his gourds. In tears, the farmer dusted his blanket and got up.

The karnam[3] who had gone before daybreak to the field now appeared before him.

'Hey! Why are you weeping? Did anyone harm you? Tell me, I am the village karnam. I can punish the one who wronged you!'

The farmer thanked God that there was at least one person who would do justice. He told him the story of his eleven gourds and then threw his blanket on his feet and holding them pleaded, 'You are Narayanamurti! Help me karnamayya!'

The karnam kicked him aside, pulled away the blanket, and, tucking it under his arm, said, 'Hey, you loafer! You gave everyone

---

1 revenue officer/collector

2 trader, vaisya caste

3 book-keeper

their share and lost my share? Do I seem lower than the talari to you? More useless than the carpenter? That illiterate mali patel is bigger to you? Go! Get my gourd and then take your blanket.' With reddened eyes, he tucked the blanket under his arm and went home.

The farmer looked at him from head to foot. 'So you are all the same, and this whole village is like that. What is this country? Damned country! How can poor fellows like me survive?' Grumbling sorrowfully, he followed the patwari[1] pleading with him. 'Orey! Take another step and I'll break your head! Watch out', said the patwari, looking at the farmer. The farmer stopped in his tracks. He wept like a child for a while.

A few women said, 'Go, son, go! Whose face did you see this morning? This village is full of maharajas like this! Don't ever come back here', they advised.

The farmer, deep in thought, set off for his village. He mused, 'Thoo! One should be born a patwari or patel. Or at least a talari. Better to die than lead this useless life! Not only did I lose my gourds, I also lost my blanket. That karnam was worse than all the others. That's why they say the karnam will continue to haunt you to the graveyard. If I don't take revenge, am I a man? But I am a poor man. What can I possibly do? That talari does not even have a patch of field. I have a field. My wife has an armlet, and I have a bullock. Am I less than the talari?... Even God needs a blow now and then to teach him! I will do some hocus pocus...'

Thus deep in thought he walked along. He reached a well. He sat on the mound beside the well, lost in thought. Suddenly an idea flashed through his head like a bright light. He jumped up and went into the village. He went to his wife and said, 'Osey, give me your armlet. Never mind; just get it. By the next Ugadi, I will get you a hundred armlets instead of one, if my name is Venkaiah.' He sold it to the patel for two hundred rupees. He took the money and went to the town that was ten miles away. He bought sherwani, pyjamas, socks, turbans, belts and badges, and so on, and hired four Arab jawans. He put the badges on them. Then, he dressed up. He hired a buggy.

---

1 village revenue officer

A couple of furlongs away, there was a big basti. Four roads crossed there. It was a big commercial centre. Officials, ministers, even the nawab, would go on that route for entertainment. The farmer got off at that village. The village well had a huge banyan tree on its bank. He set up a table and chairs under that tree. He set the jawans to guard the well.

Early in the morning, when the women of the village came to collect water, the jawans threatened them. 'Watch out! Pay a paisa per pot, and collect your water.'

The patel and patwaris came. 'Orey, we have received orders from the sarkar! Here is the firman!' said the farmer, showing them a firman stamped in Urdu. Thinking it was probably right, the village officials kept quiet.

Through the day, the collection grew. The first day, it was twenty rupees. Gradually, the income grew. It was known as the 'Marriman Pargana Sunkam.'[1] Its fame spread all around for a distance of two amadas. Weeks, months and years passed. One day, the subedar came visiting and set up tents. When his servant went for water, the jawan asked him to pay money. They returned with empty pots and told the subedar, 'Sarkar! Four Arab jawans are asking us to pay money to collect water: I told them that the water is for the subedar sarkar, and they came to stab us with their spears.'

Then the patel and patwari said, 'Huzoor, this tax is being collected regularly for the last ten years. There is a sarkar firman.' The subedar too, thinking it was possible, paid to collect his water.

One day, the dewan bahadur camped there. He faced the same fate. The Arabs did not allow anyone to climb down a step unless they paid a paisa for each pot. The dewan thought, 'Huzoorgaru must have issued a firman. Otherwise would he have the guts to collect money even from me?' He also paid the tax.

There was no limit for the farmer. When not just the subedar, but even the dewan bahadur paid the tax, the people were awestruck by his clout.

As things were like this, the nawabgaru, who was out for a hunt, decided to spend the night at the village, as it was late. Nawab

---

1 *sunkam* = tax

or not, the farmer was not willing to consider anyone. He told the nawab's servants to put down a coin before they got into the well. The complaint reached the nawab. He thought, 'Our dewanji must have ordered this to fill my treasury. I will find out after I reach the town. Now I should obey the law.' And he paid the water tax.

By now, there was a two-storey house in Marriman Pargana. The farmer owned half the lands in the village. He farmed with a hundred oxen. He gave loans for a distance of five amadas.

After nawabgaru returned to the city, he sent for the dewanji and said, 'Dewansaab, why have you created a tax for water? Is it not unfair?'

Dewangaru replied: 'I am your servant, huzoor! I also thought of making the same request to you. I also paid the tax. I thought that huzoorgaru must have issued this firman mubarak.'

'Arey! You didn't give the order. I didn't give the order. Then how has he collected money for the last fifteen years? Arrest him and bring him here', growled the nawab.

The farmer was waiting for the firman for the last ten years. He poured a thousand ashrafis into a golden platter and covered it with a velvet cloth embroidered in gold. The farmer offered nazrana to the nawab. The nawab was pleased with the nazrana.

'Kya re? Who gave you the order to collect water tax?'

'Huzoor, Marriman Pargana Sunkam came into being just like the "gyara kaddu bara kotwal hukum".'

'What are you saying, fellow? I can't understand anything you say. Explain!'

'If you promise to forgive my mistakes, then I will explain everything.'

'Alright, go ahead. We'll see.'

The farmer told him the whole story with rich descriptions.

Huzoor laughed as he heard and said, 'You are a clever fellow. Your mistakes are forgiven. Hereafter, you stay at my palace and ring the bells at night. That is your punishment.'

Soon, the farmer grew crazy. No income, no authority, nor anyone who cared about him. He had to stay awake the whole night. One night, in a sleepy state, he forgot to ring the bell at eleven.

He woke up and rang the bell at twelve. This small mistake turned the palace upside down.

Huzoor used to visit one begum each hour from eight o'clock. It didn't strike eleven, so the huzoor didn't visit the eleven o'clock begum. The next day, she sent for the bell ringer and said to him, 'Orey! Don't forget to ring my bell. I will pay you fifty rupees each month.' 'As you say, huzoor', he said nervously.

'These bells hold some secret', realised the farmer. One day, he missed the nine o'clock bell. One day, the ten o'clock, and one day, the twelve o'clock bell. For every bell that was missed, the begum of that hour would fix a salary for the farmer. He began to earn four hundred rupees a month.

After some years, the nawab came to know about this.

Thinking that he was a very smart fellow, he gifted him the village he had taxed and sent him on his way.

Do you see the power of the gourd? They say cutting a gourd is to tell stories like this!

Written 1930

Source: 'Gyara Kaddu Bara Kotwal' by Suravaram Pratapa Reddy (*Telangana Kathalu*, edited by Kaluva Mallayya, Sadanand Sarada and Chandra, Hyderabad: Visalandhra Publishing House, 2005, pp. 12–15)

Devulapalli Krishna Sastri

Devulapalli Krishna Sastri (1897–1980), born in East Godavari, was a poet, translator and playwright. Recipient of the Padma Bhushan in 1976, he is considered a leader of the romantic tradition in Telugu literature. Of his translations, one worth mention is his adaptation and translation of the Tamil *Tiruppavai* into Telugu verse. Among his works, *Krishna Pakshamu*, *Urvasi*, and *Pravasam* are well known.

Do Not Let the Winter In

Do not let the winter in
Do not let the cold come in
Do not let the blossoming spring leave, do not ever
Beware! Beware! Beware!
Beware! Beware! Beware!
Let the fury of summer fall upon you in anger
Let storm clouds batter you in heaving sobs
Do not let the winter in
Do not let the cold come in
Let chaitra[1] bring your desires into bloom
Let sarath[2] fill you with intoxicating dreams
In the winter, you stretch sleep-filled and drowsy
The cold brings destruction and death
Do not let the winter in, pray
Do not let the cold enter
Let them say I am not home
It is not possible, send them away!
As soon as you hear
The sound of age's footsteps on the street corner
Quickly say I am not home
It is not possible now, send them away!
Do not let the winter in
Do not let the cold come in

Source: 'Sheetavela Raneeyaku' by Devulapalli Krishna Sastri (*Amrita Veena*, edited by Devulapalli Venkata Subbaraya Sastri, Chennai: Rajahamsa Prachuranalu, 1983, p. 66)

---

[1] the month in spring which marks the Telugu New Year
[2] the season between monsoon and winter

Folk Song

Lifting Water from the Canal

Lifting water from the canal
To harvest a thousand measures
I have never tasted a grain, brother
Not a grain in my gruel, brother!

Lifting water from the canal
To harvest a thousand measures

As I sat on the bank after washing my hands and feet
The crow came and kicked me
Its chicks came and kicked me

Lifting water from the canal
To harvest a thousand measures

Unable to stand the nagging, I sat at the fire
The girl kicked me and went, brother
The girl's mother kicked me and went

Lifting water from the canal
To harvest a thousand measures

At the crack of dawn as I carried the pail
I fell head over heels, I broke my ribs, brother

Lifting water from the canal
To harvest a thousand measures

What a life is mine, brother
Why didn't I die that day, brother?

Lifting water from the canal
To harvest a thousand measures

Unpublished; oral

Kusuma Dharmanna

Kusuma Dharmanna (1900–46) was born in Lakshmivarapupeta in Rajamundry to dalit parents who were agricultural labourers. A qualified ayurveda physician and Telugu scholar, he was proficient in Sanskrit, Hindi, English and Urdu. Deeply influenced by Dr Ambedkar and widely read in Marxist and Gandhian philosophy, he was a leader of the dalit movement, and campaigned relentlessly for the abolition of untouchability. His song, 'Maakoddee nalla doratanamu' ('We don't want this rule of black lords'), soared in popularity on the wave of resistance to caste oppression led by him. Well known among his writings are *Asura Puranam*, *Nalla Doratanam* and *Harijana Satakam*.

Crimes that Shatter the Heart

'We are lovers of Freedom! Behind the curtain of the Congress, wearing a burqa, we can do no wrong. We do not need social reform. Swaraj must fall into our hands like a laddu.' Such wastrels who say this cannot change anything.

The horror of Kavitha village. The violence of Chettinad. The horror of Ponna Mandal in East Godavari. The injustice in Chelluru in Ramachandrapuram Taluka in the same district. The massacre in

Gajularega in Visakhapatnam District. The terror in Mangalagunta in Chittoor District. The cruelty in Eluru. Just hearing about the attacks in Jaipur State in Ramnath, our hearts are shattered. Who carries out these deeds? Isn't it Hindus and people following the Hindu religion? Why don't these leaders speak out?

The crime of the harijans of Kavitha was in sending their children to board schools which children of all castes attended. For this they were punished by pouring kerosene into their wells and burning their huts.

The crime of the harijan women in Chettinad was wearing blouses and walking on the public roads. The youth of Ponna Mandal gathered the courage to ride cycles on the streets. That was their crime. In Chelluru, the harijans took out a huge procession of Kunti Devi in a festival. That was the dreadful sin they committed. In Gajularega, a harijan bride and groom were taken in procession on a horse. That was the terrible crime they committed. Harijans committed the grave treachery of walking on the main street of Mangalagunta wearing slippers. Kicks and blows were the reward they deserved and their penance.

On Mukkoti Ekadasi day, the gods were being taken in procession and the harijan's god crossed the path of the sanatana god. That was an unworthy deed. The punishment was to drive the mala god through lanes and corners with the help of the police teaching the malas a lesson.

In Ramnath District in Jaipur State, the Hindus declared that harijans could not wear clothes with borders or shawls, that they should not cook anything in ghee, that they should not have doors to their houses, and ruled them with villainy. Earlier, harijans had to wear a pot under their mouths, a cloth and a broom dangling from their ass, and a broom tied to their feet. In the twentieth century, such terrible ordinance on not dressing, not cooking, not having doors! Is this ill fortune? Or the arrogance of the Hindus?

It seems they can carry the governor in his shoes uphill in a palanquin to Tirupati Venkateswara. In Mangalagunta, in that district, a mala cannot walk in slippers on the main road. Can we forget that Etturajulu Dasu (a harijan) who was overcome with devotion and worshipped Alivelu Manga Devi, was accused of a crime and dragged to court? It seems Pandit Malaviya will teach us mantras and make us enter temples! Does that mean that all those who flock to temples have learnt the mantras?

The cruel incidents described above are not isolated incidents that happened on and off. They are our daily experience. Our lives are dirt cheap. We cause such mental disturbance! We are not human beings! We are animals! This is sanatana Hindu religion. This is the philosophy of love of savarnas. Their ahimsa dharma.

1. Unable to bear the suffering of the harijans of Kavitha village, he asked them to leave the village (Gandhi).
2. To save their human dignity, he said harijans should leave the Hindu religion (Ambedkar).

Gandhi thought that Ambedkar was mistaken. It is natural after all to assume that everyone who disagrees with you is wrong! Perhaps Gandhigaru would say: if you can't leave the village, leave your lives!

1. Injustice is our family deity.
2. Torturing innocents is our caste occupation.
3. Using God and karma to loot is our religion.

Scales of sand

Eradicating untouchability is a part of the Congress manifesto. If mere resolutions can eradicate untouchability, why can't they bring swaraj?

As the soldiers of swaraj march into prisons and against lathis without hesitation to practice satyagraha, why does the Congress not show the same zeal in eradicating untouchability? Is that a lump of jaggery, and this a piece of ginger? Is it the Congress's intention to not create any discomfort or disturb unity, and allow untouchability to continue for another century, and after swaraj comes, start another struggle for untouchability?

The Congress, which is a puppet in the hands of the rich, has built a castle of sand with the blood and lives of the poor. It does not realise that there is a volcano under that castle. They imagine that they will always enjoy cool mountain breezes and the shimmer of autumn even in their dreams. They do not understand that the sooner they wake up, and lift the harijans who are below to their level, and treat them as equals, the better it is for their good and the good of society. So they first set up seva sanghas. These harijan seva sanghas were set up purely to douse the smouldering embers in harijan society waiting to burst forth into a fire that will destroy this world.

Scales of dung

Gandhi held forth that the other classes were indebted to harijans. They conspired to contain the raging fires in the blood of harijan youth by giving them books, slates, and student scholarships, and bind them to their slavery. They are deceiving them with sweet words and winning them over to their side. They create the illusion that the ones who are torturing them are the ones who will support and develop them.

For ages, they have confined us in a narrow trap. Somehow we escaped that. Now, they fling a few strips of meat and bones and bits of bread in our path, and drag us into the new trap of the seva sanghas. This prison is like Section 144, babu! Realise it! Wake up! Have you seen people like me speak up? They get excited, their eyes turn red, they tear their throats and they swallow in anger that the dog they raised is biting their feet. Some educated harijans, wanting to drink the water dripping from their beards, dance on a veil of illusion and ask us to forget caste. The more you study the more you learn to deceive.

Why did the world saviour Gandhi mahatma fast? Do you know? He believed that separate electorates for harijans like us would only distance us from Hindu society. So what is the task of the seva sanghas born as a result of that fast? The mahatma who grasped this separation as the essence and protested against it was hailed as great by people. The very same people set up separate wells and schools, separate temples and gods, separate names and separate villages, separating harijans even more from Hindu society, discriminating and distancing them. Was this Gandhiji's intention? Then how will untouchability go? How will the economy grow? When will rights be protected?

Have you noticed how the employees of the seva sangha who draw their salaries from the seva sangha funds love harijan youth?

Like Gandhiji milking the goat and drinking milk with the kid in his lap, stroking its head and tail and ears, petting it saying 'Oh my dear kid!', and showing his love. The love of the harijan sevakas is the same. This is called step-motherly love by the brave.

They killed our self-respect and continue to kill it. They call us chandalas—mixed blood—whoresons—widows' sons. This is the argument of the sanatanas. They say we were born when a brahmin slept with a shudra.

'Why count castes? Know the births?'

Source: 'Gundeladiripoyye Ghoralu' by Kusuma Dharmanna (*Samyavadanni Sahinchani Hinduism*, Vijayawada: Prajasakti Book House, 2016, pp. 18–21)

Kodavatiganti Kutumbarao

Kodavatiganti Kutumbarao (1909–80), born in Tenali in Guntur, was a prolific and influential Marxist writer whose work includes twenty novels, short stories, and thousands of essays covering literary criticism, cinema, science, art, history and politics. He was the editor of *Chandamama*, a children's magazine, from 1952 till his death in 1980. His writing focused on middle class predicaments, and foregrounded the importance of 'praja sahityam'. He was an active member of Viplava Rachayitala Sangham (VIRASAM)—Revolutionary Writers' Association.

New Ways

The very mention of Jogarao always infuriated me. Whatever he does feels wrong to me. Even if it was something I would support if it came from someone else, the minute he said it, I would be irritated.

Jogarao believed he was a great social reformer and the very incarnation of modernity, and asserted it too. I won't say that he wouldn't support widow remarriages, that he wouldn't conduct intermarriages, or that he would not pay greater attention to the girl widows in his village than the girls in his extended family. But I can say one thing with certainty; Jogarao had never worked for social reform that was not about women. He would never dabble in useless issues like khaddar,[1] harijan issues, et cetera. His whole focus was on child marriage, widow remarriage and education for women. Post-pubertal marriages, widow remarriages, women's education, reform and independence were the most simple matters. He was very enthusiastic about womanhood that was outside the control of men. He was dedicated to unmarried girls who had attained puberty and widows.

I know the reason for this. His wife was like a fireplace in which neither wood nor bramble would burn. A brave male who never succumbed to the charms of other women, Jogarao worshipped his wife. That worship wrecked him. Jogarao's love for reform is a result of this.

Because of him, I had a poor opinion of Hymavathi for a very long time. When that girl called him 'Babai', I would get mad. He was no relation of hers. When Hymavathi was very young, her parents were tenants in Jogaraogaru's house. In those days he had never drawn her near, or even given her biscuit. I know that he didn't go for her marriage. But within ten days of her husband's death, he appeared! Although there was no talk of shaving her head, he held forth solemnly on the evil practice and by sunset, he had decided her future.

It is true that Jogarao was very helpful in the matter of her studies. He was filled with pride every time she passed a class. Gradually Hymavathi came to symbolise his purpose. Before this, his larger goals of social reform got wiped out.

Hymavathi managed to complete her BA. With that Jogarao's plans came to a halt. Her father flatly refused to have any part in her remarriage. Jogarao was not one to give up so easily. 'Leave the

---

1 khadi

responsibility for arranging that on me, Annagaru', he said. Hymavathi's father said, 'You can do what you like. Only don't involve me in anything.' From that day Hymavathi became part of Jogarao's family.

Jogarao brought a marriage proposal for her that took me by surprise. From Suryanarayana Medhavi, the handsome junior zamindar. He had passed BA Honours and remained unmarried as if he were waiting for Hyma. I don't know when or how Jogarao caught Suryanarayana, but I do know after meeting the young man a couple of times that an educated woman like Hyma would never find a better husband. You must believe me when I say that if that marriage had taken place, I would have instantly changed my opinion about Jogarao without the slightest hesitation.

But there was an unexpected hurdle to Jogarao's victory. Hyma said she did not want to remarry.

She said sharply, 'My grandmother used to say that widow remarriages were like widows. Cursed. That is true.'

Jogarao was speechless. 'What? What? What?'

'These widow remarriages don't work. There is always some problem', she said.

'Nonsense! Even ordinary marriages are like that, if it comes to that matter', said Jogarao, probably thinking of his own marriage.

'It makes no difference how those marriages turn out. They are offerings to the deity of society! They ensure the salvation of the parents. If those marriages don't take place, girls will become untouchables. After going through a marriage like that, to go through another one! Is it not foolish to marry without anyone's support and disregard the fact that people do not approve?' asked Hymavathi in one breath.

'Why are you saying this? What does it matter to you how other widow remarriages end up? You marry only if you find a husband you like in all respects. If you don't find one you like, don't marry', said Jogarao.

'That is what I too am saying', said Hyma.

The next evening, like a juggler pulling something out of a basket, Jogarao produced Suryanarayana from somewhere!

The first day Jogarao did not pay attention to their conversation. He was watching Suryanarayana and Hymavathi with a thousand eyes. But when he listened to their conversation, his heart turned to water.

'Personally, I dislike men intensely', said Hymavathi. Suryanarayana answered gently, smiling, 'I feel the same way about women.'

The two of them discussed this for a couple of hours without any need for Jogarao's intervention or any tension. After two hours Suryanarayana rose and said, 'It's getting late. I will leave.' To Jogarao, this sounded as if he meant, the sun may rise tomorrow but I definitely won't be there.

But Jogarao was mistaken. Because Suryanarayana came back the next day. And then? The discussion started from the point it had stopped the previous day.

It didn't even sound like a discussion to Jogarao's ears. It sounded like wild dogs barking. Suryanarayana spoke against women, and Hymavathi held forth against men—between them they had stripped human nature bare. Suryam did not think, 'The person on the other side is a woman, let me be gentle', nor did Hyma make any attempt to attract or win the praise of Suryam. And she made no attempt to present the feminine aspect of her character.

Jogarao wondered about the fate of their family if these two decided to marry.

He did not like the manner of discussion or the topics they discussed either. After they had discussed human nature, they talked about love. And that, so intensely!

In Jogarao's opinion, a couple contemplating marriage must not speak about love in the presence of a third person. If they did, they should discuss it graciously, not hack it to pieces. He couldn't understand.

No sooner had Suryanarayana mentioned love than Hyma retorted, 'I don't believe in love. It is possible to live without love just as it is possible to live without a hair on your head.'

Jogarao died nearly three deaths as soon as Hyma completed that statement!

'I believe in love', said Suryanarayana loudly. 'I pity your ignorance. After wealth, love is the most important thing in the world!'

Hyma, pretending to be surprised, said, 'For the same person to speak of love and wealth in the same moment is perhaps not our tradition. Americans...'

'Dharma, artha, kama, moksha! Artha, then kama. Even the order is as I said it. So my tradition is not American. We don't need tradition. Think a little and you will see. Life without wealth is impossible. To live without love is to live without fulfilment', said Suryam.

'Why?' said Hyma.

'Till we love, we cannot understand what powers we have. Even the good in us does not surface till then. At least that is my experience. After my mother died, I became a very bad fellow. I have the capacity to tell the truth, the intelligence to decide justly, the capacity to sacrifice. The courage to speak the truth, to decide justly, are all in me, but who can I practice them on? Who will bring them out in me? I can't be like Satya Harischandra with everyone.'

Hyma said sarcastically, 'If love is so important to you, why don't you just love someone and end your problems?'

Jogarao listening to all this was simmering. He had never seen such terrible misconduct before. If someone had spoken to him like that, he would have thumped him. He wondered what Suryam was thinking about Hyma. Listening to this conversation, Jogarao was angry with one and then the other as they talked. Suryam was a useless fellow. Why was he letting a mere girl talk like this to him? How could any romance bloom if they talked of human nature and love so bluntly? On the other hand, once the conversation begins, they can love each other, their hearts can melt for each other. Jogarao feared that this was not happening.

Suryam replied to Hymavathi's question, 'There is no such thing as loving. That is the illusion that has brought forth all these tales. A man loves a woman. She doesn't love him back. He is heartbroken and dies. All tales. The truth is one lusts for another but cannot love. Love needs the efforts of both. So, in love, we don't love anyone. Someone earns our love. This has not happened to me yet. I have not earned that love from anyone. So, I have not married. I do not believe that one can marry and then love. After marrying and living together, anyone will develop some mutual affection. But that affection is not a substitute for love. Though there may be people who think so.'

Jogarao was troubled by this. It seemed false, a pretence. This was how someone who can't sacrifice for love would talk.

'Why should I try to earn the love of someone who is not willing to earn mine?' asked Suryam.

'Do you believe in morality?' asked Hymavathi.

Jogarao covered his ears. He had failed in changing the track of their conversation.

'I have a lot of faith in morality. I can't deny the faith of ten crore people. But I feel people give undue importance to morality. ('What nonsense!' thought Jogarao.) If morality is so important, why is it everyone violates it every day in life? How is it possible? And so I reject morality only if I have a very strong reason. That seems the right thing to do', said Suryanarayana.

This went on for a week. Jogarao was utterly confused. He was angry with them. He was tortured by the fact that it seemed impossible to get them on the right path. Even now, perhaps he could put them on the right path. Finally, his desire triumphed. One day as he was walking Suryanarayana out, he said, 'Look Suryanarayana! I want to tell you something. I don't know what you think about Hyma. She is very intelligent and sensible. She is not talking to you properly for some reason. She is hiding her true nature and desires.'

Suryam was surprised. 'I never thought that she was not intelligent and wise. I understood this from the very beginning. Your words put me in doubt!' Jogarao was stunned for a minute, but collecting himself quickly, he said, 'If you both get married, I would be very happy.'

'If I marry her, it will be for my happiness or hers, not for some third person's', Suryam replied sternly.

***

'You put him on the wrong track', said Jogarao to Hyma on the way home.

'What happened?' she asked.

'You did not manage to attract him at all. I tried to talk to him', Jogarao said helplessly.

Hyma laughed and said, 'Do you think he comes here daily for you, Babai?'

Jogarao was stunned.

The next day when Suryanarayana came, they took up the discussion where they had left it. But Hyma took charge of the discussion that day.

'I do not believe in morality', said Hymavathi. 'But it is not possible for a woman to live without morality. However, I have the courage to live immorally for love. If I can give up my morality for someone, then it means that I love that person. Or if any person is able to ensure that I live morally, it means I love him.'

'Rubbish', thought Jogarao. 'Not a single word has meaning or context. If you just say the word love where is the romance? It is an ordinary word.' But he simply grunted and stayed quiet.

Suryanarayana placed a cigarette in his mouth and searched his pocket for a matchbox. Hymavathi got up and brought a matchbox and lit his cigarette.

After Suryanarayana left, Jogarao said to Hyma firmly, 'When you are not willing to marry him, I don't think it is proper for you to say "I don't believe in morals, I will give up morals for love", Hyma! That is not feminine grace. Nor was it proper for you to have lit his cigarette. If your marriage was fixed, then none of those things would've mattered.'

Hyma said in surprise, 'But I am willing to marry him this minute. What are you saying?'

'But he is not ready to marry you, okay?… And may I know from when you decided you could marry him?'

'Couldn't you see that from the beginning we were trying to attract each other?'

'Attracting? Fighting?'

'What fighting? We were trying to understand each other. That is the right thing to do. Otherwise if he had just said, "I love you. Will you marry me?", what would I know about him?'

Jogarao's face fell and he was quiet. The next day, when Suryam arrived, Hyma was busy. Taking this opportunity, Jogarao asked Suryam, 'I want to ask if our Hyma attracted you in any way?'

'I must say she has attracted me. I know she will not lie to me. If I win her love, I know she will never deceive me. A man must have that confidence in the woman he wants to marry. There is nothing more pitiable than having to feel jealous of one's wife.'

'Hyma seems to like you. What could the reason be?' asked Jogarao.

Suryam thought for a while, 'It could be my money. It is not that I don't have other good qualities, but they are not equal to money. I can say I am worthy of earning love. A man without money is not worthy of earning another's love. In my family, a big man developed a relationship with a woman who was entering prostitution and earned her love. But he soon lost all his money and couldn't even feed her. I call that betrayal.'

Speechless, Jogarao asked, 'Will you be satisfied if someone looks after you well because of your money?'

'Won't I be happy if someone likes me for my looks? Won't I be happy if someone loves me because I'm intelligent? It's the same with my money. Just as my face and my intelligence are linked to my character, so is my money. Without that, I will speak differently. I will look different', answered Suryam.

Jogarao thought, 'It was my foolishness to provoke you.' He was heartbroken. He felt that Hyma and Suryam were trying to make a fool of him. He could not grasp the secret of their relationship. But he knew for sure that it was not love. If this was love, either he or they were mad.

Suryanarayana had some debts. Only propertied people had debts. As the pressure grew, he went to his village to settle matters.

From the moment he left, Hymavathi changed. She was nervous. She was distracted. She didn't reply when spoken to. Jogarao couldn't understand. At first, he thought Hymavathi was deceiving him. But as days passed, it was obvious that Hyma was suffering. Once, he even saw tears in her eyes.

When asked the reason, she said, 'Suryam did not know how much debt he was in. He will have nothing left. I saw the letter his people wrote him. What is my fate now?'

'Your fate?'

'If he will not marry me, why did you let him come to our house, Babai? Can another person ever attract me in the same way?'

'If you care so much, why don't you marry him even if he is poor? Like he said, do you care for him because of his money?'

'You won't understand. Without that money to back him, he will be like any other husband. The man who attracted me was not like other men.'

'This is utter nonsense!' said Jogarao.

In a few days, there was a letter from Suryam. 'My luck hasn't deserted me', he wrote. 'I have received an offer. The girl brings a dowry of twenty-five thousand rupees. I have not lost the right to love you.'

'I didn't understand the last bit', said Jogarao doubtfully.

Her face blooming after so long, Hyma said, 'I do!'

Written 1940

Source: 'Kottapaddatulu' by Kodavatiganti Kutumbarao (*Kodavatiganti Kutumbarao Rachana Prapancham: Kathalu 1938–1947*, edited by Krishna Bai and Chalasani Prasad, Hyderabad: Viplava Rachayitala Sangham, 2009, pp. 155–63)

Sri Sri

Srirangam Srinivasa Rao (1910–83)—'Sri Sri' to the Telugu public—was born in Visakhapatnam. A path-breaking writer and pioneer of the progressive movement in literature, he deployed a style and metre unknown till that time in Telugu literature, and shifted the subject of poetry to the human predicament in the contemporary era. His use of free verse in *Mahaprastanam* stands to this day beyond comparison. A recipient of the Soviet Land Nehru Award, he was a leading figure in VIRASAM (Revolutionary Writers' Association).

Difference

You, the fortunate ones
Love the light and hate darkness.
Bronze walls separate good and evil for you.

Your thoughts travel
only in the good room
A room built long ago
So your lives are like meals served out on leaves.
Riveted certainties yours
About good
About honour and courtesy
About conduct, superiority and values
Riveted certainties yours.

The looks from your eyes straight lines!
If the line breaks you create havoc
The ones on the other side of the line are all criminals.
To protect that border
Courts, police and armed forces
Prisons and gallows.
The border must be protected.

We are the unfortunate ones
We traverse twilights without borders
We are filled with doubts and dilemmas.
Darkness amid light
We see glow-worms in the dark
In a hundred flaws, one virtue
In a hundred virtues, one horror.
Differences, counter strokes
At each and every step
We have to cook our own food
Sometimes we don't find even a leaf.
The narrow lanes of life
attract us.

Our vision, a circular path
Without beginning or end.
Twilight beings, doubting minds
Questions, only questions
Answers never satisfying.
We have no walls
Our mission is to demolish walls.

Unrest is our very life
Agitation our breath
Rebellion our scripture.
However many thorns, stones and obstacles
The forward path is ours.

Sufficient unto you the space you inhabit
Some will even want to retreat further.

We will march forward
The world will follow.

You will die satisfied
The world will forget you.

Those who did not count troubles
For their convictions
Will join us.

Those who can switch opinions
And desire comforts
Will join you.

Written 1937

Source: 'Vyatyasam' by Srirangam Srinivasa Rao (*Mahaprastanam*, Hyderabad: Visalandhra Publishing House, 2010, pp. 55–57)

Tripuraneni Gopichand

Tripuraneni Gopichand (1910–62) was a short-story writer and novelist known for introducing psychoanalysis in Telugu creative writing in his novel *Asamardhuni Jeevana Yatra. Cheekati Gadulu* and *Pandita Parameswara Sastri Veelunama* are among his celebrated novels. Known for his progressive views, Gopichand was deeply influenced by M.N. Roy's radical humanism, and later by Sri Aurobindo's philosophy.

Hindu Pativratyam

The doctor, the pleader and the priest were arguing that even a tamarind fruit would not fall off a tree in our country because of logic, arguments and debates. Gopi sat listening.

Sastri and the doctor never got on. Brought up in very different backgrounds, neither liked the other's opinions. The doctor liked western culture. This infuriated Sastri who said, 'Praising western civilisation is slavery. Each culture has its own greatness. Did you ever read what Premchand said?

> "England is famous for its trade.
> France, for its women of leisure.
> Germany is famous for its armies.
> The Hindu country is famous for its pativratyam."[1]

What is the use of wagging your tongue without knowing all this?'

These words annoyed the doctor, but without showing his feelings he said, 'I agree with you. But pativratyam is connected to women. And to married women. Not all the women in our country are married, are they? To hang on to a married woman's chastity and

[1] wifely chastity

link it to the country is the work of old hags. It just demonstrates our slave mentality. Tell me, what are all the rest of us great at?'

Sastri had no answer. He couldn't think that fast. 'We are not sitting quiet, are we? We are guarding that chastity', he said.

'Hey! What is that talk? You have put a mighty task on men!' said the pleader.

The doctor was not quiet. Tossing his cigarette out of the window, he said, 'How? By sitting and munching peas?'

Sastri was angry. He really liked peas. So this infuriated him. But the doctor was talking away without giving him a chance.

'Let us agree that chastity is flowering bountifully in our country. But it only indicates that something has not been done. We should be able to talk about the greatness of the work we do because some of that work brings development and good to people. In what way are we great, tell me?'

'Don't say "in protecting pativratyam", babu', the pleader warned the sastri, 'because we may have to eat peas again.'

Gopi and the doctor burst into laughter.

Sastri's anger grew. 'It is because of people like you that the country is in this state...', he began. But the doctor didn't let him speak. 'But you say our country is great!' he mocked.

'In the matter of women! In the matter of women!' corrected the pleader.

Just then, there was a sound of shouting and commotion outside. Dropping their argument, all four rushed out.

There was a big crowd on the road. Women from neighbouring houses were watching the fun. They were talking to each other and enjoying themselves.

There was an old woman and her daughter in the middle of the crowd. The daughter was looking desperately for a way to escape from the crowd. Meanwhile a jatka came in from somewhere. A man jumped out, caught the girl forcibly, and threw her into the cart. She was kicking, but, pushing her feet aside, he got into the cart. The cart moved. The horse galloped. They vanished in a minute.

The mother was wailing and beating her head and mouth. 'Now he won't let my daughter live. He won't let her live.'

All this happened while they were all watching. No one interfered or questioned them.

Gopi was surprised. It seemed inhuman. He called an old man in the crowd and asked him, 'What is this?'

'That boy's wife, babu. He took her away.'

'Why the force?' asked Sastri.

'That girl was refusing to go. It is all that mother's fault. She won't send her to her husband.'

The doctor listened with interest, watching Sastri with sidelong looks.

Sastri asked, 'What more does a mother want than a daughter's happiness? Why won't she send her?'

'She is a wretched widow, babu. She uses the girl to fill her belly.'

'Ah?' said Sastri. The doctor belched. The pleader yawned, snapping his fingers.

'Yes, babu. She set up a business in this town.' And the man went away.

'Poor thing. Will he take her away and kill her?' asked Gopi feeling sorry for her.

'He won't kill her. He will protect her chastity', said the doctor.

Sastri was furious. 'What do you care what he does? She is his wife. Didn't he kiss her when he wanted to? When he wants to kill her, he will. Should he just watch quietly if she refuses to live with him?'

'So living with an unwilling wife is his funeral?' said Gopi.

'What is willingness? She is his wife, whether she likes it or not. Once she is his wife, she is his wife. Even the court will say the same thing.' Saying this Sastri looked at the pleader for help.

The pleader said, 'Yes, the court will say that. Unless she can prove threat to her life, a wife cannot live away from her husband. That is very difficult to prove. Because, in our country, fear for life and losing life do not happen at different times.'

'Then those two have no choice but to live together?' asked Gopi in wonder.

'The wife has to. No sastra can force the husband to', was the answer.

'While the wife is manufacturing pativratyam in the home, the husband will be busy buying warmth in another house', said the doctor.

'No! Peas!' corrected the pleader.

'What pativratyam! How carefully it is being protected in our country! Hindu society', said the doctor in disgust.

'Hindu society is like this. It is rotting away. We are trying to cover this up and live with self-deception. In Hindu society, father and son don't get on. Daughter and father don't get on. Daughter and mother. Son and mother, mother-in-law and daughter-in-law don't get on. Wife and husband don't get on. No one gets on with anyone else. But all of them have to live in one house under the same roof. They have to sit behind closed windows to prevent the foul smell from coming out.'

The doctor looked at the sastri mischievously and began to hum slowly.

'England is famous for trade.
France, famous for women of leisure.
Germany, famous for armies.
Famous!
Famous!
Famous!'

Source: 'Hindu Pativratyam' by Tripuraneni Gopichand (*Gopichand Rachana Sarvasvam*, Volume 1, edited by Krishna Bai and Chalasani Prasad, Vijayawada: Alakananda Prachuranalu, 2009, pp. 56–59)

Boyi Bhimanna

Boyi Bhimanna (1911–2005) was born in Mamidikuduru in East Godavari. He was a prolific writer, translator and playwright, writing in English and Telugu. He was also a freedom fighter and a follower of Mahatma Gandhi and Dr Ambedkar. Bhimanna held important academic positions and headed the Andhra Pradesh State Translation Division. He received the Padma

Bhushan in 2001. Born to a poor dalit family, his writings reflected the suffering of dalits and oppressed peoples. His play *Paleru* created a stir, and his poem *Gudiselu Kaalipotunnaayi* is well-known.

The Huts Are Burning

The huts are burning!
Oh, they are burning!

Whose huts are they, the poor souls?
They must be mala or madiga!
Who else lives in huts?

Many people may have them
It is the culture of this country!
But then—these huts
Are burnt down at least once a year

But then these huts burnt down once
Where do they come from
To be burnt down again?

Yes, that is true.
Where do they spring from?

That is the secret of our dharma
The secret of its true foundation
These huts appear
    springing up again and again
They burn and they are reborn!
How long will this vicious cycle last?
Till the secret is known to the
    dwellers of the huts!

Source: Excerpt from *Gudiselu Kaalipotunnaayi* by Boyi Bhimanna (Hyderabad: Bhimanna Sahiti Nidhi Trust, 1973, pp. 1–2)

Kaloji Narayana Rao

Kaloji Narayana Rao (1914–2002), known as 'prajakavi' ('people's poet') in Telangana, was a freedom fighter, civil libertarian and resistance poet who wrote in Hindi, Urdu, Telugu and Marathi. His major work, *Naa Godava*, brings together his poetry, short stories and translations, and is hailed as a critical commentary on contemporary political history. Kaloji received the Padma Vibhushan in 1992.

The Cycle

Dawn
To think it will never come
Is despair
To think it will remain
Is greed.
This darkness will not last
The sun
Will certainly rise again.
That light will not last
The sun
Will certainly set again.
For those who open their eyes
In the dark
The light is frightening.
For those who open their eyes
In the light
Darkness is a veritable demon.
Thus it has been
In the past.

Thus it will remain
Unchanged in the future.

Written 1951

Source: 'Punaravrutti' by Kaloji Narayana Rao (*Naa Godava*, Warangal: Kaloji Foundation, 2012, p. 35)

CHAGANTI SOMAYAJULU

Chaganti Somayajulu (1915–94), known as 'Chaso', was born in Srikakulam and went to school in Vizianagaram. He served as president of the Abhyudaya Rachayitala Sangham (ARASAM), the Progressive Writers' Association. Chaso's unique style made him popular as a writer of short stories, several of which were translated into other languages.

Soapnut Leaves

Appala Naidu's daughter Paramma and Chinadevudu's daughter Gaviri were going through the village to the fields. Appala Naidu was a well-to-do farmer. Chinadevudu owned only the loincloth on his body. So, Paramma wore a silk skirt and a rose-coloured half sari. Gaviri tucked her skirt between her legs and carried a bundle of twigs and an iron tray. Paramma wore corals on her neck. Her hands and feet had silver kadas. Her ears and nose bore golden rings.

'It's damned tasty', said Paramma.

'What?' asked Gaviri.

'Pickle!'

'From where?'

'Landlord. He gave my father some.'

Her father was Appala Naidu. So, the landlords would give pickle and even curry if he asked.

'I ate prawns with my rice', said Gaviri.

She lied. She wanted to boast.

Gaviri looked at Paramma's skirt with envy and felt her own skirt.

'Damned boast. Who doesn't know? There isn't even a grain in your house. Last night you didn't even light a fire. My father said you don't even have water to drink. She ate prawns! Prawns!'

And Paramma, swinging her arms high and low, mocked her.

'Last night we had no food? Oh, you whore! Who told you? Ask my mother. Last night we ate rice and munellam fish curry', said Gaviri. 'Her father is a big Naidu in the village. He went to the market and brought munellam for the curry and chanduvaru[1] fish for the dry curry', said Paramma.

Feeling small, Gaviri turned towards the paddy heaps. Paramma followed her, swinging her arms.

The schoolchildren in the village began their prayer. 'Mother, we think of you!' the master prompted. 'Mother, we think of you!' the children shouted, shattering the town.

Paramma and Gaviri went into the thicket. They were treading their path with care.

The mogali[2] tree's branches and roots had reached the ground.

'I am going to school on Tuesday. Master garu said it's a good day and my father agreed to send me.'

'Why this beggarly study?' said Gaviri.

'What do you mean "why study"? Listen to how they are singing!'

'Master garu asked my father also. "Why study for one who is a coolie?" my father asked.'

'Yes! Your father is a coolie. Mine is a Naidu!'

Gaviri felt her throat choke with grief and her eyes filled with tears.

The chameleon made a big sound in the heap of leaves. The oleander tree leaning on the mud wall was in full bloom and had

---

1 *munellam* and *chanduvaru* are varieties of fish

2 fragrant screwpine (kewda)

shed half the flowers in the thicket. Para picked four flowers and put them in her hair. Gaviri also picked a few and thrust them into her hair. She felt her small pot-sized knot of hair.

'Bale, Para, see! I have such a pot-sized knot. There is no hair on your head', she said, looking at Para.

'Why do I need that coconut fibre? See how much oil I have applied. There is no oil in your hair', Para said.

The schoolchildren were still praying, tearing their throats. Para began to hum with them.

'Sarasvati', said the schoolchildren.

'Saraspati', said Para.

'Namastubhyam', said the schoolchildren.

'Namattubbem', said Para.

'You can sit here and sing. I have to gather wood', said Gaviri, going towards the paddy heaps. Para went after her. Gaviri was eight years old. But she bore a mountain-load of family burdens. Carrying a small pot on her head, she had to go the temple pond and carry all the water for her family. Carrying a basket, she would go to all the groves and thickets and collect dry leaves, sticks and thorns needed for cooking one meal for the family. Gaviri bore all that responsibility.

There were bunches and bunches of green gram in the neighbouring fields. Paramma plucked a few branches and was eating the gram. Gaviri's stomach was burning. She had not had a grain since that morning. She had not eaten the previous night either.

'Olemma! I am hungry', she had cried that night.

'Oley, don't cry. There is nothing in the house', comforted her mother. She cried herself to sleep, hungry.

Gaviri was a coolie's daughter. She didn't have the guts to steal from some field and eat. Even small thefts by the poor became huge crimes. What well-off people did was just shrugged off. Paramma was plucking plants and eating them along the way. She was fearless.

'If they see, your head will break', said Gaviri.

'Who will see? Even if they do, I am Appala Naidu's daughter. Their face, what will they say?' said Para.

Gaviri's stomach was burning. She imagined a bowl full of gruel and a dry chilli to go with it. Where would it come from? Her father, Chinadevudu, was a coolie. If he brought something home, they could eat at night. Or else, they slept hungry. Gaviri's eyes filled with tears.

The soapnut tree had shed leaves across the path. Gaviri forgot her hunger when she saw those leaves. Soapnut leaves were the thickest leaves of all. A few leaves would fill her basket. She dusted the leaves, collected them in the basket and pressed them down. Her duty for the day was over. The basket was full. Her heart grew light, and both of them went homeward.

Paramma set out talking loudly. They reached Kambhukta garu's paddy heap. They were walking past the heap under the tamarind tree. Something fell with a plop in front of them.

'Olemma! A scorpion!' yelled Para, startled.

'Not a scorpion, it's a crab', said Gaviri.

It must have fallen from a crane's mouth, thought Gaviri, looking up at the tree. The crown of the tamarind tree was full of cranes. It was as if the tamarind had bloomed white lotuses.

'How many tamarind bunches', said Gaviri. Paramma lifted her head to look and her mouth watered. She threw stones and three tamarinds fell. She bit into one and tucked the other two into her silk skirt.

'Oley, Para! Won't you give me one?' asked Gaviri.

'If you want, you pluck them', said Para.

'Oley! Oley!' begged Gaviri.

'Those stones', Para pointed, and went away.

Gaviri lifted her head to see the tamarinds hanging like sickles.

Fearfully, Gaviri threw a stone. That stone fell down with a thump.

Frightened by the sound, she looked in four directions.

Paramma got into the fields in search of green gram. Gaviri threw another stone.

Although no fruit fell, a big dry branch slipped from the tree and fell down.

Gaviri hooped in joy. She cried in joy, and breaking the branch, she stacked it in her basket.

'Who is there?' came a shout from the paddy heaps. That shout sounded like thunder to Gaviri.

She looked at the paddy heap. Kambhukta garu stood in front of her. Scratching her head with one hand and not knowing what to do with the other, Gaviri was bent like a bow. Bhukta garu looked at her with angry red eyes.

'For the fire', said Gaviri, shivering.

Bhukta garu went at her. He saw the soapnut leaves and the tamarind twigs in her basket. He raised his foot, shod in a wooden sandal. He kicked the basket forcefully. The leaves and basket flew away. Gaviri, shivering, picked up the basket and went to pick up the leaves.

'Whore! You are still picking', he growled. He had no idea how valuable the rubbish Gaviri had collected was. The rubbish Gaviri gathered was precious for Chinadevudu's family. That rubbish was enough for a day's fire. That Gaviri knew. Although she was eight, she knew its worth. Her heart was fluttering for that rubbish.

'Babu garu, I will never come again', she begged. Bhukta garu looked around. He found a reason.

'What have you hidden behind that rubbish?' he asked.

'I didn't hide anything', she said. He poked the pile with his stick. A pile of dung appeared. The theft was out. He hit her on the back with his stick and said, 'What is this?'

'Ammoyi, I am dead! It's not mine, baboyi', she said.

'Whose else, you whore?' And he hit her again.

Gaviri didn't understand. Even though she was saying no, he was hitting her. She was shocked that he couldn't understand what he was being told.

But her tears gave her courage. She was not a thief, and so she was brave. She stopped crying and reddening her eyes.

'Not me. Look at my basket and my hands.' Her basket and hands were not stained with dung. The field hands had done that job. But Bhukta garu didn't have any sense. He hit her again with the stick. Although she told him firmly, he hit her.

'Oh, you bastard!! It's not me! Olemma, it's not me. You bastard!!'

Starting with abuse, she moved on to swearing. Gaviri began to swear. She kept abusing Bhukta garu who had buried many great people!

Bhukta garu removed his sandal and threw it at her. It hit her ankle bone with a snap. She fell down, her face in the mud. She curled up and struggled like a chicken with its throat slit.

After crying bitterly, Gaviri opened her eyes. It was getting late. The schoolchildren were reciting their tables. 'Three times seven is twenty-one', they were shouting. They were singing the tables.

Gaviri looked at the paddy heap. There was no one there. She picked up the soapnut leaves that had fallen. If she left the leaves, there was nothing for the fire. Whether her parents brought food to cook on the fire or not, Gaviri must bring something to feed the fire.

'You bastard. No one wants your tamarind twigs', and she left them behind. She put the basket on her head. Her leg was burning. Then she bent and looked at her leg. There was a swelling on her leg where the shoe had struck. It was reddish.

'Olemma', she went weeping into the thicket. The schoolchildren were still reciting their tables.

'Sixteen sixes are ninety-six', one was shouting.

'Sixteen sixes are ninety-six', all of them were singing together.

Written 1943

Source: 'Kunkudaku' by Chaganti Somayajulu (*Noorendla Telugu Kathalu*, edited by Mudiganti Sujata Reddy and Sangisetti Srinivas, Hyderabad: Potti Sreeramulu Telugu University, 2011, pp. 190–94)

VATTIKOTA ALWARUSWAMY

Vattikota Alwaruswamy (1915–61), born in Madaram Kalan, Nalgonda, was active in the communist movement in Telangana, and was jailed for his political activity by the Nizam's government. He was a leader of the Andhra Mahasabha in

Nalgonda, and of the library movement. He was a publisher and a writer. His novel *Prajala Manishi* is particularly well known.

Man of the People

A frightened Venkatadri left Nizamabad and, on reaching Dhimmegudem, described the situation in detail to Rambhupal Rao. Listening to the terrible crimes thrust upon Kanthiravam and Komarayya, they were horrified. Rambhupal Rao went to Hyderabad to talk to the Arya Samajis.

Venkatadri talked to Chandrayya every day. Talking about this and that, he gradually convinced him to think of Rambhupal Rao as someone he could trust. Because they trusted Chandrayya, other farmers too began to look upon him favourably. Basically, the tensions caused by Komarayya's land dispute changed into a feeling of enmity towards Muslims. They also turned on the harijans and harassed them for the loans they had taken as labourers, and the extra grain they had received with wages earlier. They stopped calling women to labour in the farms or for any other work, and yelled at those who came. The conversion occurred exactly during the cropping season, and took a toll on the economic life of the harijans. The support from the anjuman[1] went down. The anjuman preacher went now and then to Nizamabad and stayed longer and longer, and came rarely to Dhimmegudem. The hut built for the preacher gradually collapsed. First the palm leaves, then the sticks, and finally the rafters, all fell down. So, the preacher's house was there only in name. He began to stay at Hyder Ali's house. Hyder Ali found it difficult to bear him. The pressure of the converted grew gradually. Hyder Ali also went to Nizamabad and consulted the anjuman leaders, but the plans and schemes of the anjuman leaders did not look as if they would yield immediate results. If the villagers behaved like that, it would amount to social boycott. So, the anjuman leaders told Hyder Ali that he could bring such accusations against the villagers. When this was revealed to the harijans in the village, they were afraid that the enmity in the village would grow.

---

1 (Urdu/Persian) congregation (of believers)

Komarayya, acquitted of the charge of waging war on the state, reached Dhimmegudem. Following Kanthiravam's instructions, he brought Parandamayya with him so that they could run a night school, a library, and a bhajan group in Dhimmegudem. Parandamayya was a close friend of Kanthiravam and his companion in all matters.

Rambhupal Rao, who went to Hyderabad, brought an Arya Samaj preacher called Vijayadevu with him to Dhimmegudem. Rambhupal Rao's self-confidence grew when he heard the preaching of the Hyderabadi Arya Samajis. As an elder of the village, he wanted to use all his power to stop Hyder Ali's games. That way he would not only regain his earlier influence in the village, but also be known for his social service. This thought calmed him.

One day, when Hyder Ali was not in town, Rambhupal Rao called all the harijans into his gadi.[1]

'You became Muslims hastily and so you are suffering the consequences. You must have understood Hyder Ali's deceit by now. I know how much hardship you suffer each day. How can I as the lord of this village stay quiet seeing you, who were born and bred in this village and live here, suffer for food? I will talk to all the farmers, and see that you get back your work and your jobs as before. You have nothing to fear.' Rambhupal Rao sermonised, and asked his servants to measure out five seers of grain for each of them. Immediately, Vijayadevu performed a purification ceremony and converted them back to Hinduism. Then, taking advantage of the situation, he preached to the harijans.

'With a tradition of lakhs of years and spreading knowledge to the whole world, that you who belong to the Arya family should take to another religion is unfortunate. To forget dharma and greatness, just to fill your bellies temporarily, is a matter of grief. At least now that God has given you good sense, we should be grateful to Parameswara.'

The harijans looked at each other's faces and, with kumkum bottus[2] on their foreheads and bags of paddy on their shoulders,

---

1 landlord's mansion

2 vermilion mark on forehead

went home. They got back their jobs and their wages. Begari[1] started again. They returned to their old state.

Hyder Ali was stunned when he saw the changed circumstances after he returned. He was afraid to even go to the harijanawada. Holding his head, he sat at home without moving. Hyder Ali stayed away in Nizamabad with his family for some time.

This disturbance, this boastfulness, the violence, accusations, law courts, arguments, Hindu-Muslim religious preaching, brought about a change in the lives of the villagers—a peculiar mindset, a way of thinking and a consciousness. With the help of Parandamayya, Komarayya set up a library and ran a night school and bhajans. Vijayadevu began to live in Rambhupal Rao's gadi. Now and then, he would give a sermon in the library. An important part of his talk would be about the government's corruption, religious bias, and, because everything was becoming Muslim, how Hindus were growing far away from their dignity and culture. Vijayadevu would keep going to Hyderabad now and then.

In some time, the situation returned to normal. The consciousness of the villagers grew. Parandamayya won the appreciation of the people. He became an intimate friend and mingled with all. The peasants began to whisper to Parandamayya about Rambhupal Rao's administration.

Parandamayya thought that he should try to use Vijayadevu, who was close to Rambhupal Rao, to raise these matters. Rambhupal Rao's habit of taking bribes, mamool,[2] bullying peasants into working without any rewards, and particularly Komarayya's land issue, which was a very important matter to clear.

Once, when Vijayadevu came to the library and was chatting, Komarayya came and raised the issue with Parandamayya. Komarayya went and sat beside Vijayadevu.

'Sir, the peasants want to discuss some matters with you. They feel that the people will benefit if you open your heart to their problems. Rambhupal Rao as the village head is doing many unjust things. You may or may not have noticed. You are very fond of Rambhupal

---

1 bonded labour

2 a routine bribe

Rao and he trusts you. The people have been paying bribes and mamool since their grandfathers' and great-grandfathers' times. That is because of the people's ignorance. But things have changed. If you can talk to Rambhupal Rao about this, wouldn't it be good?' Parandamayya said to Vijayadevu.

Komarayya added, 'He swallowed my land unjustly, ayya.'

Vijayadevu thought deeply. 'Alright. I will definitely talk to him. I will do everything in my power', he said.

Vijayadevu said to Rambhupal Rao, 'See, sir. I want to say something. You called me here and asked me to serve the people. A man like you should conduct himself with some kindness and justice. The people will be happy. You have property and wealth. You are comfortable. If you think of the conditions and people's concerns, and give up bribes and corruption, it would be very good. If you consider Komarayya's land issue, it will seem as if we are taking care of our people. What do you say?'

As soon as Vijayadevu began his conversation, Rambhupal Rao felt as if centipedes were crawling all over him. Vijayadevu was good to talk to the people, but to dare enter a matter that concerned him was misconduct stepping beyond Vijayadevu's power.

'Have you finished? Or is there anything more?' asked Rambhupal Rao in a voice of authority.

Vijayadevu saw a new note in Rambhupal Rao's voice and also a slighting tone. He looked at Rambhupal Rao in astonishment. He said, 'Among the things I placed before you are matters that have already come to your notice.'

'These are village matters. If you enter this, there will be no limit. Compared to the expenses we incur, the bribes and mamool people give us do not even add up to the sweat on our palms. However, it is better you don't get involved in matters like this. I also do not like you going to the library. I've been meaning to tell you this for some time', said Rambhupal Rao harshly.

Vijayadevu felt as if he had been slapped. His self-respect gushed forth. He was about to say something.

'What more did he complain to you?' Rambhupal Rao questioned.

'If you think these are complaints, then I will not raise these matters with you. I will follow the path that I like', Vijayadevu rose, pained.

'This is like biting the hand that feeds you', said Rambhupal Rao.

Vijayadevu did not feel like standing there anymore. He took his clothes and belongings and said, 'I am taking leave now. I have no place in your house. Namaste.' And he left the gadi and walked to the library.

There was no one in the library. He turned over the books. Then he saw a book called *Rigvedadi Bhashyabhumika*, and turned it over. He opened it and began to read it seriously. The contents inspired Vijayadevu. He wondered why the Arya Samaj had not worked towards such a perfect system.

Parandamayya came and questioned him.

'I broke my relations with Rambhupal Rao. I don't intend to set foot there again.'

'It's gone so bad? Is it what we thought about?' asked Parandamayya agitated.

'This is our fault. What is the use of blaming others? This is the result of our closing our eyes', asserted Vijayadevu.

He gave the book *Rigvedadi Bhashyabhumika* to Parandamayya, and asked him to read the part that had interested him.

Parandamayya read with interest. His face brightened. 'We never read this book. It is a great book', he said.

'Till we create a perfect system like that, there is no use in anything we do. If Rambhupal Rao is so arrogant and anarchic, it is because the village folk are not united or aware of their responsibilities', he said.

Source: Excerpt from *Prajala Manishi* by Vattikota Alwaruswamy (Vijayawada: Visalandhra Publishing House, 1978, pp. 124–29)

Bucchi Babu

Sivaraju Venkata Subba Rao (1916–67), who wrote under the pen name 'Bucchi Babu', was born in Eluru and studied English literature. A novelist, short-story writer, essayist and playwright, he worked at All India Radio for two decades. His novel *Chivariki Migiledi* opened new pathways for the novel in Telugu literature.

What Is a Blade of Grass Worth?

In the western sky, the yawning red sun moved on to another world. The rest, unable to leave the light, groped towards darkness in a stupor. The stars sparkled in fear. The canal snaked its way into the darkness like a black serpent. Dayanidhi, sitting on the grassy banks of the canal gazing at the sky, smiled. The breeze fondled his body, awakening desire, rousing his blood, making it flow along new paths—the senses dimmed. Eyes stopped looking and the western sky revealed itself, its gash waning. The skies had stopped seeking the night; the stars shone fearlessly; the canal had stopped twisting its tail like a black serpent and grown calm; the blades of grass swayed gently; nature tranquil, in a state of total surrender; and he—all united into oneness, oblivious of reason or purpose.

Plucking a blade of grass, he wrapped it around his little finger. He lay down on the grass that seemed to cluster together with bent heads fearful of the breeze. His collar, moving in the breeze, tickled his ear.

'It is late. Come home, babugaru!'

Time, hour, place, home—where will these bonds go? Dayanidhi sat up.

'Home? Where are you coming from, Narayya?'

'I am taking the cow home. Get up, let's go. Ammagaru will be waiting for you.'

Dayanidhi got up and pulled his shirt down. He pulled out a blade of grass and threw it in the water.

'There was a big row at home in the afternoon, after you left. Father and your elder brother had a fight. He said, "If mother stays here, I won't stay. Either she or I should stay in this house." Father shouted at mother. Bhulakshmammagaru left by the five o'clock train. After Bhulakshmammagaru came, brother has been agitated.'

Dayanidhi did not speak… Narayya was trustworthy! Because he had worked in their house since he was young, it was alright for him to know the family quarrels. But it seemed undignified to discuss these matters with him.

'Narayya! You go home. I will stay a little longer and come.'

'Ammagaru said in tears that you had not even drunk your coffee in the afternoon, and asked me to look for you and bring you home quickly. Why did you come away in the afternoon? Kamakshi's daughter has not come back yet.'

Dayanidhi could not understand how he knew about this matter. He began to think. Kamakshi must have told him. Or else mother might have told him…

'Narayya! When is she coming back to town? Anyway… you go. Tell her I will go for a walk and come after an hour.'

Narayya tied the calf to his waist, removed a bidi from his turban, and lit it.

'Abbayigaru! You won't get angry, will you? I will tell you something. Why don't you marry soon?'

Narayya had not lost the capacity to laugh. There were no experiences in his life that he could sort out as happy or sorrowful. The night his wife eloped with Chandranna, he got ten people together and played 'catch me if you can' on the bank of the canal. In the morning, he went to Chandranna's house for a cup of hot tea. When Madhavayya's horse got sick, he was so worried that he did not even eat both his meals daily. When Lala sahib's goat's foot was swollen, he kept it under his cot and massaged it all night. He would laugh at whatever happened to him. He would weep for others' woes. That was Narayya's nature. Though he was worried about the events in Dasaratha Ramayyagaru's house, one of the many reasons for him to laugh was Abbayigaru coming to the canal bank.

Dayanidhi laughed to himself. Narayya knew everything. He was an old fellow and couldn't pretend he didn't know.

'Come, babugaru! There will be insects and bugs in the dark. Come quickly.'

Narayya left with the cow. The flock of cranes were shining in the moonlight. Some bird stirred the water. The grass blades were shivering lustfully. The trees in the distance, cloaked in darkness, began to whisper. The smoke from Narayya's bidi swirled to the moon. The moon shone dully, like a face heavy after an afternoon siesta in summer. Slothfulness. The moon stretched itself across.

Effortlessly walking into the town, Dayanidhi entered the yard of Kamakshi's house. There were no people in that lane. Three huts and two tiled houses. He stood like a shadow at the steps and saw his shadow on the door.

His shadow looked really good. His nose which looked so good in the shadow, looked so odd in the mirror? Komali's shadow must have fallen so often on that door… In that same place, he put a finger in his hair and shook it. How many times Komali would have walked on those steps! Why couldn't he turn into a step! He laughed to himself. When the shadow laughed, he was startled. Some noise came from his throat.

'Who is it? Mangamma, did you get the tamarind? Wait, I am washing my hair.'

He stepped back. So they came back in the evening. He peeped through the gaps in the door. He felt like someone who had committed a crime. He wondered what someone peeping from another door who saw him peeping like this would feel. When we think we are not observed, we do many things. We wonder what people will think if they see us, and we are afraid of doing those things. Our morality is a crack-in-the-door morality, he thought.

Source: Excerpt from *Chivariki Migiledi*, 'Gaddipocha Viluventa' by Bucchi Babu (Hyderabad: Visalandhra Publishing House, 2007, pp. 1–3)

Potlapalli Rama Rao

Potlapalli Rama Rao (1917–2001), born in Taatikaayala village in Warangal, was a progressive poet, playwright and novelist who enriched the intellectual environment in Telangana through his work. He was active in the freedom struggle and the Andhra Mahasabha in the 1940s, and his writing was a powerful critique of the Nizam's government and the feudal order in Telangana. *Chukkalu*, *Atmavedana*, *Aksharadeepti* and *Naalonenu* are among his best-known works.

Village and Forest

The sun was burning hot. The earth burnt, without a blade of grass, looked like a burning ghat. Under that sun that blazed like fire, I walked. The sun had drained all the strength in my body. My body was weak with thirst. No sign of water anywhere to quench my thirst.

'I am so angry.'

There was nothing else on my mind. In the distance, there was a village under green trees. Seeing those green trees and human dwellings, I felt new life, as if I had drunk water. I entered the village, stopped before a house, and shouted, 'Thirst!'

'Which is your village?'

He asked me that first! As if that were more important than thirst! I was too thirsty to tell him my name or village. I did not answer.

He stood still, as if to say he would not give me water if I did not tell him my name.

I did not like his standing like that.

I stood awhile and went to another house.

'Who are you?'

Again, the same question.

I did not like hearing the same question again. I grew a little angry.

'I am thirsty', I said.

'Why don't you answer when asked who you are?'

'Does it matter who, ayya… to give water?'

'Can't you say who you are?'

'For thirst what does it matter who it is?'

'Why does it bother you so much when asked who you are?'

I went from there to another house.

'What is your name?'

Again, the same question. I grew angrier.

'What does it matter who?'

'No! What is your name?'

'Some name!'

'What ayya? Tell me.'

'Abba! Name! Name! What does it matter what name?'

'Why are you so irritated?'

'Why do you weary a man who is dying of thirst for his name?'

I left the village in anger. After I left the village, I was angry at my own stupidity and impatience.

Because the village was gone and the forest had come. Where would I find water in the forest? Even if they did not need my name or village, the bushes and creepers were not going to give me water. I did not know what to do. I walked on like a mad man. My body was going out of my control. My legs began to tremble. I felt as if death were overpowering me, and my eyes began to darken. I was filled with the fear that I might die in the forest. Suddenly, I saw a small stream. I felt my departing life come back in the shape of the stream. I was overcome with happiness.

Travellers had made a pond by the water. I dipped my head and drank the water as if it were nectar. I was so happy to have found some water to quench my thirst. As I drank more and more, I worshipped that silent mother who gave me life a million times. But what made me most happy was that the pond did not ask me my name or my village. I felt this was something out of the ordinary, and was filled with unearthly joy.

Written 1953

Source: 'Ooru-Adavi' by Potlapalli Rama Rao (*Telangana Kathalu*, edited by Kaluva Mallayya, Sadanand Sarada and Chandra, Hyderabad: Visalandhra Publishing House, 2005, pp. 103–04)

KANCHANAPALLI CHINAVENKATARAMARAO

Kanchanapalli Chinavenkataramarao (1921–92) was born in Panagallu in Nalgonda and studied law. Active in the Andhra Mahasabha during his student days, he wrote poetry, essays, stories and plays. He practised as a lawyer, contested and won in the 1952 elections, and served as Deputy Speaker of the Legislative Assembly. His poetry collection *Aruna Rekhalu* and his short stories *Maa Vullo Kudaanaa* are well known.

Feast

The new revenue inspector (girdavar) had hardly gotten out of his car when the patel[1], patwari and other staff came to receive him in the courtyard. Within half an hour of his arrival, a syce of a big horse arrived followed by the chef (bavarchi) with cooking pots, et cetera. Twelve washermen came and unloaded these things. Girdavar saab had many advisors, and his right hand Chanda saab also reached there.

Chanda saab was the unpaid servant for all the revenue inspectors who came. His advantage was that he could eat good meals with free chicken curry. To every village, he was like a prime

1 village policeman

minister to the girdavar saab. The village folk gave him some small gifts of money along with the meals. This way, along with free meals, he used to get at least hundred rupees a month. The girdavar had no burden. If every girdavar had a Chanda saab, he would never lack the pomp or respect due to him. With the view that he was a source of income, every girdavar would recommend him to his successor when transferred to the next post.

The girdavar was doing his work. The patels and patwaris were all with him. It was twelve o'clock. Rats began to run around his stomach. 'Bring the food', he said to the bavarchi. 'The provisions have not come, sarkar!' said the bavarchi.

'Where did the potters and washermen go? If they had been sent to the komati houses, the provisions would have come. Don't you know this much, shameless fellow?!'

'Chanda saab and I went around. The komatis said that they would give the provisions only if we pay first. Not otherwise.'

'Why should you go around? Isn't that potter son-of-a-dog there to go around? This seems to be a peculiar town.'

'They also said that they would work only if they were paid.'

'The komatis and the workers seem to have come straight from London. I have not seen a village like this from the time I was born.'

Chanda saab came forward and said, 'Sarkar! This is a motherfucking village. The people in this village have become badmashes. They don't care for anyone's word. There is no control or order. Is it Arya Samaj or what? In Gulbarga, there was an Arya Samaji. I made him say "haro hara". These games won't work with me.'

The patel added, 'This is not the village of old. It is ruined completely. The custom of vetti labour on the farms for the landlords and for us is gone. The custom of making cow dung cakes is gone. When people like us came, we got some grass for the oxen. When big people like you came, the komatis used to give gram as fodder for the horses. It's all gone. Even the landlord, who is like Dharmaraja, is engaging servants to do his work. If that is the plight of the landlords, what is the chance for people like us? It's all topsy-turvy.' He poured out his woes.

The seth began his woes. 'The last girdavar was also a good man like you. Ask Chanda saab. These villagers used to fight with him also. That he had calculated the levies wrong, excused those who bribed him, and kept taxing the really worthy people. They gave a complaint against the girdavar saab. They said that is why he was transferred and that this victory was theirs.'

Patwari: 'The tahsildar is a just lord. He became a tahsildar from a clerk. He knows all these matters. Fortunately, we had someone who knew our difficulties; otherwise, we would have suffered a lot of hardship.' He was drawing out his words.

Then the patel intervened and said, 'Sarkar, it was our patwari's cousin who lit a spark in this village.'

'If he was your fellow, couldn't you control him? I am hungry, bhai', said the girdavar.

The patwari said, 'We don't get on with each other. He is trying to get me suspended and dismissed and grab the patwarigiri from me. That's why all these tricks.' The patwari threw in a clever remark in the middle.

Girdavar: 'Alright, we can see to that later, but what about my food? I will never allow the habit of paying for my food to enter my life. This is a matter of my pride.'

'Then I shall send you food from my house. Or if you want, you come. You can eat and leave', said the patwari.

Meanwhile, a pot-bellied man with a pyjama, sherwani and rumi topi appeared, saying, 'Adaab! Adaab!'

The patwari said, 'He is the landlord of our village. He is a very good man. In the past, if you mentioned his name, even the birds wouldn't drink water. He would keep everything in control.'

The dora continued, 'That is all an old story. In this kaliyug, evil has increased. Good times are ending. The apocalypse is near. Butter is fast drowning in the curds. Soon the whole world will drown. Everywhere you look, there are villains.' Then, as he was talking philosophy according to habit, he suddenly switched and, moving to polite enquiries, asked, 'Where are you coming from?'

'Even with people like you, the village is getting ruined while you watch. If every village becomes so badmash, even our authority will not survive. I can't think how my goods will pass through this village.' With hunger pangs in his belly, the girdavar showed his anxiety.

'Arey! Is it like that? Why didn't you tell me, pantulu? You could have come to my bungalow. Come to my house. You can have breakfast. We can talk about all matters there. Come along, Chanda saab', the dora invited all.

Thinking that his misfortune was over, the girdavar pricked up his ears and reached the house. The patel and patwari also followed the girdavar to the dora's house hoping that they could also get some share of the girdavar's feast…

Written 1947

Source: 'Daavatu' by Kanchanapalli Chinavenkataramarao (*Kanchanapalli Chinavenkataramarao Kathalu*, edited by Elikatte Shankara Rao, Hyderabad: Kanchanapalli Sahitya Protsahaka Samiti, 2012, pp. 43–46)

Devarakonda Balagangadhara Tilak

Devarakonda Balagangadhara Tilak (1921–66) was born in Mandapaka in West Godavari and educated in Visakhapatnam and Chennai. He lived and wrote in Tanuku, on the banks of the Godavari. A short-story writer and poet, his poetry anthology *Amrutham Kurisina Ratri* immortalised him in Telugu literature.

Letter from a Soldier

I am well here—
   you too there
Old mother, the old cot's legs
Our little boy
   The crane in the lake…

Now it is night, midnight
I can't think of anything
    There is a fear in me
The white frozen snow
    fringes the darkness of night
Far away in the next tent
    the sound of the corporal's boots
As if someone had fallen from a straw heap—
The snores of soldiers sleeping in the silence
Like the plea of dead souls.

Abba, it is cold!
    A cold that freezes the blood!
Even if I smoke a long cigarette
Lindel (the sin costs a rupee)
Lindel clutched to my chest
or its alcoholic liquid drunk
    the chill won't go.

My fear will not go
    Again in the morning
I have to cross deserts, rivers and forests.
Hide in trenches
Aeroplanes above
    Sten guns in hand
We are cardboard soldiers
Moving when wound up
March!
One, two, three, shoot dead! Who
You or me
Send a cablegram
c/o so and so
(Your son dead.)
In the unconsciousness of the anaesthetic
The spine stiffens like a stick

War, war
In Libya, in Berlin and in Stalingrad
Selfishness ran amok like a mad dog.

Abba! Shivering cold
All are sleeping
All dying
The clock striking the hour after midnight
Hits my face like a flame
I am no longer the man I was
I have no values
I have no feelings
Killing, being killed
like twirling my moustache
have grown into a habit.

Under the visible uniform
A great despair, a savagery
Secret, like the river under the bridge
Like quicksand one cannot escape
I am disgusted with myself
And so I will kill again and again
    I will drink again and again
Anything else, no one will approve.

It is daybreak
Faraway on the Alps
    the snow melts like grief
The rising sun rocks
    like a silver ship on the sea
When will I come back to our village!
Will I see you?

When your beautiful white smile
    ripples down your neck like a necklace
and your moist eyes
    open up like a peacock feather.

How long! How long!
These thousands of miles between us
Have turned into ages
Now goodbye, my dear!
Sleep comes heavily and darkly
Yonder before the tent
The sentry like a tombstone.

There
The sound of the corporal's boots
Like water swirling in my belly
Take care, my dear, take care
You, the children, the lizards, all.

Reply soon, my dear!
How long I wonder
Goodbye! Abba! It's cold!
The cold cuts like a knife through my heart
You touch my body with warmth.

Source: 'Sainikudi Uttaram' by Devarakonda Balagangadhara Tilak (*Amrutham Kurisina Ratri*, Hyderabad: Visalandhra Publishing House, 2006, pp. 21–23)

Rachakonda Viswanatha Sastri

Rachakonda Viswanatha Sastri (1922–93), known as Ravi Sastri, was born in Visakhapatnam. He went on to study law in Madras, and set up an independent practice. As a short-story writer, he focused his literary energies on sensitive portrayals of the lumpen proletariat. A founding member of Viplava Rachayitala Sangham (VIRASAM), he was imprisoned during the Emergency. His story collections *Aaru Saara Kathalu* and

Aaru Saaro Kathalu, and his novels *Rattalu-Rambabu* and *Raju Mahishi* are particularly well known.

Justice

A sudden stink of arrack.

Court.

Loud sounds of a market.

Court.

A snake pit of lies.

Court.

A highway to the prison yard.

Court.

(The distress of orphans. The muted groans of the helpless. The flowing tears of the poor.

That is a court, I feel like saying. But many will criticise me for writing sentimental sob stories, tearjerkers.)

It is half past eleven. Broad daylight. Light shadows in the magistrate's court.

The magistrate sits on the bench, his head swirling with knotted thoughts.

Outside on the veranda, there is the chatter of people. The sound of loud voices. The odour of bodies. The stink of stale clothes.

The magistrate is young. The shades of youth have not yet left his face. Fine lines on either side of his lips but no wrinkle on his brow yet. He sits lost in thought. It is as if midway he has forgotten where to go. As if he is wondering whether he is on the right path. As he thinks, he scribbles on a sheet of paper. Then, he stops and sits looking towards the ceiling.

A few black coats are sitting in front of the bench. Five or six red topis are standing. Behind the bench, the government symbols shine, piercing the darkness of the court. From one wall, the honourable president with a determined look, and from the other, Sardar Patel looking sternly on. The fan is caught in age-old cobwebs. They flutter with the fan, but do not fall off.

Even as the magistrate gazes at the ceiling, the clatter of two boots falls on his ears. The clatter of the boots suddenly stops.

The magistrate's eye, descending, falls on the sub-inspector's salute, on his smile while taking a seat after the salute.

'Isn't this your case?' asked the magistrate.

'Which one, saar?' asked the sub-inspector.

'That case', said the magistrate, pointing to a girl.

A girl was sticking like a lizard to the wall behind the inspector. From a distance, she looked like a girl, in the darkness. At close quarters, she seemed to be about twenty-five. As the public gaze turned on her, she seemed a bit ashamed. Quickly, she suppressed the shame. That shame was playful like lightning during the day and frightening like lightning at night. All the people in court were amused by that bashfulness. She drew her sari around her head like a veil. The veil covered half. Her breasts were full and magical. The rest of her body and her face revealed the truth. There was no life in that body. Her face had no touch of charm or brightness. She was like a string of faded flowers cast away in a third-class compartment.

'She has not even a quarter seer of flesh', thought the magistrate.

'Is this case ours?' the inspector asked the head.

'Yes, it's ours. You were there when we caught her', the head whispered, coming near.

'This case is ours, saar', said the inspector, addressing the court.

Turning to the head, softly he asked, 'Is she admitting her guilt?'

'Right. That's what it seems like from what she said to us.'

'The charge sheet says that you caught her with the arrack?' said the magistrate.

'Yes, saar! That's right, saar!' he said to the court. Turning to her, 'Emey! So you are admitting the crime?' the sub-inspector asked her.

She looked strangely bashful again. She stood there rubbing the red nails of her left hand against the red nails of her right. She was wearing a skirt with blue flowers, and her red half sari moved over her chest and head very slowly in the breeze of the fan. Her hair, roughly tousled, was like the fur of a black street dog.

'What is this shyness? Why don't you answer?' asked the sub-inspector.

She raised her eyes and looked at him. He saw her eyes, but did not notice that they were moist.

'They are not ashamed at night, saar! Only during the day', said the inspector, turning to the court.

'You! Girl! What work do you do?' asked the magistrate.

Everyone laughed loudly at the question.

It was just a month since the magistrate had joined duty. The pleaders had decided that he was a 'crazy bastard'.

'He won't let go. Doesn't know how to give and take! He says truth, truth! And pesters us. There is no case in the world without some imagination. When this whole world is an illusion created by God, one can only draw illusion from illusion. Justice! Righteousness! Truth! He is like the fellow who said, "Tell the truth! Tell the truth!" and wringing his wife's neck, jumped into the well. If you want truth and justice, I have to cohabit to give birth to it. Where will this truth and justice come from? If there is justice in the case, why are the police here? Why all these pleaders? Why these courts?' thought the head—he had just been made permanent—pacing around the veranda a few times.

'What, girl? What work do you do?' asked the magistrate again.

Everyone burst into laughter again.

The magistrate was puzzled. He came from a well-to-do family. But despite his affluence, he didn't mingle with people even in the days of his practice. When he didn't have a practice, he read books. He wrote poetry secretly. He had a large double-storeyed house in Kakinada. A new house in Hyderabad. He had fields, well-watered orchards. A good account in the bank. A job worthy of a man. A good son. He had no siblings, but if he had, he would have been a good brother. A loving husband, he was a good father to a daughter who was like Daisy Irani, Shirley Temple or Vasanthi. No one had ever said so far that he was not a very good fellow.

And so he simply couldn't understand any of this.

'What is her work? It is that only', said the head to the court, concealing a smile.

'Hey! Aren't you in that Nookaraju's company?' asked the inspector. She nodded in assent.

'What is that company?' asked the magistrate.

'"Company" doesn't mean company, saar! It's a dignified way of saying a company of whores!' said the inspector softly, approaching the bench. The magistrate bit his lip. When he realised the facts about the accused, he was filled with revulsion. He wondered at his own revulsion. After all, she didn't look like a virtuous woman in a story. Yet, when he saw the reality, he was nauseated.

'Last night, in a lane beside the house of landlord Nootakadu, you were caught with a drum of arrack, and you are charged by the police of committing a crime under the Madras Prohibition Act, Section 4(1)A. Are you guilty?' he asked, according to practice.

She shook her head in reply.

'Don't shake your head. Say it in words.'

'I accept the charge', she said.

'Did you commit the crime, then?'

'I have accepted the charge.'

'Did you commit the crime?'

'I have accepted the case, babu garu.'

'Did you commit the crime, then?'

'I have not committed any crime.'

'Then why do you say you admit the case?'

'I am admitting the case, saar.'

'Do you understand what it means to admit the case?'

And so the dialogue continued between her and the court.

'This case will go on till daybreak. He is like the cussed husband who will neither listen to what he is told nor give up till you tell! Just keep watching what happens.' There was a murmured grumble across the hall. The bench clerk leaned back, stretched out his legs, and sat watching. The hands of the clock on the wall were moving slowly.

'Did they find a barrel of arrack with you?' shouted the magistrate finally. His forehead was glistening with sweat, and the veins on his forehead turned into bright green lines.

'They didn't find arrack on me! They arrested me saying I was drunk!' said the accused suddenly.

'Come on!' said an old man. The people near the windows laughed heartily. One young lawyer sat down, fed up.

The magistrate was shocked.

'What did you drink?' he asked weakly.

'Beer, gin, brandy, whisky. Whatever they gave me. Where else will I get it?'

Her eyes reddened moistly.

'Didn't you get arrack?'

'I drank it.'

The court looked at the inspector helplessly. He questioned his head with a look. The head cleared his throat and approached the bench. His voice was sweet, loud, clear, and dignified like one who recited the Puranas.

'The day before, an American ship came, babu garu. The whole batch descended on the town. After suffering on the ship, how will they feel when they see a town, babu garu? They would have wanted to celebrate a little. In that celebration, they drank and got her drunk. And instead of just leaving, they brought her to our doorstep, and left her as she was at the doorstep. Imagine her ruckus on the road! It was a job to get her to the police station. She is like a fox, but when she was drunk, we can't describe the obscenities that rolled out of her mouth. We sent for the proprietor. He just sent her clothes but never appeared. He is scared of a ruckus. It was such a problem to get her dressed and bring her here in the morning. What could we do? It's a fact that she was drunk, but we also found arrack.'

The head's face looked as if all the difficulties and problems of the department had manifested at that moment.

It was obvious that there were a series of questions in the magistrate's mind. That he could not decide what to do was clear.

She had not committed any crime. Yet she admitted guilty to the case. This was a problem.

All problems. No one will allow this to progress smoothly and properly.

Suddenly, from the eyes of the accused, teardrops began to roll. Whether it was remembering the sun's rays on the thatched palm roof, the muggu[1] on the mud floor in front of her house, or the youth whose eyes met hers at the temple on the river bank, or the dark hour of the first time she lost her virtue, who knows what came to mind. She leaned against the wall in the court and sobbed loudly a couple of times.

Someone said, 'No crying in court.'

---

1 drawings made with rice flour at the entrance of a house

'You get drunk and dance, and come to court and cry', shouted the inspector.

The magistrate said in irritation, 'Don't threaten her.' Because she had caused his irritation, he was even more irritated with her.

'Not just anyone, even if the American president comes, thinking he has come for that, she will ask him how much he will pay. She is that type, saar! She will not care a damn even if we say we will hang her! Tears!' said the inspector.

'What is this drinking? That too, a woman. Tcha!' said the magistrate.

'It is kaliyuga, saar!' said the head. He was old enough to say this. He had grown grey in service.

'Saar! You can abuse me. Say whatever you feel like! But I am telling the truth, believe me. These whores—don't think I've used a wrong word—she is that! That is why I said it. If the government gives people like that a vote and gets elected—what government is that, saar? In the times of the Englishman—'

Before the inspector could finish, the head interrupted: 'In those days, not just at a jawan, if someone raised an eye and looked at even a recruit under training, that was it, babu garu! He would be caught immediately and locked up. It was the reign of Sisupala. The white man used to kick and rule us. So it all passed happily', said the head. He even let out a timely sigh in memory of those bygone happy days.

'These people won't give in unless you kick them, saar!'

'But now do we have the guts to kick, babu garu? They attack us even if we kick a dog! Telegrams to Nehru garu himself. When the station is packed with stray dogs, we just salute them and stay quiet, babu! That is the condition. If the policeman is afraid to lay a hand on the accused, then what government, babu garu!'

'We need dictators, saar!'

'They should be there and they should not stop us, babu garu. People like this should be beaten with a rod. Last night, on the road, you didn't see the ruckus she created. If you had, you would have sent her off for six months at least.'

The magistrate felt as if someone was pulling him down rapidly from the sky. He tried to imagine how she had behaved last night.

He couldn't believe that women could behave so badly. This woman was also human, after all. He was surprised.

'She is human like us, after all', he said in a feeble voice.

The inspector said, 'Saar, leave my case aside. But is it fair for you to say that there is no difference between you and her?'

The head said sympathetically, 'Babu garu has a very soft heart.'

The magistrate felt that his feet were floating and at the same time dragging him down. He remembered the advice of an elderly man. He had asked him, 'How many cases in your court per month? On an average, five hundred. You may have the patience to dig five hundred mountains one by one, and may even have the energy, but where is the time? Give it a thought.'

The magistrate remembered the advice and finally turning to the inspector asked, 'Then these companies you mentioned, why don't you remove them?'

'We are removing them. But then they begin to graze the roads, saar! What do you want us to do? They are such a terrible nuisance to us, I need a whole week to explain to you. If they are kicked out of the companies, there is no one to take them', the inspector said.

'Who will take these terrible whores, babu? When we ask them to find a living and quit this work, they will die rather than give it up. That is their life. Catching them is our life! To each their own livelihoods, babu garu, isn't it?' said the head philosophically.

All this while, the accused had been sobbing quietly. But when she heard the word 'life' six or seven times, some nerve in her brain must have caught fire. She rushed forth and began to weep loudly and shout.

'Not for me, babu! Not for me!' she began. 'I don't want this life! Kill me! I don't want this life. I cannot live this life. This low life, degraded life, I can't live it. The food I earn with such hardship, do you think I can eat it in peace? If I eat, I vomit, have stomach pains, headaches or faint. My body is weak, filled with poison. Days are without a moment's comfort. Nights are sleepless. You saw last night. Head babu saw. Ask him. Babu! How many were there? How were they? Shall I die without drinking? Tell me, shall I die? I will die. Who will weep for me? Will you weep for me? Who will weep? Do I have mother, father, or siblings to weep for me? If they were all there, why would I lead this life? If they were there, I too would be like the daughters in your house. Why this dog's life? See, babu, see! I have no shame. Look! Don't feel shy! Not one or two. So many in one night, so many bit me, wounded me, and drank my blood last night. So many pleaders, so many jawans, and so many lords of justice, there are so many. Last night, which of these babus came to prevent this? Tell me! Who came? Who didn't? Don't let me live like this any longer—just kill me. Hang me from that threshold. Stamp me down with your feet into the earth. Two pieces of wood are enough to make a handful of ash. Take the handful and scatter it to the winds. Stab me. Fling me into the sea. Just kill me. Kill me!'

And she ran towards the magistrate.

So many people in the court found it difficult to hold her back and restrain her. Slowly, she calmed down and sank against the wall.

'See, babu? How she pounces on you?' said the head.

The magistrate couldn't bear to look towards her torn blouse. He felt nauseous.

'She rose like a storm suddenly', said an old lawyer.

'Just keep watching, and soon she and her likes will throw us all to the winds. Just keep watching', said the inspector.

The magistrate said, 'Let it be. I will let her off under a first offence.'

'There are three more old cases that she has admitted to, babu garu!' said the head.

'Will she pay the fine?'

'Her proprietor hasn't come, saar! He won't come now.'

Finally, the court said, 'One month' for all the four cases.

'Fair!' said the head.

The magistrate began to call the other cases briskly.

Written 23 April 1961

Source: 'Nyayam' by Rachakonda Viswanatha Sastri (*Rachakonda Viswanatha Sastri Rachana Sagaram*, edited by V.V.N. Murti and M.V. Rayudu, Bengaluru: Manasu Foundation, 2007, pp. 442–44)

Kalipatnam Ramarao

Born in Ponduru, Srikakulam, Kalipatnam Ramarao (1924–2021) was a schoolteacher by vocation and a widely respected writer of short fiction. Kara Master's stories, although relatively few in number, are beyond comparison. A member of the Viplava Rachayitala Sangham, he set up Katha Nilayam, a library and storehouse of literature in Srikakulam, to bequeath the wealth of literature to future generations.

The Hero and the Super Hero

During the Sri Rama Navami celebrations, the Ganjipeta rowdy and the Allipuram ustad were caught in a tug-of-war. Both were beating each other up furiously.

The Ganjipeta rowdy was just that much. Unless you wore inch-thick glasses, you couldn't see the man. But he was still hanging on like a thin vein.

The Allipuram ustad was as big as a tree. If he chose to, he could pick up not just two or three rowdies like that but half a dozen and crush them into lime without bones. Why was he hesitating? There were people all around.

Who were those people? They were the youth who would join anyone teasing girls and boast the next morning of their bravery; after roaming all day behind the painted tigers and bearing their tails, they would go to the liquor shops without a paisa to buy even a cup of tea, these weary former tigers; when the women in the house send them out to sleep on the street, sleepless, they set out to watch the celebrations in the marketplace, these hollow tigers; youth who set out for combined studies and leave the books in their friends' homes and take to the streets; rickshaws without customers, ringing their bells; dishwashers in small shops—these were the people gathered there.

I was the only one a little better than all of them.

I did not set out to watch the celebrations. When I heard that a James Bond movie was playing in Minerva, I had dragged my feet for two miles and gone for the second show. I went and found the booking was closed. Oof! Anyway, since I had come, I took to the main road and after visiting a few tents was returning home grumbling because I had lost my sleep. Then, I saw this stunt scene.

What is this? What is happening? But no one answered. Out of ten people, one man answered, 'It seems to be a fight over a girl.' 'Oho!' I looked around, but there was no girl in sight. Yet another said, 'When this fellow and that one were thrashing each other up, that other fellow came. He pulled them apart and then he caught him and got him thrashed by the other fellow. So, because of his anger and knowing he couldn't fight him, this fellow is fighting that one.' So he gave me a small clue.

This fellow is the Ganjipeta hero. That fellow is the ustad. The fellow who started the trouble slipped out long ago. I shouldn't say it but I was furious—not with the fellow who was doing the beating, nor with the fellow who was being beaten up, but with the people who were watching.

Yes sir! If you and I are fighting, we should settle our quarrel ourselves. Why let another fellow interfere, with the public watching quietly? Not just the ustad, but the great-grandmother who brought him forth would sink into the earth. But no; they were watching as if it were a cockfight or rams fighting. Was it an equal fight? Not even that—if equals were fighting, for some poor people, this would be ticketless entertainment; I would have let it pass.

That fellow was huge and strong; the Allipuram ustad was more than six feet tall, no less! For every blow, this Ganjipeta youth was turning three somersaults; but he wouldn't fall and stay quiet. 'You son of a whore! You beat me? You are beating me because I am small! You came to release me, and beat me! I will see your blood yet…' And he kept attacking the Allipuram ustad again and again. And when he was kicked, he would fly out and fall some distance away.

What can I say? When I think of his courage even now my skin prickles. Great courage. The man was not even a fourth of the ustad. You wondered whether he was even a tenth of him. The ustad was six feet tall. He was probably a man who had trained well, eaten to burst, and exercised well—one huge chest, another huge thigh, he was like an elephant. This fellow was a young man, but a Ganjipeta character who had shelter and food only every other day. Was it a simple thing for this fellow to fight with that fellow? Besides he had already been battered a little by the first fellow.

But the fighting spirit comes to people like that sometimes. What kind of time is that? Justice should be on your side. The other fellow should play foul. If you question him, then he begins to attack. The spectators should sit back as if there is not even an ant bite. You should understand that people afraid of the other's strength remain silent. The fellow's tyranny grows as he sees the people's cowardice. That is when a great fighting spirit emerges. Then, even a kitten turns into a tiger cub. He leaps and stretches his paw like a tiger cub aiming at the elephant's forehead.

Even if you are at fault you can fight, but the minute you get a chance you get ready to settle.

If two are fighting, you don't have to ask anyone who is at fault. If you do, this one will say it is that one, and that one will say it is this one. Without asking, just stand by and look at their faces—you will be able to tell correctly who is at fault.

That's why my sympathy was with the Ganjipeta rowdy, not the Allipuram ustad.

Every kick of his seemed to land not on the rowdy's side but on my ribs. Every time the rowdy fell down and got up, I would say 'ammayya' in relief. This fellow's blows did not land on that one. But if they did, I felt like clapping loudly. Sometimes I felt that I should also attack the ustad come what may. But it wouldn't work. Why? Because my terylene clothes will tear. I had never fought ever. But he was an ustad. Fighting is his business. What is the point in putting a life that is comfortable into hardship? Then, I would think… There is no need to surpass him. Even if equal, since there were two of us against him, we could have beaten him. I had never felt like that before, but at that moment, I was irritated that I had never exercised and had felt ashamed of getting into street fights.

Kothapeta Sandow[1] came at that exact moment. Have you ever seen Kothapeta Sandow anytime? If you see him once, you can never forget. That was his build. Six and a half feet tall. A chest that was sixty inches wide. Where will you find a man like that in India? Maybe his body was built on scientific lines. If he lifted his elbow and smashed even a thirty-ton stone, it would become powder.

But many people there didn't know that he was Kothapeta Sandow. A few worldly-wise sages like me, a few may know, and his two pupils who were hiding behind the crowd. That the Allipuram ustad knew, there is no need to add.

He arrived like Siva summoned by Narada when Nara and Narayana were in battle. He asked, 'What is this?', looking around at the ones who were fighting.

The people who saw him wondered who he was and looked around to see where the Narada who brought him here was. I thought the story had peaked.

By then the Ganjipeta hero, who had eaten mud a hundred times and was finding it difficult to rise the hundred-and-first time: 'Son of a whore! I will die if I need to today, but I will see your blood first.' And he stood up staggering. When Sandow appeared out of the blue, he peered at him with hazy eyes, as if to say 'Who is this fellow?'

'Come you ass-licker! I'll see which whoreson will come in the way!' the ustad said.

Do you know the funny thing? Till now the ustad had been using his hands and legs freely, but had not opened his mouth. Now, seeing Sandow, he said this.

Either noticing this, or because of the way Kothapeta Sandow turned his head on hearing that, the people felt a stone on their hearts. Why talk of everyone, even I felt it was good to slip away from there.

But the Ganjipeta rowdy wouldn't go down! He looked exhausted. He retorted word for word. But even though he tried

---

1 muscleman (the eponym is a reference to bodybuilder Eugen Sandow)

he couldn't gesticulate when he spoke because his hands and legs wouldn't move. It was only because of the municipal lights that we were able to watch him—I don't think one could bear to see his face in broad daylight. But the power in his throat remained.

'This whoreson came to relieve me and is beating me up. He caught me alone and is kicking me. He is practicing his ustad tricks on me because I am a small fellow.' … 'He is planning to kill me.' And, crying out loudly, he ran and leapt into the sky!

Then Kothapeta Sandow—Who? Not the Allipuram ustad who was fighting till then, but Kothapeta Sandow, who had just come—went swiftly and caught his right hand. The crowd scattered screaming, like anthills scattered by the rains. Twisting the hand that he had caught backwards he said… to whom? To the Ganjipeta rowdy, who was being beaten up—what did he say?

'Now calm down!'

'Tell that fellow!'

'Not him! I'm telling you!'

'Why don't you tell that fellow, Sandow! Tell him! I know that you are Kothapeta Sandow. I know you have an army. I am suffering the blows. He is the one who is kicking! Not just me. He is also challenging you! If you have guts, fight—not with me, with him. Or move aside', he said with a yell.

For a second there was pin-drop silence. 'Then, let your word stand', and holding the twisted arm and the man who was like a corpse, he pulled him back and threw him far away. The rowdy spun around thrice and fell into the iron arms of the Allipuram ustad. After flinging him there, knowing where he would land, and as if he had done what he deserved, Sandow left without even glancing back.

'Then what happened?'

'What will happen? Sound of war and battle. The Ganjipeta rowdy, protesting the neutral attitude of the people, began to appeal to the people in his language. The people were furious, and each laid a hand on him freely.

'On whom?'

'Who else? On the Ganjipeta rowdy.'

'...'

'Yes. He should at least think of it. Or listen when he is told. Why didn't Sandow support him? Was it because these two could not beat up the Allipuram ustad? Why do they need his help? If he says "Hmm", his followers will finish him off—not one ustad, all four in a row!'

Then? Was it all finished? Are there no more ustads in Allipuram? Will they wear bangles! If he had thought of helping people in distress and supporting the underdog, he would have to challenge all the Kothapeta Sandows in the ring.

If he did, heads would fly. The police would come. Would it be one trouble? It would be a second world war. All the big shots in the town would have to be involved.

In that one second of pin-drop silence, Kothapeta Sandow had assessed all these points. So, he settled that row peacefully and cleverly. Otherwise, there would have been a huge row. But there is a small point here.

'That is this. If the danger was to him, would he have left it like that?'

He would not leave it. True. He would have summoned all the people of his area. He wouldn't even have to call them. His followers would jump into the fire even before he summoned them. That is the attraction of big power. We may think anything, but at any time at any level, this difference between big and small will be there. Take electric power. Unless there is a generator, how will the heaters, engines and lights burn? If the main is knocked out, how will the rest work?

The logic of Kothapeta Sandow will not be clear to us, but if we understand, then it will seem the right one. If you ask me, that Ganjipeta hero needed those honours. Otherwise, he would be in danger.

'Yes, guru! Such people think that the people will not watch quietly when there is injustice. When they start talking about big words like justice and dharma, and fall into difficulties with big words, they start creating crises, wondering how to bring other people in.

'Once they understand the people's attitude, they will never try these crazy tricks. That's why, for his own good, I also struck him.'

Andhra Jyothi, 5 April 1968

Source: 'Veerudu-Mahaaveerudu' by Kalipatnam Ramarao (*Kalipatnam Ramarao Rachanalu*, edited by V.V.N. Murti and Rachana Sai, Hyderabad: Progressive Publications, 1999, pp. 449–61)

ARUDRA

Arudra (1925–98), born in Visakhapatnam, is remembered as a chronicler of the history of Telugu literature. His thirteen-volume encyclopaedia on Telugu literature, *Samagra Andhra Sahitya Charitra*, spanning ten centuries from the ninth century to the twentieth century, was published between 1965 and 1968. Arudra was closely associated with the Abhyudaya Rachayitala Sangham (the Progressive Writers' Association), and he translated the Tamil *Tirukkural* into Telugu.

August 15

A broken charkha in a corner
This day that comes flaunting
The burqa named Gandhiji
Is evil and intoxicating arrack

Hunger in the middle of the ocean
Why don't you anchor life?
Which leader even knows
The people's pulse?

That flag flapping on a hunched mast
Fills the country with despair
Where is this freedom you seek?
It is the same old tale you hear

It will not stop the fight with hunger
It will not quench the burning anguish
Misery and unhappiness a crore and a half volts
Wherever you turn, you see nothing but revolts

Can the wind ever blow free
Today as our fate is blazing?
Not a trace of green fields in sight
But the jails are filled to bursting at the seams

To dream that the nectar Garuda brought to free his mother
Would liberate our motherland, a mere illusion
Our rulers have licked the holy rushes clean
Till their tongues split and forked

The elephant has devoured the wood apple
Leeching it of its sweet pulp
If you don't agree, well, let it pass
Our freedom is but a wild fig teeming with worms
Our poverty but a festering ulcer

Written 15 August 1948

Source: 'Augustu 15' by Arudra (*Arudra Rachanalu Kavitalu: Vipula Sankalanam*, Vijayawada: Kwality Publishers, 1985, p. 52)

Aluri Bairagi

'Bairagi' was the pen name of Aluri Subbarao (1925–78) who was born in Itanagaram in Guntur. He wrote Hindi poetry from a young age. His major Telugu poetry collection, *Nootilo Gontukalu*, introduced humanist trends in Telugu poetry. Bairagi wrote about the suffering of the working classes and of the poor, about women in prostitution, and about hunger. His works touch upon the contradictions in the human condition.

Girl at Play

The morning light of autumn
A golden peace covers mountains, trees and housetops.
On a deserted street, a breeze softly wafting
    lifts her luxuriant tresses.
A solitary girl goes along playing merrily
Humming some strange tunes to herself.
The tips of the sun's rays lighting on her dark locks
Like rainbows, electric sparks.
Miniature images of a hundred thousand suns.
Butterflies fluttering over a bed of blossoms
Like a word unforgettable
Like a tender note in a melodious song
Like an invocation of golden blooms
    to the invisible goddess of dawn
Like an idea gleaming through the vastness of intellect
Like a blessing of Mother Nature
    that girl wafted along.
To which shore in the ocean of life will this little paper boat float?
What storm or cyclone lies in wait? What lies beyond the veil?

Golden fragrant child!
Ten years hence I will not remember you! Time will not halt till then
But the morning light of this autumn
Fragrance mingled with morning mist
Unheard melodies, notes of the divine veena
Will conjure a hazy image lingering in my heart
A footprint in the boundless sands. A single wave in a mighty river!
But oh, where is the traveller?
Where is the path through the water?

Source: 'Aadukontunna Balika' by Aluri Bairagi (*Agama Giti*, Hyderabad: ABC Prachuranalu, 1998, p. 62)

DASARATHI KRISHNAMACHARYULU

Dasarathi Krishnamacharyulu (1925–87), born in Chinnaguduru in Warangal, was a poet recognised for his virtuosity even while he was a student. Closely associated with the communist movement, he was an important figure in the resistance against the Nizam's government and the Razakars, courting arrest for his political activism. His revolutionary poetry, his translations of Mirza Ghalib into Telugu, and his popular lyrics in Telugu cinema made Dasarathi a household name in the region.

It Belongs to the Peasants

Sacrificing their lives
Clearing dense dark forests, creating good fields
Telangana belongs to the peasants
Who burnt down their bones to ash

And ploughed fields
Filling the nawab's treasure chests with gold.
Telangana belongs to the peasants
It belongs to the peasants alone.
Can it remain under the rule of the old fox?

Oh, you demon Nizam!
Never have we beheld another king like you
My Telangana, a veena worth a crore of gems
You have cut its strings and cast it into the flames.

Source: 'Raitude' by Dasarathi Krishnamacharyulu (*Dasarathi Kavita*, Secunderabad: Mahaandhrodaya Prachuranalu, 1977, p. 15)

Dasarathi Rangacharyulu

Dasarathi Rangacharyulu (1928–2016), born in Chinnaguduru in Warangal, was active in the Telangana Armed Struggle in the 1940s. His contribution to Telangana literature includes essays, stories, novels, and his interpretation of the Vedas. His most well-known works are the novels *Chillara Devullu* and *Moduga Poolu*.

Janapadam

Narrow path, cart tracks, uneven ground. On either side of the path in the green fields the crops had grown tall. Carts were moving along. The first cart was full of armed police; in the second cart, Balaramayya; after him, more carts. They were also full of armed police. The carts were moving slowly. The bullocks were walking heavily along. The sun had just reached its peak. Balaramayya was anxious to reach his village quickly. He was returning after two years to his village—to his kingdom.

The cart went over a boulder. It bumped up and down and rocked. Balaramayya was greatly disturbed. He always kept two pairs of bullocks to draw his cart. Once harnessed no one could stop them. When he set out, the whole village would hastily move out of the way. A washerman would run before his cart. Behind him another would run carrying his luggage on his head. If he couldn't run, he was as good as dead. Once the amin[1] and he were going together. What happened to the washerman in front, no one knew. Why he walked slow, no one knew. The bullocks raced ahead and stamped him down. The cart wheels went over him. The cartman said he was dead. He told him not to stop the cart. The body lay there. That was how he ruled in those days. But that authority withered away in a moment. It vanished into thin air. He had to leave the village. Now after the Police Action, and because the police were with him, he was able to return to his village. The Nizam nawab was a weakling. He was not able to give him protection. The Indian government was good. It was giving him police protection to go back. Didn't he wear khaddar after all!

Balaramayya peeped out of the cart. The crops were tall. They were ready to eat. These fields were all his but for two years he had not got a single grain. The armed people had come. They distributed all the lands. He thought the lands would not come back to him. They prepared the fields. This year the harvest would come without expense or labour. The harvest was all his. The lands were all his. He must take revenge on those who had distributed it. He must enslave the tiller. He should rule again.

'Could he rule?'

The words in his mind spilled out. There was no one in the cart—no one heard. Why did he get that doubt! He should fatten the police! He saw two jars of arrack in the cart. Would it do? In another cart the goats bleated. In the old days, if he wanted, a hundred goats would be cut before his gadi. But who would give a goat now? If needed he would get them, he decided.

The carts were going along. They reached the entrance to the village. The police shifted their guns. They aimed without a target. And shot. They entered the village. It was filled with fear. The

---

1 police inspector

houses were like nests without birds. There was not a squeak or sound. Not a person to be seen. It was forlorn. Deafening silence. The carts drove through the village. One dog howled. Another growled. Hearts pounded.

Source: Excerpt from *Janapadam* by Dasarathi Rangacharyulu (Hyderabad: Navayuga Publications, 1976, pp. 1–2)

Madhurantakam Rajaram

Madhurantakam Rajaram (1930–99), born in Damalcheruvu in Chittoor, was a master of the Telugu short story. A teacher of Telugu in a zila parishad school, his prolific writing, first published for the most part in newspapers, portrayed globalisation in the Rayalaseema region and its impact on the social order. Rajaram wrote around 300 stories, in which he foregrounded the complex contradictions of life and the centrality of humanist values in understanding adversity and the human predicament.

Exile

'Ayya! Great man! Are you here, sami?'[1] I looked around fearfully at the bus stand. I stared around at the bazaar. At the hotels I gulped and stared. Everyone says this is 'a town, a town!' For my lot it is a jungle. I said 'Ayya!' I said 'Sami!' I said 'Devara!' There was no lord to listen to my woes.

I sat in the same place and stood in the same place for three days. 'Is this what you have done, God?' I said, and dragging my feet walked here, here where these four roads meet, and I saw you.

[1] *sami* = sir

I came to life. I wanted to tell you my tale and came and fell at your feet. I know your heart is a pot of milk. It is a silver pot. You will open your ears and listen to my tale. You will open your eyes and see my state. 'Orey, Gangadu! Is this your story?' and shed a teardrop. I have that faith, that is why I am telling you.

What, sami? I don't know how old you are. But I was forty-one or forty-two in last year's Ganga festival. In all this time, I have never come here and seen you. I saw your pictures in books and pictures on the walls and thought you would look like this. I recognised you as soon as I saw you. This town is new to me. These people are new. Their talk is new to me. Their tricks are also new. I am like a mountain goat that has been let loose in a market. They call the forest 'wilderness', but the forest is far better than this town. There you can graze on leaves or weeds, eat fruit or roots. One can drink the water in the stream and sleep under the cool shade of a tree. It is not like that here! Tcha! They will not let you do any work you want to. If I want to pull a rickshaw, they won't let me get one. If I want to lug bags, the men who do that work will not spare me without a kicking. I thought I would clean wells, but here each house has a tap and there are no wells left. What am I to do? The whole day my life is barren as a stone. In the nights, just see my troubles! They don't let you sleep on the pyols. They don't let you step into the choultries. All the temples are closed and locked. Not finding any place if I stagger around the streets, the police think I am a thief and chase me. If I enter the by-lanes to avoid those virtuous men, the dogs set on me barking 'Laow! Looow!' Three nights have passed like this. This is the fourth day. Just as it was falling dark again, you appeared.

Perhaps you will ask 'When you can't do any work why did you come so far, you mad fellow?' My sami! Don't say that to me. If the fox toughens, it becomes a man they say! If a lizard toughens, it becomes a chameleon. If a crab fattens, it will come out of the shell. I did not come out because of pride. If you want more ask Pasala Poli Reddy from my village. Ask Pinapedda Rayappanayudu. Ask the temple pujari. If you don't want to ask such big people, ask the boys who graze the cattle in front of the village. I have never coveted another's property. I never shirked work. I never broke my word. What do you want me to do? Tell me! Though I have not committed even a small mistake, I left my village, left the house I built, left my wife and children, left all who were close to me, and throwing a cloth on my head I was forced to come like this. Why? That is the story, ayya. That is it, sami, this Gangadu's story!

On the road that leads from Rayavaram to Racchaladoddi, east of Dalavayyapetta, as you cross the Sigamakulagutta, you can see it—that is it, sami, my village. It is called Porakala Baylu. In the hills around, the reeds grow widely. That is how it got its name. If there is even a little rain, water flows for three months. There will be paddy sprouting along the mountain stream. Near the lake that the Pancha Pandavas once drank water from, there are sugarcane fields some distance away. Go further and you see golden fields of groundnuts; around this there are mango groves. I'm not saying this just because it is my village but you will say 'this is a village' if you see our Porakala Baylu. If you throw four stones together, won't they fall either near or far from each other? There are four villages like that. Where the kapus stay it is Kapuru; where the kamma[1] nayudus stay it is Kammapalem; the malas live in Malapalli; and the madigas in the madiga hamlet. Doesn't a village need gods? There are—in the north, Mankallamma; in the forest path under the maddi trees where the cattle and sheep sleep, Katamarayudu; between Kapuru and Kammapalem, there is the Bhajan temple of Rama. Why speak of those stone gods who don't move? There are only three gods who—sitting, moving, speaking—look at justice, speak dharma, and safeguard the village! You can find blossoms on a fig tree; but if Karnam Mallayya draws a line, you cannot find a man who will cross it. You can find a rabbit's horn; but if Manegaru Rayappanayudu gives an order, you cannot find someone who will disobey it. You can find a white crow; but if President Poli Reddy glares, you cannot find a man who will not tremble in fear. Perfect order, without disturbing the distance between higher and lower, there was dharmarajyam reigning in Porakala Baylu. I don't know what god cast eyes but a problem arose there.

The problem was nothing but the panchayati vote!

---

1 *kapu* and *kamma* are landowning castes

What is it you don't know, sami? Take the Ramayana and there is only one Rama. There cannot be two Ramas. Take the Bharatam and there is only one Bhima; there can't be two. Our village is the same! From the birth of the panchayat, Pasala Poli Reddy was the president. What after him, you may ask! Why, isn't his son Sina Nagi Reddy there? We had no such fears. We are not the kind who search for ghee holding butter in the hand.

But who knew that the rulers would suddenly bring a crazy rule? One day at dusk, my president, Poli Reddy, sent for me. Folding my hands, I stood at a distance. 'What ra, Ganga! Do you know why I sent for you?' said Poli Reddy. 'I drive cattle and eat lumps; what do I know, sami? You only must tell me', I said.

'Nothing ra, Ganga. Times are changing. The rule today won't be there tomorrow. Now a new one has fallen on us. It seems none of us should be the president of the panchayat. It seems we should have one of you. It won't do if we refuse. They will not agree. I have talked to the Karnam and Manegaru. They would also like to have you. I'm saying that you should be the sarpanch of our panchayat...'

I was stunned. 'Sarpanch? What is that, sami? I never heard of it', I said. 'That's all, fellow. They pour old arrack into new bottles. The word "president" has become useless. Now one should say sarpanch. Both are the same. You are now the president of our panchayat. Do you understand?'

My body grew wooden. Words wouldn't come from my mouth. 'What is this strange thing, my father!' I thought and opened my mouth. After I was born and grew to understand, I had never heard of something so strange. But I... Asadi Gangadu, I, who did the work with my hands that the great ones told me to do with their feet—just because some government fellow said something, will I become sarpanch at one stroke! You tell me. There is the goddess in the temple. If we give her a sari, it should be a Kanchi silk. Or else a Dharmavaram silk sari. But you don't wrap her with an old quilt. Can you have such extremes anywhere? At any time?

Not just that. I tried to tell him a lot. But he wouldn't hear me. 'Alright, Ganga! Why have a band for a wedding that is over? You are sarpanch. That's all. Do you even know how to sign? First do something about that.' And he got up and went inside.

It was as if a stone had fallen on my head. I worried that when there were so many great men in the village, this curse had curled around my neck. If tomorrow some officer should come and say 'sign on this paper', what would I do? I had learnt letters with difficulty in the night school when I was twenty. I borrowed a pen from my neighbour and wrote carefully. The boy laughed fit to split his stomach but wouldn't tell me what was wrong with it. In the end I learnt. It seems I wrote two letters instead of three. He mocked me, 'Gandu, Gandu', and I couldn't raise my head.

What shall I say, sami? Even that bad day came. Officers wearing suits and coats landed in the village. 'There is a meeting in the school. They are asking you to come', said someone who came running. My heart was beating hard and I went and stood there with fear. After talking to Manegaru for some time, the officer came forward and said, 'Come! Come sarpanchgaru. Come and sit.' And he showed me the chair. When President Poli Reddy, Karnam Mallayya, Manegaru, Rayappa Nayudu, and all the village elders were there in a row, did I need a chair? 'No! No, I'll stand here', I said. He was in no mood to listen! He sat on me till I sat on the chair. My legs were trembling. My whole body was sweating. My mouth was dry. After that, for half an hour what happened there I cannot tell you clearly. Pasala Chinanagireddy, Pacchipulusu Chengayya, Kadiri Saranappa, Muthirevula Nancharu and five or six others came and sat as 'members'. We put thumb impressions where the officer showed us. He asked us to take the oath and we recited the words he read out. 'It's done. It's done. You are the panchayati sarpanch', said all of them loudly. Why I became and what I became, what do I know? Only that god knows.

All I know is that when I went back the mud walls of my hut hadn't changed. The straw roof hadn't changed. The door which was a thatch hadn't changed. The gruel pot in my house hadn't changed. The gruel inside it hadn't changed. My wife's old clothes hadn't changed. The dirty clothes my children wore hadn't changed. But they were all saying that I had changed…

That night after we had eaten our meal and gone to bed, Rangi asked me, 'What is this, mama! You are a sarpanch now. Will they give you a salary?'

'If they were giving, someone would have said so. It is doubtful that they will.'

'Let it go. They pay or don't pay. After becoming a sarpanch, how can you go for coolie, mama? You stay at home. I will go to work and bring back two lumps of food. One for you. One for me.'

I felt like crying. A woman earns and I sit at home swatting flies? Tchi tchi! Is that a life?

It was dawn. All the folk in the village set off for work. I was the only one left on the string cot under the tree. Because I was a sarpanch and shouldn't work.

I should curse the god who gave me a boon I didn't ask for and tied up my hands and legs. What is the use of blaming human beings?

Not one or two days but a month passed in this way. One day I said this is not it, and went to the village square. All three maharajas were sitting there.

'What ra, Ganga! Are you well?' asked Karnam Mallayya.

'What well, sami? No one in the village calls me for work. The house doesn't run on a woman's labour. I don't have ten rupees to buy notebooks for my son who is studying. I am going mad. I can't pass my time like this. I came to tell you and go. If you allow me, I will go to some Rayavaram or Racchaladoddi, do some work and earn a few rupees...'

'Orey! Orey! Don't do such a thing', said Pinapedda Rayappa very emphatically. 'If people say that the sarpanch of Porakala Baylu is doing coolie work in our village, where will we hide our heads? If you can't manage, go to Chittoor. It's a town and no one will bother about you. Karnam, what do you say?'

'Yes, yes, that's true, Ganga', said Karnam Mallayya. 'You may have to be present for a samiti meeting once in two or three months. Never mind. Just find a big man, talk to him and send us his name. Suppose you speak to Javilangadi Subbaramayya, we will write to 'Asadi Gangadu, care of Subbaramayya' when there is a meeting and you go back after the meeting. What ra, Ganga, do you follow?'

I nodded as if I had understood.

That's all, sami. The next day I left and came here! There is no shortage of important men here. Only I couldn't find a single man who would listen to me. Now I have found you! If it comes to that, who is more important than you to us? They say you worked all your life for our good! It seems it was you who named us harijans! After three long days of searching I have found you. I am truly fortunate.

'Asadi Gangadu, c/o Mahatma Gandhi, where four roads meet, Chittoor.' If my people write I will get the letter, isn't it?

What sami? Why don't you answer?

Written 1981

Source: 'Agnyata Vasam' by Madhurantakam Rajaram (*Madhurantakam Rajaram Kathalu*, Volume 1, Hyderabad: Visalandhra Publishing House, 2008, pp. 282–88)

C. Narayana Reddy

Popularly known as 'Cinare', C. Narayana Reddy (1931–2017), born in Karimnagar, was educated in the Urdu medium and learnt Telugu on his own. He was conferred several awards for his literary work, including the Sahitya Akademi Award, Jnanpith Award and the Padmabhushan. A multi-faceted bilingual literary scholar and popular lyricist in Telugu cinema, Cinare's *Adhunikandhra Kavitvamu: Sampradayamulu-Prayogamulu* was a path-breaking study of Telugu poetry.

The Wounded Sun

These days the sun is rising late
In the fear that the bloodstains
On his body will be seen.
Karmasakshi, witness of man's actions!
Wherever masjids are destroyed by conspiracies

After all it is his ribs that are broken.
Wherever a temple is burnt by religious fanatics
it is his face after all that is charred.
Universal witness, the sun is smouldering with grief
That while filling their lungs with his light
they are spilling the poison of hatred on all
That burying the universal soul between four walls
they dance the deathly dance amid skulls.
God, a transcendent presence
is a formless radiance
beyond vows and summons.
Do you dare imprison that boundless power
in the cells of narrow minds?
Do you dare fill the breeze of dawn
with foul smells?
Will you throw dung heaps in sparkling streams?
What is it that is not the target of the evil look of evil minds?
They break the spine of faith that stands erect
when branches sing united in friendship
They chop the tree at the root.
Universal witness, the sun
trembles fevered and frantic.
Are these the children who toddled and fumbled
on their thresholds in his morning rays?
Did these toddling feet turn into crowbars?
Did these hands that ate butter turn into drawn daggers?
You inhuman demons
who have lost your minds in the name of faith
With those very hands bring to a close
the final act in creation
The annihilation of the sun.

Written 28 December 1992

Source: 'Gayapadda Suryudu' by C. Narayana Reddy (*Drukpadham: Kavita Samputi*, Hyderabad: Laya Charan Prachuranalu, 1994, pp. 50–51)

Life Has Grown Lighter

Life has grown lighter far than cotton
I never knew until stung
Of black death lurking behind white cotton.

Written 1998

Source: 'Doodikante' by C. Narayana Reddy (*Raitu Kavita*, edited by Papineni Sivasankar, Bandla Madhava Rao and M.V. Rami Reddy, Guntur: Muvva Chinnabapi Reddy Memorial Trust Prachuranalu, 2004, p. 117)

Sivasagar

Born in the Krishna district, K.G. Satyamurthy (1931–2012), also known by his pen name 'Sivasagar', was a leader of the Communist Party of India (Marxist-Leninist) and an unparalleled revolutionary poet. He co-founded (with Kondapalli Seetaramayya) the CPI-ML Peoples' War Group, and spent years underground. A long-time leader, his expulsion from the party inaugurated a serious debate on Ambedkarite philosophy and caste in the Naxalite movement. A prolific writer and philosopher who drew from his personal and political experience with revolutionary politics, Sivasagar was an icon of the dalit movement and a leading figure in contemporary Telugu literature. His published volumes of poetry include *Udyamam Nelabaludu* and *Nelavanka*.

Immortality

The dying seed
    promised a harvest.

The little flower falling off
    smiling, promised a crop.

The forest as it caught fire
    promised a raging conflagration.

The setting sun earnestly promised
    a sunrise.

Immortality is exquisite.

Embracing time
It promised another world.

Written 1985

Source: 'Amaratvam' by Sivasagar (*Sivasagar Kavitvam, 1968–2004*, Hyderabad: Bahujana Book Syndicate, 2004, p. 181)

Vasireddy Seetha Devi

Vasireddy Seetha Devi (1932–2007), born in Chebrolu in Guntur, belonged to the first generation of women novelists with a keen feminist sensibility and a deep understanding of the roots of women's oppression. Fighting off social constraints that obstructed her education, she went to Madras, studied Hindi, and worked as Director of Jawahar Bal Bhavan. Among her novels, *Samata*, *Rabandulu-Ramachilukalu* and *Matti Manishi* (translated into fourteen languages by the National Book Trust) are particularly well known for their sensitive portrayals of social and political contexts in Andhra. When the government banned her novel *Mareechika* in 1982, she challenged the ban in court and secured its release.

Vultures and Parrots

'That's alright, Dharmayya. I agree, Sekharam is doing some good work. He has laid roads, good. He has brought electricity, very good. He is going to build a school. Even better. But I hear he is going to build houses for harijans…' and Chalamayya paused.

'Why? That alone is not so good, is it?' asked Paramayya.

'Aha! Why not? It is excellent! Right in the middle of the village, on Raosaheb garu's land he is going to build the houses.' And Chalamayya looked at Paramayya's face as if to say 'What do you think now?'

'Really! Avva! Is there such a thing anywhere? Is he going to bring them here right into the middle of the village?' asked Paramayya in astonishment, looking at Dharmayya.

Chalamayya was delighted that after so long Paramayya was actually agreeing with him.

Janakiramayya was shocked and stood staring at Dharmayya's face.

'Really? Is Sekharam also building houses for harijans?' Dharmayya asked, his face alight with happiness.

'Really! Aren't you the one who made Ranganna sarpanch last time and grew horns on their heads? Sekharam himself told me this. If they are brought into the middle of the village, will there be anything left? Won't the whole village become a melting pot of spit and dirt! Already their eyes are on top of their heads. Will they listen to us now? Will they show any respect?' said Chalamayya.

'Right. Where is the respect of the past? They sit squatting under the tree. They don't even rise when we pass by on the road. They walk right in the middle of the road in front of us', said Paramayya, struggling to light a cigar.

'Now with this Sekharam gadu's support they have grown more brazen. What work has that Sekharam in those mala huts? He is always there, rubbing against them and roaming about with them', said Chalamayya.

'Yes, Dharmayya! This is no good. Shouldn't there be some difference between right and left? Let him build houses for them. But why not build those houses in their own gudem?[1] If you tell him then Sekharam will listen', said Janakiramayya meeting Dharmayya's eyes.

Dharmayya yawned. He looked at Janakiramayya for a moment.

'Janakiramayya! I didn't think that you too would talk like this. Is this the advice you give me after being my friend for so long? Are they not human beings like us? How can one human being be kept apart from another like this? Is there a greater injustice than this? So many great leaders are lecturing about the atrocities on harijans in meetings. We have been listening to these sermons from Mahatma Gandhi's time. But what have we actually done for them? Except for a few… who have been educated and managed to get good jobs after independence in this long period of twenty-five years… how much change has there been in their lives? What is the place they have been given in society? Everyone goes up on a stage and shouts that caste must go.

'But what is happening? As education, politics, knowledge, wealth and civilisation grow, caste pride is also growing. There are attempts to build harijan colonies in every village. They have built them in many villages. But where? Far away, outside the village! They stamp "harijan" and build them. That means you build solid houses and lull a people just waking up back into a deep slumber for generations to come! Why don't they build those houses inside the village? Why call it a harijan colony? If not we and our children, at least let us ensure that our children's children can intermingle and live together happily', said Dharmayya, shaking in anger.

'Look Dharmayya! Say what you like. On this matter we will not agree! Sahukar Ramayya is grinding chilli and pepper after hearing this. He says he will see how Sekharam works as the sarpanch.

---

[1] hamlet

None of the board members will agree. We will file a petition to remove Sekharam from that position!' Chalamayya said, reminding Dharmayya that he was also a panchayat board member.

Dharmayya went pale.

'Yes, Dharmayya! Tell Sekharam. Let him build the houses outside the village like in all the other villages. What is he going to prove by putting them in the middle of just our village? Anyway, how is this going to happen? It will just generate more hostility', said Paramayya.

'Yes, Dharmayya! Remember what happened six years ago? Because there was no water, with your encouragement, he told them to draw water from Ranganna's well. With that, the village turned into a battlefield. How many heads were broken? Finally who suffered most?' asked Janakiramayya.

Dharmayya fell deep into thought. 'Alright, let us see. I will talk to Sekharam after he comes.' Dharmayya agreed reluctantly.

Chalamayya's eyes glittered with pride. Paramayya's face was full of the pride of victory.

'I take leave', said Dharmayya, moving forward feebly.

After walking a few steps, he turned and looked back.

The three were standing under a tree.

***

Sunanda cheerfully went about her work, travelling from village to village, crossing bunds of fields and canals. She visited the harijanawada, bathed children, taught them hygiene, spoke to the women. 'There is so much to be done', she thought to herself. With support from gram sevikas, she set up night schools for adults. Sunanda's confidence and her carefree demeanour while she went about her work drew respect from some elders in the village, and angered many.

In a few days, Sunanda realised that it was far from easy to work in a village and change the perspectives of villagers.

When she spoke about family planning, the women would look at her strangely. They would talk back. Yet, undeterred by their words, Sunanda put all her energies into convincing them.

She spoke to them about nutrition, held cookery shows, and encouraged women to join the mahila mandalis in large numbers.

It did not take Sunanda long to understand the shocking goings-on in some villages. She found that eggs from the hatcheries set up by women's groups were not reaching the target groups. She went to these villages on the day eggs were to be distributed and made sure they were given to children, pregnant women and new mothers. She made surprise visits to balawadis to see if the midday meal given to children was good. If it wasn't, she would write a complaint against the teacher.

In a very short time, Sunanda became an irritant for some people.

Some men in the village would glare at her angrily. Others would mock her. Yet others would find fault—'You did not do this. You did not do that.' Even though deep down she was troubled, Sunanda did not let it affect her work.

The sarpanch and the mahila mandali president of Chintalapalem were very angry with Sunanda.

She sensed what the sarpanch wanted, but she kept pretending she did not know. The mahila mandali president was the sarpanch's wife. When Sunanda heard that one of the two sewing machines given to the mandali was in the sarpanch's house, she had it brought back to the mandali. Since that day, husband and wife were furious with her. They raised all kinds of allegations. They spread rumours about her character. Sunanda ignored it all.

The sarpanch of Gogulapalli was a man of letters. The mahila mandali in that village was also really good. The sarpanch and women of the village held Sunanda in high regard. When she went there, the sarpanch's wife would not let her eat anywhere else. Normally, Sunanda would never eat in anyone's house.

It was late. It was drizzling. But Sunanda set out for the headquarters from Chintalapalem. Degalamarri was three miles from there. There was no road to the village. Vehicles would not ply in the rains. Not wanting to spend the night in that village, Sunanda began walking on the bund bordering the fields. The peon did not accompany her that day. He was on leave.

'Where to, amma, sevika? To Gogulapalli?'

Sunanda looked up with a start. Standing in front of her on the bund was the Chintalapalem sarpanch. Sunanda was furious.

'How dare you address me like that?'

'Why? Aren't you a sevika?'

'No. My designation is Extension Officer. If you must address me, that is how you should address me with respect', said Sunanda.

'Come again? You are an officer? What officer? An officer who travels by foot? Why the offence? In Telugu, they say mukhya sevika.'

'Once upon a time. It is because people like you humiliate us by calling us "sevika, sevika", that the government has changed our designation.'

'Abbo! That is a long tale indeed! Let that be. It is getting dark and it is drizzling. Where have you set off to alone across the fields? To Gogulapalli?'

'That is none of your business. Move out of the way', said Sunanda, angrily.

'Why so much anger when I speak the truth? Will you sleep there the night?'

She caught the veiled meaning in what he said. 'Yes', she said defiantly.

'It's okay. Why don't you sleep one night with us?'

'Shut up!' Sunanda shouted.

'Why are you jumping up and down? What wrong did I utter? I only said why don't you spend one night in our village', and the sarpanch laughed sarcastically.

Sunanda felt like pushing him off the bund.

'Make way!'

'What if I don't?'

'Don't try to be too clever'.

'Why are you behaving like a maha-pativrata? Is the Gogulapalli president better than me?' and he grabbed Sunanda's arm.

Sunanda pushed him hard. Unable to hold himself on the slippery bund, he fell into the field.

Sunanda steadied herself and walked on. She did not turn and look back.

After a long day, working on government programmes without respite, Sunanda was exhausted. This incident broke her spirit. Her face looked wan. She managed to reach home.

She threw herself on the bed without dinner. She remembered Janakiramayya's words. Can she really do this work? She now understood how difficult it is for girls to travel from village to village on work. But there is no choice. There is no alternative to facing the challenges.

Sunanda slipped from thinking into sleep.

***

'Look, Ramamurthy. Divert all the remaining funds to the works', said Narahari to the BDO, referring to the samithi's estimates.

'You want me to divert the whole amount?' the BDO asked just as Sunanda walked in.

Narahari's face paled. 'What, Sunanda? What do you want?' he asked in a sugary voice.

Without answering Narahari, she said to the BDO, 'I am going on a visit to Rabandulapadu Mahila Mandali.'

'That's good, go', said the BDO. 'I am going to Chilakalapadu. You can come with me in the jeep', said Narahari.

'I have a programme with the mahila mandali in Rabandulapadu. The balawadi is being inaugurated today. They will all be waiting for me', said Sunanda.

'Inauguration of a balawadi? How come you didn't tell me? Where did they get the funds from?' Narahari shot the questions at the BDO.

'Oh! The five per cent allocation from the General Fund for women and children has not been spent for three years. A large amount has accumulated. Sunanda submitted this proposal. We sanctioned it when you went to Delhi', said the BDO.

Written 1985

Source: Excerpts from *Rabandulu-Ramachilukalu* by Vasireddy Seetha Devi (*Rabandulu-Ramachilukalu: Vasireddy Seetha Devi Sahityam* 5, Hyderabad: Visalandhra Publishing House, 2003, pp. 40–41, 102–04)

Kolakaluri Enoch

Kolakaluri Enoch, born in 1939 in Vejandla in Guntur, is an award-winning short-story writer, novelist, poet, playwright, and literary critic. He is a leading figure in the dalit movement. Enoch was among the first generation in his family to secure an education. A professor of Telugu literature at Sri Venkateswara University, he went on to become its vice chancellor. Enoch's writing portrays the lives of dalits, the working class, and agricultural workers.

Sunrise

It was a small village in the corner of this Telugu country. Ravadu was not a man, he was a machine.

Like the sun, he would pierce the field and return to rest at home at night. He would bathe the field in sweat and mark it with his blood. He would tend the field with a mother's tenderness.

The village had never seen Ravadu's face. His children had not seen it. His wife had not seen his face. The sun had not seen it. The field had seen it.

He would bend to work, walk with bowed head, and cover his face when sleeping; that was his practice.

Even the field had not heard Ravadu's voice. Silence was his daily practice, his life practice.

A child's scream was kept hidden in the cave of his heart by a rakshasa. It could not be heard outside. When there were four people around, even Ravadu's heart would not beat.

There were no tears in Ravadu's eyes. No tears. No anger. A stone does not become hot in the sun or cold in the shade. Not even stone, cotton.

The five elements distributed Ravadu's body among themselves even while he was alive. By some oversight his bones were left. And one doesn't know why, but they were moving.

When he came home, the whole village was buzzing. Sita was dead. She had hanged herself. Some fellow had caught her hand, she didn't listen even when told—people were gossiping.

Ravadu slept as usual that night. In the morning, the sun was in the field.

Ravadu was a child of the earth. That acre of land was his whole existence.

When he washed his hands and legs and sat for a meal, he did not see his daughter's serving hands or feet. The food did not come. There was no word that there was no food. Ravadu didn't bother; he went to sleep.

There was no fire lit. There were grains. The girl was not there. She had eloped. She was carried away. Two versions. What proof was there for Ravadu to believe that the girl had not been stolen?

If it came to that, what beliefs did Ravadu have?

Didn't many villagers go when they heard that they were building houses in the hills and were giving lands?

He set out for the field and saw his son lying in a pool of blood in front of the house. Blows! His heart was beating. He won't die, the stubborn fellow. A strong life.

The villagers gathered. 'When we said "don't quarrel with the people in the village", did he listen?' The ones who had some life and patience were weeping. Those who were able to, were going about their work.

But Ravadu was not there. He was roaming over the field with the sun.

The light at home was flickering. Hiding the light in his eyes with a cloth, as he listened to the sagging cot's tales, the sound of bangles and toe rings.

He knew that sound. It was his. The sound of his blood! His heart!

Ravadu rose from his sleep. The sun came out at midnight.

Before him, his daughter! Full nine months. She caught his feet. He stroked her head.

That morning the sun rose at home. It set in the field.

By the time he reached the village, it was noisy. The cry of a newborn. Loud women. A male child. The mother died.

Ravadu saw his grandson. He saw his daughter. He saw his grandson and his daughter. He saw the dawn setting.

In the arduous mission of raising his grandson, Ravadu was turning the child into a sacrificial animal.

'It looks as if you won't die till he dies', said the barren woman next door as she carried the child away.

'Stop. Beat him. Stab him. Kill.' He could hear shouts from a distance. Men carrying sticks, canes and bamboos were coming across the fields.

They are probably killing a pig, thought Ravadu. Panting, choking and foaming at the mouth, his son came running. He didn't get the blows. He came to the field. Saw his father. Fell at his feet.

The fallen one didn't rise. The sticks did not let him rise.

Blow after blow. Ravadu got a few. The sticks didn't cease till it was clear that this was not a human being but a clump of mud.

Then the men didn't wait. They left. The son's body was bloodied. Ravadu's clothes had blood. The sun's hands were stained full of blood.

The ancient Ganga in Ravadu's eyes, the Patala Ganga brimming over.

Wet! Moist! Sticky! Rain! Ceaseless! Tears! Blood! Bloody tears! Tearful blood! Wonder! Tears in Ravadu's eyes!

He dug the grave slowly. He laid his son down leisurely. He wiped his face. He threw some mud. He buried him.

This body was rich manure. The field would bear well. The village would feed on this corpse.

For many days, the sun rose in the field. He died there. The village was like a graveyard, and his house, a coffin.

Ravadu set up his hut in the field. Three bamboos and a thatch.

Pot, dish, pan, rice pot, water pot, and vessels. A shiver in his veins, a fire burning in his bones. Ravadu's ailments.

When the noonday sun high up was looking on, Chintayya came and coolly gave him the deadly news, 'This field is mine.'

Ravadu should have asked, 'How?' He didn't.

He should have looked at him and asked, 'What?' He didn't.

Silence.

A loan taken long ago. A hundred rupees. It had crossed thousands. It had crossed thumb impressions and gone to court. The stamp came to life. It walked into the field.

Ravadu couldn't stand. He collapsed. He couldn't sit. He just slid down. He embraced the earth. He embraced the earth as if he was embracing his children, relatives, mother and father. He embraced the earth.

There was dust in his mouth.

Chintayya dragged Ravadu out of the field.

The field that had drunk his blood and sweat sat without moving.

With his son in its belly, it was silent.

The sun that bore witness was beating down on his back.

Ravadu was born upside down. He grew up with his head bent. As he grew older, his head lowered closer to the ground. Now it was ground down.

For his devotion, the earth showed her kindness, drenching his body and mouth in sludge.

Sitting down slowly, resting his hands on his knees, holding his waist and rubbing his spine, Ravadu stood up.

He stood up since he had no work that needed him to bend.

As he straightened up, his spine crackled. Trembled. Moaned. Screamed.

His bent head stubbornly refused to lift. It grew tight. It got pulled. Slowly it got looser. It turned. And allowed him to hold his head erect.

He opened his eyes wide and looked ahead. His eyes darkened. He looked around. He looked impatiently. He looked in all directions.

How much happiness! Earth, sky, horizons. The earth was so beautiful and so boundless—he was born on this earth. He grew up here. How fortunate! The air he breathed—the heart's soulmate—how comforting it was!

He walked. With each step, what strength to his feet! What joy! He began to realise what he had missed all these years.

He looked at his field. His body was going out of control. There was a house in name in the village.

For a week, the sun did not leave the house, during day or night. This week there was no sleep in Ravadu's eye.

That morning, Ravadu was born on the bank of the village lake. The sun, just born, was thrashing about the village lake. Who would save the sun!

In the morning rays, from the bank of the lake, Ravadu surveyed the whole village.

Strangely—it looked new.

Wonder—he felt revolted.

Miracle—fury.

It grew dark. The matchbox in his pocket touched his hand. It rustled. He took it out and struck.

Ravadu's face was visible in its light. It was not the old one.

The sun that had set rose in Ravadu's face at midnight. A red, burning, flaming face. The sun was burning.

Holding the matchbox tightly, Ravadu roared loudly. The lake echoed it. No words were heard. Strange. Ravadu was talking.

He left the bank and going into the village, he shouted.

'These lives shall not be burnt down like this anymore. These lives shall not be burnt down like this anymore. These lives shall not be burnt down like this anymore!'

Written 1998

Source: 'Suryudu Talettadu' by Kolakaluri Enoch (*Noorella Telugu Kathalu*, edited by Mudiganti Sujatha Reddy and Singisetti Srinivas, Hyderabad: Potti Sreeramulu Telugu University, 2011, pp. 431–35)

Kethu Viswanatha Reddy

Short-story writer and literary critic Kethu Viswanatha Reddy was born in 1939 in Nagammarangasaipuram in Kadapa. His stories draw on the realities of rural society in Rayalaseema, the region he belongs to, known for its chronic drought and factional politics. Viswanatha Reddy retired as Professor of Telugu studies at B.R. Ambedkar Open University. As a teacher, he is known to have opened new pathways to the teaching and learning of Telugu literature.

The Earth We Trust

As I get off the Rayalaseema Express at Erraguntla, before me the CCI cement factory. As I get off the bus at Chilamakuru, on the road on either side, the bustle of the new cement factory that the Coromandel people were building.

Chilamakuru, which had never seen jeeps or cars before on the road, now had jeeps and cars passing to and fro. Bearing stones to the site of the factory, lorries plied on the uneven roads. With the stones, there were men and women in the lorries.

There were new shops along the road. Shops which had never stocked more than Charminar and Scissors were now stocking brands like Red Wills. Only brandy shops had not yet come. Vegetables, provisions, eatables, teas, coffees, clothes, soaps and pastes were available in a single shop and also in separate shops.

The road was bustling with people who had come for the bus, loafers, factory hands, and the people connected with them. The changes that agriculture, commercial crops that had depended on the rain, and stone mining had failed to bring in all these years, were visible now. The Grameena Bank in the midst of this change. People speaking two or three languages in the middle of these changes.

There was no one from my village on the road. I got off the road and took the path to my village—through the fields.

Fields all around. Hundreds of acres of fields. Mother Earth had been changing hands. An earth fractured into several fragments through sales and family partitions. The earth goddess, 'Bhudevata', between the bunds.

Although the fields had been cultivated, the seeds had not taken root… The fields were barren. Gazing at the skies looking down on the drought, the barren lands seemed to say 'they ploughed barren lands'. No rains. No crop.

There were no millets. No oilseeds. No groundnut crops either. What use any crop? Here or there, barely a foot high, like a dying child, the gram crop dried to straw. By now, if only two or three rains had fallen on time, the fields would have been gleaming green, covering the bunds. Now, one could see only the bunds. Like the future of their lives!

Again drought. A drought that was part of famished lives. Have lost count of which drought this is. Would remembering solve the problem?

The earth below my feet was like a street with burnt down dwellings and cattle sheds. The sky above was like a pile of ash. A cloud here and there in the sky—like cotton buds broken by the harsh sun, starved for rain, scattered by the winds. Not a crow in the sky. I did not pass a man in the scorched path. At the time of the southern breeze, winds like during gales.

We never thought the drought would be so unbearable this year. The news in the papers and the announcements and the promises that so many made came to mind. Ever since I can remember, there has been no change in the announcements and promises.

In such terrible circumstances, what had I come from Hyderabad to achieve? The minute Angadi Subbarayudu's letter came, did I have to rush all the way here? Need… Necessity…

The two acres I had inherited and sold to my kinsman Veeranna was a continuing bond to my village. My last bond to the land. If my work was done in these two or three days, I would be cut off from this land.

Four years ago, Veeranna offered to buy my two acres of land that was beside his field. Instead of selling my land that was part of the common well to another and creating problems for Veeranna, I felt it was better to sell it to Veeranna. By the time Veeranna sold his four acres of outer fields, his debtors surrounded him. What he had left was two thousand. He put that two thousand in my hand and got the deed written. He promised to clear the rest as soon as his two-year-old lime trees bore fruit. Till then, it was decided to give it on contract. Since then, he had neither paid me nor registered the land. I needed the money. My third daughter Prasuna's marriage had been fixed. There was no reply from Veeranna. I thought I would go some other time, but there was a letter from Angadi Subbarayudu. Saying that Veeranna had stopped farming. He had sold the lime patch. He was ruined. Subbarayudu was ready to buy my two acres!

There were no details in the letter. It was like dried fibre. I didn't know what happened to Veeranna's lime trees. I didn't know why he sold them. Although it was a battered livelihood, I didn't think it would be this bad.

My wife pestered me when she saw the letter. As it is, it was a daughter. I felt embarrassed because this was a tangled affair. Even if I wanted to lease the land, I would still have over a thousand rupees advance that I had taken from Veeranna. Would Veeranna let go of the land? Will he take back his advance? How could I ask him to take back his advance? What of my need? How to meet my need in these times of drought? What was Angadi Subbarayudu's plan?

I was disturbed. The village drew near. I remembered the fields, ponds and hills I had roamed during the monsoon and harvesting season when I was young. Attachments don't break at once. Knowing that land prices will not rise in a drought-stricken area, how long I had postponed selling the land! It was possible because I could live on my salary. What would have happened to me in such a place if I had no education, no job? It is scary to think of it.

Under the platform below the neem tree at the centre of the village, Pullayya who was always there was not to be seen. That old man used to abuse people who lived on salaries. I heaved a sigh of relief. Half the people of my village who would normally be seen on that platform were not to be seen. When I was a child, there were peddlers who brought all kinds of wares to the village on carts, and the women and children would crowd around them with trays full of grain. The children used to spin their tops. They would play games with cloth balls. We children would listen to stories till late at night, and would tell stories too. I heard that storyteller Yerikalayya's father had died. I would earlier see at least some of my other friends on this platform. Now two boys are looking at a matka[1] chart. I could not recollect whose children they were. They did not recognise me. When I come only once every two or three years to look around the place, how would anyone know me? It has been more than twenty years since I left the village.

The other half of the village who would be seen near the village temple were not to be seen. Sanyasis, mendicants, sadhus, soothsayers, street performers, leather puppeteers, would all gather here. We would learn puranic dramas. For some years, the school was in the temple. Goats were sacrificed before the temple. Frogs would be married there for rains. The Virata Parvam would be read there. Bhajans were sung there. The panakam[2] for Sri Rama Navami was prepared there. The full moon after the sprouting of the new crop was first sighted there. That was where we squabbled over toys. People who were new to the village came there, and their introduction to the village was there. That is where the Reddis and revenue officers disembarked. It was there that I first heard one man read *Kasinathuni Andhrapatrika* while others listened. I listened to their discussions. In the days when I was studying for SSLC, I heard about Congress and Communist politics. Only the boulder on the stone platform on which the national flag was hoisted since the day of Independence was lying in a corner, much like the temple—in ruins.

During the harvesting season, this was where each one's harvest was discussed. The panchayats on the cattle that had entered the fields were also held there. Thieves were punished there. The good

---

1 a form of gambling

2 a jaggery drink prepared especially on Sri Rama Navami in South India

and bad of the village was also discussed there. My father had gambled and lost his house and thirty acres in that temple.

Some boy sitting at the temple asked, 'Did you bring today's paper?' 'Whose paper?' I asked.

'Who gets the paper in this village? I thought you may have bought one.'

'I have yesterday's Telugu paper', I said.

'Give me that', he said, and took it.

I couldn't understand whether this was a thirst for news or an educated fellow's hunger to read. There were no people on the street.

It was as if the whole village had migrated. Except for children, there were no adults even on the front porch. Should a village change like this?! Maybe they were huddling in their houses without any hope. Even the community life driven by superstition during rainless days was not visible now.

Veeranna was not home. His wife was winnowing millet rice. She was startled to see me. She went in hastily and brought me water to wash my feet. She put out a string cot, and spreading a torn mattress, she asked me to sit. I sat.

Ramalakshumma asked about our welfare. Looking at the condition of their house, I muttered my answers.

'I will just come, bava', she said, and went out. The house didn't look like a farmer's house. It was like a house rented to a schoolteacher. There were no bullocks. There were no implements there. No cattle. No straw on the attic. One or two chickens were roaming around. It was obvious that Angadi Subbarayudu had spoken the truth. It looked as if Veeranna had given up agriculture.

Ramalakshumma came with something hidden in her sari. She said, 'Wait, bava, I will bring some coffee.' She picked up some twigs and went in. She brought some coffee after half an hour. Jaggery coffee, smelling of smoke. I could understand her trouble.

'Is Veeranna not in the village?' I asked.

Ramalakshumma did not speak for a while. Then, because she couldn't escape, she spoke choking, 'After returning from Proddatur, he has been going to the cement factory. Many people in our village are going these days. There is no end to this story, bava.'

Her throat grew hoarse. I didn't ask another question. But I didn't understand what coming from Proddatur meant. I thought I would ask Veeranna after he came.

'I will heat some water, bava. There is no water in the pot. I will bring some water, wait.' And picking up a pot, she was about to leave.

'I will go into the village and come. Don't cook for me', I said. I thought she would insist and left without waiting.

It was not yet ten o'clock. Veeranna would not return before evening. I was hesitant to go to anyone else's house. I couldn't decide what to do if I had to stay in the village for two or three days. Looking at Veeranna's house, it seemed terrible to stay with them and expect them to feed me. He was a clansman, no doubt. There were other relatives like him, but we had bad relations with them while my father was alive. This hostility went back to my great-grandfather's days. After that there were differences over the share of water from the well. They did not break each other's heads. But they fought like dogs near the well. They let their harvest wither. They allowed the near-ripe lime trees to wilt. They would meet at weddings and funerals. Kin during auspicious occasions and shared blood during polluting occasions—that's all. Then back to normal. But because I was educated, and employed, once my father died, they did not have any differences with me, so we greeted each other. They invited me for a meal when I visited the village. I decided that I would pay for my food and eat at Angadi Subbarayudu's house.

Subbarayudu was sitting in his angadi.[1] It was his home and his shop, where he kept kerosene drums for the oil engines stacked on a platform.

He would not have invested even a thousand rupees on the shop. He was bare-chested. He was wearing a soiled, torn pancha. His beard had greyed. The man was reeking of poverty. He had keys hanging from his waist thread. Watching him sell his wares made it clear that the self-sacrifice necessary to earn wealth is beyond the ken of ordinary men—it is only renunciants who can achieve it.

Seeing me, he put a plank across the wooden box in which he stored grain and asked me to sit. As he catered to the children

---

[1] shop

who bargained for five paisa and ten paisa worth of bamboo, nuts, balloons, et cetera, he enquired about my welfare. He asked me slowly, 'Should I get rice cooked or do you have to go to Veeranna's house?'

'Get it cooked', I said.

He went in and told his wife. She came and enquired after me and went in. Subbarayudu said slowly, 'Veeranna asked me to take the land.'

I said, 'Let Veeranna come, we can talk.'

Before these words could finish, my paternal uncle's son, Munireddy came. He fussed because I hadn't gone first to his house. 'I was just about to come', I bluffed. He said, 'Come and eat.' Subbarayudu said as if in jest, 'He will eat here now. You can cut a chicken for the night!' Munireddy said, 'Come and drink some coffee at least', and forced me to get up.

Munireddy anna gave me coffee and spent two hours talking about the village, disputes, politics, the state of education, and national politics. That was all bluster. The bragging of a man who thinks he knows everything. But he asked me nothing about myself. Unable to bear this, I told him why I had come. The first thing he said is, where is the need to sell land. Then, 'What do you spend your salary on? How much have you saved? How much insurance do you have?' and so on—a hundred questions. I told him about Prasuna's wedding. He asked about the boy's education, job, dowry and everything.

Then he said, 'In this terrible drought, how will the price be good? You may have to give it to Subbarayudu cheap.'

Then he said, 'Well, that bargain will be after Veeranna comes.'

Then he told me Veeranna's story.

'He brought a bad name to all of us. All the other kapus in the village also got a bad name. What is our lineage? After all, he was a relative who was hurt; so I asked him to stay in our house and work. He was greedy and didn't agree. He listened to those useless Kamanuru people and joined a bogam[1] company. At least then it would have been okay if he lived respectably. He sold those two

---

1 a hereditary caste of performing artists (musicians and dancers)

acres and went off to Chilakaluripeta without settling all his debts. He brought two bogam women who disappeared saying they were going to the backyard. He was ruined in all ways. I don't know what happened. They say he fell out with his brothers-in-law. He came back to the village recently and joined the cement factory. As if the drought was not bad enough, this cement factory has ruined the farmers. The cement factory pays fifteen rupees per day. If you ask the farmer to pay that much, where will he get the money? Now, even if we are willing to pay five rupees, no one is willing to come. Even women have got used that. They get ten rupees. We will have to sell all our lands. The days are not far when the coolies from our village and neighbouring villages buy up all our land…'

Munireddy anna did not know how much land coolies had bought. If people like Angadi Subbarayudu were coming forward, this meant they were indifferent people. Whatever the anxieties of Munireddy anna, who owned fifty acres, my mind was deeply disturbed on hearing Veeranna's story. Fifteen years ago, he was a farmer with twenty acres. He did not have a single bad habit that I knew of.

I told Munireddy anna that I would come back in the evening and left for Subbarayudu's house. On the way I saw another relative who said, 'You fellows with jobs, and those wretched coolies—look at what you are doing.' He was not a big farmer. He was at one time a big farmer. The arrogance of the bygone days had not yet died in him.

I went to Subbarayudu's house. We sat for food.

'I thought your mouth must be tired of rice, gruel is far better. So I didn't get rice made.' Whatever Subbarayudu's miserliness, I didn't mind gruel. But I had lost the habit for the chilli in it. There was no ghee.

A thin buttermilk. If Subbarayudu didn't live like this, he could not afford to buy the land of people who were losing it. I didn't know whether to pity Subbarayudu or feel contempt for this growing greed for money.

I was not used to an afternoon nap. I felt like sitting near the temple for a while.

When I reached, there were four more examining the paper I had given in the morning. It was as if they had found something rare.

One boy came and sat beside me. I recognised him. Pullammanayudu's son. He said he was studying BA. It was like he was talking to someone else.

'There should be a government announcement that Kadapa district is a drought area… Will this area be drought-stricken only if some collector or minister makes an announcement? This is a country without shame. So many years after Independence, they are still not able to sort out scarcity of drinking water. Why won't we respect Telugu Desam Party? Congress will only come to its senses if all the farmers vote for Telugu Desam this time.'

The boy who took the paper from me in the morning replied, 'Congress is like the Hindu religion. Historically it has swallowed all other religions; in the same way, Congress will swallow Telugu Desam and a lakh other parties. We saw Janata then. It is the same now. What we need now is not parties that will swallow others. Nor parties that will get swallowed.'

'Your communist talk…'

'Your… talk…'

I did not know how to argue with people who were reaching for the stars. Behind that anger, their frustration was clear. It did not seem to me that they understood that frustration is not politics. The boy who compared Hindu religion to the Congress was intelligent. And sincere. Pullammanayudu's son lacked that quality. His politics was like kite-flying. I wanted to tell them what I thought. Subbarayudu's son came and said, 'Father is asking you to come.'

'You were in the temple so long? Useless fellows gather there at sundown. All these young fellows who have had their lands sold to study BA are unemployed and spoilt. They play matka or abuse people.'

What can one argue with Subbarayudu? He abused them for a while and then turned to me. 'What should we do?'

'Let Veeranna come… Or you tell me. If Veeranna has no objection, you can take the land', I said. Subbarayudu began to narrate all his troubles. He showed understanding about my need for money. He told me about the situation in the village. Even someone like Munireddy had a debt of forty thousand rupees, and he gave me details of the debts of others. He told me how nobody was willing to buy land in our village and gave me details of different families. He said they could not find labour. And finally he said, 'I cannot give you a naya paisa more than six thousand. You can check with your Munireddy anna if you like.'

For the land that I sold for ten thousand four years ago, Subbarayudu was offering me six thousand. Was this an increase in the value of the rupee in Subbarayudu's eyes, or a decrease? A little earlier, when someone bargained for a piece of coconut, he said, 'When prices are shooting up, what should I say?'

I said, 'Let Veeranna come. We can talk at night.' 'Okay, let him come. What is the hurry?' Subbarayudu said dragging his words.

It was evening and Veeranna returned. He said chicken-shicken and fussed about arranging a meal. I told him that Munireddy anna had asked me to come. Ramalakshumma remarked sharply, 'Why will you eat in a poor man's house?' What could I say?

I told Veeranna the whole matter. After listening to me, he said casually, 'Sell it to Subbarayudu.' He brought the deed that he had hidden inside and gave it to me. I didn't know what to say. In the end, collecting my thoughts and summoning my courage, I said, 'I will somehow manage Prasuna's marriage. What has to happen will happen. Let it be. You keep the land and work it. You can pay me when you are able to.'

'What do you mean? When will I be able? You are so educated. Are you mad? Do you want me to trust the drought? Or trust Subbarayudu? What should I do if there is no share of the well? If he refuses to run the engine for hire, what should I do? I have no bullocks. No ploughshares or other implements. What should I look to and take the land? If you have to sell the land to me, of what use is it even if you wait for twenty years? I still have to pay Subbarayudu fifteen hundred… then government loans…'

'Even now?'

'Aaa… That's why I went to Proddatur, unable to deal with these loans. I did what no farmer does. I carried water for the bogam company. I carried food packets for the bogam women. I brought brandy, arrack for their customers. I sent bogam women to the police. I was beaten up in the false raids… And I thought I would set up my own company and was deceived. I realised I was no good there. Unable to live there, I died daily of shame—afraid that I would meet someone I knew. In the end I came home… Even if I have no land, I can labour. Now there is the factory—for many people like me.'

'It is only a matter of two or three years. Once the construction of the factory is over, there will be no use for someone like you. That is why…'

'You want me to come back to farming? I don't want any land. There is another thing you don't understand. Assume I work on the land. I will still owe Subbarayudu, the government and you. Subbarayudu will charge me interest on his loan. And he will take the land. The two acres that you want to give me will go towards repayment of Subbarayudu's loan. He is unwilling to give more than six thousand. You cannot do anything about it. You just have to hand over the land. I will not get a paisa from the advance I paid. Subbarayudu will keep that and adjust it against my loan. Since Munireddy anna is also in debt with Subbarayudu, he will nod for everything. What can you do? What can I do? What do you say?'

What could I say? That night the land deal was finalised. Munireddy anna made the deal final for three hundred more.

Subbarayudu said, 'I will give you four thousand now, and in the next months I will give you two thousand. I would have paid you all, but your Munireddy anna borrowed money from me saying he was in difficulty. Over three months I will cut the thirteen hundred that you owe Veeranna. I will give the two thousand seven hundred to you.' I agreed.

These accounts would never finish.

My last link with the land and my village was cut.

We chatted past midnight about the village and the factory. Veeranna told me a lot about the factory. He told me how the local leaders were cheating the farmers in land deals with the factory. He told me about the skirmishes between Tamil coolies and Telugu coolies, about the strike, about the union that was started recently, and about the strike to increase wages.

It was dawn. I set off with the people going for factory work. What work did I have here? I thought I would go to Tirupati and tell the groom's family that we could not have the wedding soon, and return to Hyderabad.

Veeranna was walking ahead. Along with him, there were more than twenty farmers who had sold their land because of the drought. Walking in the direction of the factories that had sprung up in the lands of drought…

The ashen sky above, the shade of cement mixed with bone meal.

Somewhere far away in the distance a red spot…

Written 1982

Source: 'Nammukunna Nela' by Kethu Viswanatha Reddy (*Kethu Viswanatha Reddy Kathalu: 1998–2003*, Hyderabad: Visalandhra Publishing House, 2009, pp. 113–21)

Bojja Tarakam

Bojja Tarakam (1939–2016), born in Kandikuppa, was a dalit advocate for civil liberties and human rights, as well as a poet, philosopher and political activist. A staunch Ambedkarite, he founded the Dalit Mahasabha, and was the senior public prosecutor in the Chunduru dalit massacre case. Tarakam was a prolific writer, and his books include *Naalaage Godavari* and *Brazil Prajala Bhooporatam*.

The Voice of the River

When you asked me to sing
I could not
I could not speak
You did not see
    the scars of police lathis
    on the songs that sprang from
    the depths of my despair
I used to sing
in solitude
When I met you
I raised my voice to yours
    and sang with you
You wanted my song
    to be heard by all
And you took me to the people
Seeing the people
Seeing the voice of the people
Seeing the joyousness
And blazing energy of their hearts
The frightening soundscape of the starving
Seeing clouds of mercy enveloping
    the unfortunate and miserable
My blood vessels swelled
    and burst forth ringing
    echoing like the wind
    tears pouring forth
I spread words
    and threaded songs
They became waves and waters
    and streams
When people burst forth in the water
    and began to flow
They choked my voice born of the river
You did not see the scars of the police lathis

When my lips come alive
The sounds that struggle in me
    are the broken voices of the people
Hearing that you will swell forth
In ecstasy and wonder
    like the Ganga
Then I will be
    the Paramasiva that bears you
The song stirring on my lips
    will become the pallavi in your throat
    echoing in tens of tens of voices
    traversing tens of tens of tens of waves
    from one mouth to another and another
    as waves of wind
I will sing again
Then lathis cannot
    choke my throat
Lockups cannot
    shut my mouth…

Written in Central Jail, on 27 January 1976

Source: 'Nadi Puttina Gontuka' by Bojja Tarakam (*Nadi Puttina Gontuka: Jailu Kavitalu*, Hyderabad: Janapada Prachuranalu, 2015, pp. 27–29)

P. Sathyavathi

P. Sathyavathi, born in 1940 in Kolakaluru near Tenali, is a feminist short-story writer and translator. Her collection of stories *Sathyavathi Kathalu* and her translation of Simone de Beauvoir's *The Second Sex* into Telugu are particularly well known. She received the Central Sahitya Akademi Award in

2020 for her translation of Revathi's autobiography *The Truth about Me: A Hijra Life Story* (2004), titled *Nijam Cheptunna: Oka Hijra Atmakatha* (2016).

A Nameless Girl

Malacchmi sits at the threshold. In her hands, silver anklets and gold earrings. Eyes brimming with tears. She has been sitting here for six months. Sometimes the madam whose house she worked in stops by in her car and says, 'Come Malacchmi, let's go to my home.'

Malacchmi snaps back, 'I cannot work anymore, amma. Didn't I tell you to look for someone else? Why don't you listen?'

'Not to work… Just come so we can talk.'

'What will you talk? You have hundreds of chores. Roaming around with candles and other things. Why would you want to talk about my girl? I won't come to your house', and she turns the other way. The madam sighs and goes away. Of late, Malacchmi gets irritated with anyone who speaks to her. All attempts to bring back her old self fail.

Malacchmi sat leaning against a pillar on the police station veranda, clutching her head in her hands. Her husband and son were talking to the SI inside. She kept wiping her eyes and looking in from time to time.

Soon they came out. Her son's employer, Ravindra Babu, also came out with them. He looked at Malacchmi and said, 'They have written down a complaint. They will bring her back. I will keep checking from time to time.'

'Come! Let's go. There is nothing to be gained sitting here', grumbled Malacchmi's husband.

The son drove his employer's car away.

Malacchmi hoped he might say, 'Poor things! Drop them at home.' Was he mad or what? Dragging her feet, she set off behind her husband.

He was walking fast. She followed. Her legs were aching. She hadn't eaten for two days. She hoped he would say that they could take a rickshaw. But he was walking away fast. When he was angry, he always walked fast without looking back. Malacchmi had ten rupees tucked away in her waist. There was no cycle rickshaw in sight. A shared auto came along and, stopping it, she got in. She thought of asking him also to get in but he was too far ahead. To each his fate, she thought as she took her seat.

No sooner had they reached home than the neighbours accosted them, asking what the police had said.

What would the police say? Didn't they know?

'Okay! Carry on! Make yourself some tea and cook some rice. It's all God's mercy! How much can you weep?' He took the towel off his head and, shaking it, threw it on his shoulder and left. A golden girl! Which evil demon had carried her away?! She was taking tuition because her English was weak. The girl who had gone for the private class disappeared without trace. Overcome with sorrow, Malacchmi sat on the threshold, wailing loudly.

Yesterday when she and her son went without Ravindra Babu garu to lodge a complaint, that police bastard said, 'She must have eloped with someone. She will come back in four days after roaming about. In the meanwhile, you can harass us!' But did he write a complaint? Four rings on four fingers, a car, ironed white clothes—without all that, why would he write a complaint?

'You are still sitting on the doorstep. Get up and light the fire. One has to suffer one's karma. You brought it on yourself. What is the use of crying? Go! Go and cook some food. If you don't eat, you will faint and die!' said Malacchmi's husband.

Malacchmi didn't speak. Nor did she get up from there. He went himself, lit the stove, made some tea, and gave it to her. When she refused, he scolded her into drinking some.

'What is the use of crying after doing what you did?' he shouted. Then, 'Poor thing! What can you do? You thought it was for the best. If you sit crying, no one is going to beg us to eat! Come on!' he coaxed her.

Meanwhile her son who had come said, 'They will find her, amma! Stop crying. My saar also said he would keep checking, isn't it? Tell your madam also. She has a sangham, isn't it?' Malacchmi got up after a long time. Her eyes were still watering.

The madam Malacchmi worked for came. She wanted to find out why Malacchmi had skipped work for three days. Grasping her hands, Malacchmi wept copiously. 'Thalli! Tell your sangham people and find out about my girl', she said. The madam said she would, but asked 'Are you planning to come back to work soon?'

'I can't, thalli', she said, and telling her about her daughter, began to weep bitterly. 'Don't worry. Nothing has happened to your daughter. She will come back.' The madam left with these comforting words.

A week passed! Ten days passed!

One day there was a message from the police station, and bowing to the picture of God on the wall and slapping her cheeks, she ran to the police station.

'A body was washed up at the Bandar Lock. Langa and odni. Hanging earrings. Go see if it is your daughter.'

'O my mother! It shouldn't be you! It shouldn't be you!' she said, and went there. It was not Malacchmi's daughter. Her heart sank. Wonder whose daughter she is! O my mother!

A girl on the rail tracks! A head. A torso. Langa odni, hanging earrings. 'That girl is not my girl, swami.'

'We brought the Telugu girls caught in Bombay. One girl said she was from this place. See.'

'Not our girl, naayna!' We are dying. Breathless from running from the police station to the canal edge to the rail tracks. Corpses every two-three days. Why are so many girls dying, O lord! What has happened to them? Why can't they just eat, roam and be happy? What affliction is this?

'Bodies are still coming in. Your daughter has been missing for many days, isn't it? These are new bodies. She must have run off with someone. Just shut up and keep quiet', say relatives and neighbours.

And Ravindra Babu garu had work to do. How many times could he ask the police? As for madam, she had meetings and dharnas and candlelight processions. Is our trouble the only thing for her to worry about?

'We should leave the burden to God and do our work', said Malacchmi's son. 'When I protested and yelled and said she shouldn't study, did she listen? Both mother and daughter went on like cacophonous crows that she should be eighteen. I want to study, nanna! I want to study, nanna! Now what happened? The study is gone and the girl is gone', said Malacchmi's husband, beating his head.

In his anger, he shouts at his wife. She weeps and cries bitterly. Again, he comforts her. He feeds her. The son gets into the car as soon as he wakes up. Then he gets back only at ten in the night. As soon as she finished her tenth class, Malacchmi's husband said, 'Let us get her married to her cousin Veerabhadram.'

'I won't marry him even if I have to die, nanna! I can't live in that village. I want to study. I am only sixteen. If you get me married at sixteen, they will put you in jail', the daughter said. Quarrels and more quarrels. Only quarrels… Veerabhadram is a good lad. His mother is good. He has a house. He has leased a field. Malacchmi sang her bit. As if her daughter was going to study a lot and become a collector.

It was college. So some decent clothes and slippers within what we could manage! Did we deprive her of anything? She was also a good girl. Not a single male friend. The police searched her books and clothes. Nothing wrong anywhere. Except for her notes and lessons, no love letters. Everyone had a cell phone but she didn't. She had asked for one a couple of times, but they didn't buy her one. If only they had, then she might have called her brother if she was in danger. When he thought of this, the father trembled like a leaf.

'Maybe it would have been good to buy the girl a phone, Lacchi', he said, sitting beside her and wiping his eyes with his towel.

'Maybe it would have been good if we could have persuaded her and got her married, ayya', said Malacchmi.

'What is the use of this stupid Inter except to pass time? What am I doing after studying Inter? These studies are a waste', said the son. About three months after the girl went missing, her friend Nagamani was removed from college and married off. Now it was right to get girls married early.

Malacchmi who used to work with ten hands found that her ten hands were dead. She looked daily at the silver anklets and three-gram earrings she had bought secretly for her daughter from her back-breaking labour… Malacchmi's refusal to work affected the income of the household. What her husband and son brought in after their expenses was barely enough.

The identification of corpses was still going on. 'Please leave us now, swami! We can't come anymore. It is six months already', said Malacchmi's husband with folded hands.

'What is that! One month to fall in love and marry! Living together for three months. Pregnancy for three months. One week to leave the girl. Then two days to die', laughed a seasoned policeman. If someone had spoken like that in front of Malacchmi, she would have hit him and gone to jail. Her husband just listened and, leaving with folded hands said, 'We want the girl, not a corpse. Don't call us hereafter.'

'Yes! But what is happening to these girls who don't elope, or fall into canals, or come home? Why don't four women or four men sit and discuss this on TV? Is there a fuss only if city girls die? I will light candles for my own girl.' And Malacchmi lit seventeen candles and placed them in front of her doorstep.

Written 2017

Source: 'Peru Leni Pilla' by P. Sathyavathi (*Navya Vara Patrika*, 18 April 2017)

Varavara Rao

Varavara Rao was born in 1940 in Chinnapendyala in Warangal. He was a lecturer in Telugu at CKM College, Warangal, and later its principal. Rao set up the Sahithi Mitrulu (Friends of Literature) and published the literary journal *Srujana*. He was part of the Tirugubatu Kavulu (Association of Rebel Poets) that emerged to offer support to the Srikakulam movement, and a founder of Viplava Rachayitala Sangham (VIRASAM). VV is a prolific poet, literary critic and translator, whose writings from jail—written during several spells of imprisonment over four decades—are particularly memorable. He translated Kenyan writer Ngũgĩ wa Thiong'o's prison diary while in jail.

Encounter in the Waking Fields

1

The wind is blowing
The fishing hook
scents the fish swimming in the water

The wind is blowing
The foxes
smell the paddy stalks
lying in the field

In the fading darkness
the rising moonlight
peeps over the clouds
Birds nestling in the bushes in the hillocks
catch the eye of the khaki patrol

In fear of civilised jungle justice
Nestling in the arms of the forest, Bhukya
comes home for water
The pulley drops the bucket
into the well
startled at the sound of the jeep raid

2

In the hour that the whole earth is cracked
Parched for a drop of water
Some spring sparkles
Some clouds burst
Gathering resources for the sowing season
From streams, canals and wells

The ploughshares wake up
The barren fields stretch their arms

In the movement of the sprouting seeds
The mud smelt of creation
The earth pungent with the pounding of gunpowder
And the smell of exploded muddy hides

If water is to flow in the fields
The people who shed blood through sweat
If they are to enjoy
the sweet scent of paddy
They realise that they must shed blood
Blood that flows like water
Blood that is tears
Spilling it
till it overflows
They know it now

Now, to water their fields
in spring and summer
The peasantry is arming itself.

Written 12 April 1985

Author's note: Written on the encounter killings of five Naxalites while they were asleep in the rice fields on the hillocks of Kondapur, Vemulavada taluka, Karimnagar district.

Source: 'Melkontunna Polalato Encounter' by Varavara Rao (*Varavara Rao Kavitvam*, Hyderabad: Svecchasahiti, 2008, pp. 365–66)

K. Siva Reddy

K. Siva Reddy was born in 1943 in Karumuruvaripalem in Guntur. He was a lecturer in English literature at Vivek Vardhini College, Hyderabad, retiring as principal of the college. A prolific, award-winning poet with seventeen collections of poems published between 1973 and 2009, Siva Reddy is known for his commitment to peoples' movements and progressive politics. His poetry collections include *Mohana! O Mohana!*, *Kavisamayam*, and *Aame Evaraite Matram*.

The Hanging

Be ready for everything
We walk through mountains that crumble
Treading paths that dissolve without warning
We swim rivers
    not knowing if we will reach the other side
    just as far as the eye can see
    only as far as the hand can reach
A boundary that does not look like one
Injustice that seems like justice
Daylight that is like darkness
Darkness that is like daylight
Grasping two banks with both hands
Where is the warrior who cleaves
    the waters like a knife?
Who will inscribe four lines on the river
    that refuses to be calm?
In a time where you know not who will do what
    let us be ready for everything
Some plan is in progress

to make us know ourselves
From the gallows
Will Srinadha speak
Or will Siva Reddy speak
In a court that claims there are no executions
when the plot to hang you has already begun
we must be prepared for everything.

Written 18 April 2017

Source: 'Uriteeta' by K. Siva Reddy (*Navya Vara Patrika*)

Singamaneni Narayana

Singamaneni Narayana (1943–2021), born in Bandamidapalli in Anantapur, was a short-story writer whose stories focused on the agonising experiences of farmers in the arid lands of Rayalaseema. A literary critic and editor, he was a widely respected writer and social activist. He was instrumental in offering critical support to writers from Rayalaseema and consolidating the distinctive literature of the region.

Crocodile Face

Getting off the bus, I put down my small suitcase and, wiping my face with my handkerchief, looked around. Except for the bus that dropped me, there was no one in sight. I stood looking at the iron signboard fixed on two sticks at the edge of the road that said 'Venkatapuram: 2 km', and glanced at my watch. It was about ten o'clock. The sun blazed cruelly, with the fury of a landlord attacking dalits.

I was posted to Venkatapuram Elementary School as a 'Secondary Grade Assistant'. I received the posting order three days ago. I got this job two years after I had finished my BEd. I was selected after passing the written and oral test conducted by the zila parishad.

'You got a job through the reserved quota! You SC fellows are really lucky.' When an upper-caste friend in my village said this, I was disgusted.

'It is not your merit. It is your caste's', he said, spewing envy.

'So, why haven't you, born into an upper caste, got a job till now with your merit?' I asked him seriously.

'What do you mean "why"? It is because of your reserved quota fellows…' he said, and I felt like slapping him hard.

I was troubled that whole day. Those words of my friend were not new to me.

'We have had freedom for so many years. If reservations continue even now, the ones with merit will be swept into the mud.' I have been hearing this since my college days.

'SC, ST castes are being offered many educational opportunities by the government. Free education, free meals, books and clothes; isn't that enough for their development? They should use these opportunities and compete. But to use caste without any merit to knock off good jobs is a social menace.' When a lecturer would shoot off like this, I would get furious.

I had seen many such filthy mindsets in my student life. I had faced many of these sarcastic statements full of disdain in several situations.

I was born far from the village, in an old hut in a harijanawada of about thirty huts, twenty-three years ago. My childhood was full of difficulties and humiliation. I have no hesitation in talking about this today. Anyone born into the family of a bonded labourer who swept dung and rubbish in farmers' houses, emptied dirty water, and worked like a slave, was born into a life full of troubles.

My father was a servant in a big farmer's house. I am told my grandfather was also a servant. Come to think of it, what else would my ancestors be but bonded labour? When I was six years old, studying in the first class of our village elementary school, my father died. It was no ordinary death. He was drawing water from a well when a nail came off and he fell into the well along with the rope. His head broke, his body was in pieces, and he died a cruel death. When I think of those times, I begin to shiver even now.

My grandfather was alive when my father died. My mother, I, my brother and sister: this was our family! It was difficult even for this small family to survive. My mother did all kinds of work. She would work as a coolie. She would do the dirty work in farmers' houses without straightening her back. She would stitch slippers. She would carry an axe on her shoulder and clear thorny bushes. She supported the family single-handed. I still remember how bitterly my mother wept when my grandfather suggested that I should be taken out of school and sent to graze cattle for some farmer. I still remember my schoolteacher Dayanandam garu. He was a Christian, and he was like his name. 'Don't take your son out of school, amma. You don't know what lies in the future. He is intelligent enough to study. I will manage it.' When he said this, my mother touched his feet. That scene is still before my eyes. In the fourth class, Dayanandam teacher, teaching a lesson on Ambedkar, said, 'My son! In this country, you can change your religion but caste is permanent. A man like Ambedkar, disgusted by the caste system, became a Buddhist.' Those words haunt me even today.

There was no high school in my village. I joined a high school four miles away and stayed in the SC hostel. I owed this to Dayanandam teacher. My high-school teachers were all very indifferent to the boys in my hostel.

Deep in thought, head to the ground, I walked along when I sensed someone standing in front of me and looked up. In front of me was a sixty-year-old man, with an old sheet on his shoulder, bent with stick in hand. He was unable to stand straight.

I barely took four steps and there were people walking around; women sitting in front of their houses; lying across the path were two buffaloes; standing between them, looking at me curiously were some dogs; I could hear music from the radios in the houses I passed; the noisy chatter of men standing before a beedi shop—signalling to me the bustle of a village.

There was a small shed beside the beedi shop. It could be a hotel. Leaning against the shed, a neem tree. In front of the shed, in the shade of the tree, two long benches, with a couple of people drinking coffee.

Since I was new to the village, they observed me carefully and in silence.

I walked up to the shed and sat on an empty bench with my suitcase. The man in front of me greeted me, 'Which is your village?' He wore white clothes and looked like an educated man. Probably four or five years older than me.

I introduced myself in four words.

'Oho! It is you. They informed us in the mandalam office a few days ago that they had posted a teacher in our village. You seem to have travelled a long way', he said.

I smiled.

'I think this is your first appointment. You got a job at a young age', he said, as if complimenting me.

He then asked for a mug of water from the hotel. I washed my face.

'Will you eat some tiffin?' he asked.

'I ate in the morning in town. Coffee will do', I said. Sipping my coffee I asked him, 'What do you do?'

'What is there to do? Farming. I failed Inter and stayed on in the village', he said laughing.

Suddenly, a man came there in haste, removed the towel that was wrapped around his head and threw it on his shoulder, and sat down on his knees in a corner of the hotel. He was perhaps fifty years old. He was thin and dark like a dried berry. A dirty banyan and a waistcloth that barely reached his knees. He had wrapped an old paper around his stick. Sitting, he stretched out his skinny hand, took a glass that was in the corner, and called out 'Sami', bending towards the hotel. A few minutes later, the owner of the hotel came out and poured some water into his glass and went back. The man gulped down the water and kept sitting. After two minutes, coffee was poured into the glass, and he sipped it slowly, blowing on it. He then waited for water to be poured into the glass again, washed it, and put it back in the corner. He loosened his waistcloth and counted some change before he walked off briskly, as if on work.

I understood who he was and what his actions meant, and grew very disturbed. I wondered if I too would have to take the glass if it became known who I was. I was agitated.

I stopped the man I met there from paying for my coffee, and paid for it myself.

'Will you show me the way to the elementary school?' I asked him, getting up from the bench and picking up my suitcase. 'My house is on the way. Come with me', he said and I walked along.

As we walked along, he told me about his village. It was a small village with less than two hundred households. There were no good harvests for the last two years. There was no water in the wells. Families depended on coolie work. Six months ago, there had been heavy rain. The roof of the elementary school had collapsed in that rain. It was an old building. Since then, the school was being run in the Anjaneya Swami temple. For years, the authorities had promised to appoint a second teacher. 'After so long, you are the second teacher.' He kept chatting along the way.

When I heard the school was in the Anjaneya Swami temple, I was agitated and stopped walking. I remembered the Anjaneya Swami temple in our village. Our Anjaneya Swami was famous in all the surrounding villages. Someone or the other would keep coming and performing betel leaf puja in the temple.

We used to crowd around the temple as school boys. My friends would go in, but I would stay outside nervously. The devotees would break coconuts and throw a few pieces at me from a distance.

As I grew older, I thought a god who can't be touched by us is untouchable, and would laugh to myself bitterly. When we passed a few people on the way, he introduced me. 'This is our new teacher.'

When we turned a corner, he pointed to an old building and said, 'This is the elementary school whose roof collapsed. Nobody knows when they will repair it.'

The village was full of narrow lanes and bylanes. There were small stones strewn across the path. I walked beside him. The sun was blazing.

We walked along a large street. As we turned the corner, we saw the Anjaneya Swami temple in a wide open space.

'That is the temple. That is the school', he said.

I stood there astonished by that temple. The children were sitting in groups on the steps and platforms in the shade. I could see them clearly.

In front of them, before the temple, in the blazing, merciless sun, a man was saying something, gesturing with his hands. He had a small towel on his head. His cheeks were covered with streams of sweat. There was a small stool curled up helplessly at his feet. Wearing a thin cloth and standing erect, he looked like someone performing a fiery penance amidst five fires. Like an old thumma[1] tree that had grown on its own from the ground, withering away with no water, he looked miserable to me.

When I stopped, the man beside me stopped and said, 'You have to take lessons here, saar.' 'That is alright. But who is the man standing in front of the temple?' 'He is your fellow teacher. He came here a year ago', he said in a tone that implied 'Can't you understand that much?'

'But what is that? Why is he standing in the sun and teaching?' I asked with a quaver in my voice.

'He is a harijan, saar, a harijan. It is unavoidable.'

When he said that so normally, as if it were an ordinary matter, a fire raged in my belly, my heart pounded, and my body was ablaze. I stood there smouldering. After a few moments I controlled myself.

I looked at his face calmly. 'I am also a harijan', I said in a firm voice.

Written 1995

Source: 'Makaramukham' by Singamaneni Narayana (*Singamaneni Narayana Kathalu*, edited by Vedagiri Rambabu, Hyderabad: Sri Vedagiri Communications, 2012, pp. 140–47)

---

1 babul tree

Cherabandaraju

Cherabandaraju (1944–82), born Baddam Bhaskara Reddy in Ankusapuram in Hyderabad, was a Telugu teacher in a government school in Hyderabad. He was one of the Digambara poets of the late 1960s, and later, one of the founders of VIRASAM. He earned wide acclaim for his revolutionary songs. He was imprisoned in 1971 under the Preventive Detention Act, and again in 1973 under the Maintenance of Internal Security Act, and finally implicated in the Secunderabad conspiracy case for inciting armed rebellion against the state through his songs. He died young, and is remembered for singing the revolution as few could.

Vandemataram

O my beloved motherland
You are mother, father and god
Yours the virtue of heaving in the beds of tyrants
Yours the beauty of one who has pawned each limb in the global market
Yours the youth of one who slumbers forgetfully in the arms of the wealthy
Swooning unmoved whether people spit at you or cast mud at you
You are the Bharati who stands patiently
While rats and bandicoots dig at the roots of crops ripe for harvest
You are the evergreen land that does not reach people's mouths
Vandemataram! Vandemataram!
Stitching flags from the clothes on your body
Boldly you parade naked
Yours the wretchedness of a cat with burnt paws
Roaming on terraces built on borrowed money

Yours the grief of being unable to comfort
Children who spring at your shrivelled breasts
Yours the elegance of woman starving, blazing with hunger
Taking to the streets in borrowed finery
Amma Bharati! Whither are you going?
Vandemataram! Vandemataram!

Written June 1968

Source: 'Vandemataram' by Cherabandaraju (*Cherabandaraju Kavitalu: Patalu*, edited by Varavara Rao, Vijayawada: Peoples' Books, 1982, p. 5)

AKKINENI KUTUMBA RAO

Akkineni Kutumba Rao is a novelist and film maker known especially for his sensitive portrayals of the working classes. He was born in 1946 in Choutapalli in the Krishna district. His novel *Sorajyem* explores caste and depicts the subjugation of dalits in rural Andhra—the first to focus on village life after Unnava Lakshminarayana's *Malapalli*. His *Karmika Geetam* tells the stories of the urban, industrial working class in Telangana. An award-winning film director, Rao's film *Bhadram Koduko*, which focuses on the injustices of child labour, is particularly well known.

Sorajyem

Sorajyem stood without saying a word.

'Why don't you speak? Where were you dying all this time?'

'I was in the field—the ridge broke.'

'The ridge broke... You just sat there, you wretch.'

When the coolies were all returning from the fields, Paddalu thumped her daughter a couple of times.

Sorajyem ran across the bund, crying.

'I will break your legs, just you wait', said Paddalu, following her, but the other coolies cooled her down saying, 'Let her go. Why do you get behind her?'

[…]

When the circus arrived next to the big school, Sorajyem ran there to stare in wonder at the bear and the monkeys.

Bodi and Sankurathirigadu were running into the village.

'Oley, Bodi! Voley, Sankurathiriga! Come let's look at the bear, come soon!' shouted Sorajyem.

Hearing Sorajyem call, they stopped running and came crying to Sorajyem. Sorajyem, who was full of excitement, saw their tears and said, 'But why?' with a sad face.

'My brother has been tied to a tree, it seems. And they are going to beat him', said Bodi and began running again. Sankurathirigadu ran crying after her.

After pausing for a moment, Sorajyem also ran after both of them.

Jojigadu was older than Bodi and Sankurathirigadu. Six months after Sankurathirigadu was born, their father had died in the field when the bullock cart overturned. He was working as a farmhand for Nallachantabbayi garu when he died.

Jojigadu was only eight years old when his father died. His mother put him to work for Nallachantabbayi garu as a young farmhand. She used to work for wages, sometimes in kamma houses, sprinkling the yard, pounding paddy, and making cow dung cakes.

A few people were kind to her because she was a poor widow whose husband had died.

When Bodidi, Sankurathirigadu and Sorajyem reached the tamarind tree in front of Nallachantabbayi's house, there were many doras there.

Sovi garu who was passing that way in a bullock cart called out, 'What happened, Peddoda?'

'Nothing much… It's a mala fellow. He stole something it seems at Chantannayya garu's house. They have tied him to a tree', he said.

'Slipper the bastard so that he doesn't do it again and again', said Sovi garu as his cart turned the corner.

'The thieving bastard's hands should be broken', said Mohana Rao garu who was right there.

'Arey, Pesadu, why waste time needlessly? Get a measure of sugar, throw him down, tie his hands and legs, and sprinkle the sugar over his whole body with a few drops of water. That should teach the bastard a lesson for all his next lives… Go soon… get it…', Malleswara Rao garu said.

Sundarayya garu, who was hurrying, turned that way and asked, 'What did he do, this fellow?' addressing the others there.

'It seems he stole', a few of them replied together. All of them said 'it seems'.

'He is no bigger than a finger, this son of an ass. Tomorrow when he grows up, will he obey? He will become the gang leader of the Gudivada taluka. Look at his eyes! The rascal has rogue eyes. Take a sharp hatchet and strike the thieving bastard.' And, turning to leave, he sprang back at him in rage and slapped him on both his cheeks. Now Jojigadu, caught in this unexpected happening, till then dull as yam with tears in his eyes, burst out weeping loudly. Hearing his weeping, his mother started howling loudly. Jojigadu's sister, his brother and Sorajyem all began to cry.

All the doras hissed in one note.

'Stop that rogue weeping! Damned weeping!' they shouted.

They stifled their crying.

Sundarayya garu, leaving in a hurry, stopped at the turning and shouted furiously, 'Don't let the thieving son of a donkey go! Pulp his hands and feet. Let the son of a donkey complain to who he will!'

Hearing this, Bodidi, Sorajyem and Sankurathirigadu burst into tears again.

'Pesadu babu, just let him go this once, babu. I will die and be born in your belly. He is not the kind who steals, oh my father, my father.' Jojigadu's mother ran and clutched the feet of all the men there.

Nallachantabbayi garu rolled his eyes angrily. 'Then do you mean I did it and put the blame on him?... You thieving whore! You! — your mother! You should be tied to a tree and thrashed. You filthy whore!' And he leapt up. 'Arey, Mohana, fetch a rope from the shed. We will punish this fellow. He will tell us whether he really stole or not', he said in a rage.

Mohana Rao hurried into the Nallachantabbayi garu's courtyard and brought a rope.

They untied Jojigadu from the tree and hung him from a branch. Two or three caught the other end and pulled. The rope tied around his stomach tightened and Jojigadu gasped. He screamed in agony. The mother collapsed in a heap. She lost consciousness. The children surrounded her and wailed inconsolably.

Pesadu babu looked here and there and threw some straw under the branch. Someone poured some kerosene on it eagerly. Mohana Rao set the straw on fire. It burst into flames.

They kept yelling, pulling Jojigadu so that the flames touched him and missed him.

Some of the doras said, 'Stop it now, that's enough', and hurried away, leaving it to the boys.

Meanwhile, someone came running and whispered something in Nallachantabbayi's ear. He became like a monkey treading hot coals.

'Aaa... Let them come! Which whoresons will come? Arey, Pesadu! Gather our youth. The mala whoresons are coming with sticks. Let us see how far this will go! Are you listening?... Here, get some kerosene and pour it on this fellow. Let us see what those bastards will do!' he said, jumping up and down.

Jojigadu's mother became conscious and began to run madly here and there.

'Babu! Ayya! I hold your feet... Save my son!... Ayya! Ayya!' She kept falling at everyone's feet.

Bodidi, Sankurathirigadu and Sorajyem were weeping loudly. Pesadu hurried into the house and came out with a bottle of kerosene and poured it over Jojigadu. Some spilled on the flames below and flared up spreading to the kerosene on Jojigadu's clothes.

The mother ran and embraced her son and fell unconscious.

Bodi, Sankurathrigadu and Sorajyem stopped weeping and stood staring madly in horror.

The rope that held Jojigadu snapped and he fell on the ground. By then he was dead. From the time he was tied to the tree, it was all over in a quarter of an hour. The minute they realised he was dead, people slipped away one by one.

By then some malas and madigas had come from Malapalli and the fields.

Except for Jojigadu's mother, Bodi, Sankurathirigadu and Sorajyem, there was no one else.

The people who came were furious.

Some ran to Gudivada police station.

Some stood guard over the body with sticks.

The police arrived before dark.

That case went on for six months. Nallachantabbayi sold an acre of his land. Four boys from Malapalli were jailed. For killing Jojigadu in a fight near the field.

[…]

Following cattle with dung baskets, gathering bramble from thorny thickets, hopping around the fields in rain or shine… Sorajyem no longer liked these tasks.

Seeing children cross the lake bund with slates, books and bags on their way to school, Sorajyem wanted to go to school.

The voices of children in school reciting 'amma', 'aavu', 'illu', 'eega' together after the master, the noisy rush of children out of their classes at the sound of the toilet bell, the lunch bell… these scenes brought joy to Sorajyem.

She asked her father if she could go to school.

Yenkadu has learnt to laugh a strange laugh these days. Whatever anyone asks him, he laughs like that.

If his wife says, 'There is no broken rice. Go out and try to get some', he laughs as if to say, 'Why do we need broken rice?'

'What is that wretched laugh? It is okay if there is no rice, but don't laugh that wretched laugh', snapped Paddalu.

That day, Tirapati said 'Orey ayya, I don't want to work as a farmhand any more. The doras are burning us alive. Get an acre or two somewhere. We can work on the land for our living.'

Yenkadu replied with his crazy laugh.

'Acres, he says, acres. Where are the acres, ra? How will I cultivate the land?' said Yenkadu, falling on his string cot, laughing long and hard.

Tirapati is only now understanding the ways of the world. His grandfathers were farmhands. His fathers were farmhands. He is a farmhand. If he marries tomorrow, his sons will be farmhands. His grandsons will be farmhands.

There were five or six people in Malapalli who had land. And how much? An acre, acre and a half. Only Durgadu had two acres. Great property! If a man has some means, he leases land from one dora or the other; the hapless ones do not even have that.

Tirapati was crestfallen when he heard his father say 'How will I cultivate the land'.

There was a change in the mala youth after Jojigadu's murder. Tirapati was leading the way.

These days after they return from work in the doras' houses every evening, the youth gather in the Mala Rama temple and talk about the injustices they are subjected to.

That is why he told his father he did not want to be a farmhand but wanted to work independently—and his father laughed his mad laugh.

'It looks like he has gone mad, amma', said Tirapati to Paddalu.

'I don't know, ra. I too feel the same way. Oh god! Some misfortune seems to be upon us', said Paddalu groaning loudly.

'"I want to go to school"... You fool, do you think you are a dora's child? What will you do going to school? Will you become a teacheramma? Will you become a nurseamma? Osey, may your belly burn...' And Yenkadu cackled, repeating this to himself.

Sorajyem was so scared, she did not mention school for the next four days.

Then again one day, when her mother returned, she grumbled, 'Oley amma. Let me go to school.'

Paddalu was overcome with grief hearing her daughter's words. She drew her close with tears in her eyes, silent.

Her husband had lost his mind. Her son was clashing with the doras. She had an asthmatic cough. How can this damn girl study?

Can one just talk one's way to sending her to school? Clothes must be bought. Books must be bought. She is already eight years old. If I send her to someone like Anasuyamma's house, she will be able to live her life.

'Live your life in labour. Why do people like us need to study? Will it feed us?' she said, trying to reason with the girl.

Written 1981

Source: Excerpt from *Sorajyem* by Akkineni Kutumba Rao (Hyderabad: Sveccha Prachuranalu, 2012, pp. 63–69)

AMMANGI VENUGOPAL

Ammangi Venugopal (b. 1948) is a playwright, short-story writer, literary critic, and translator from Vikarabad. He taught in government colleges in Karimnagar, Medak, Nalgonda and Mahbubnagar, eventually retiring as a principal. His poetry collections include *Minugurulu*, *Pacha Bottu-Patancheru*, and *Bharosa*.

Dry Leaf

When there was conspiracy in high places
the farmer little knew that the waterfall
would not turn into a canal to water his field.
He only knew to plough with his spine
Only to scatter seeds erasing

the lines on his palm
After all this
His parched eyes could not realise
the harvest of his dreams
Hunger, the year-long single season
The stream ran dry
The field was pledged
But to tear it asunder and sell it
The field held generations of souls
Where do you want me to migrate?
When you painted my desolate lifeline green
and called it the green revolution
Do you know
what the dry leaves said?
Unfortunately
the farmer understands the tongue of the dry leaves.

Written 1988

Source: 'Yendutaaku' by Ammangi Venugopal (*Raitu Kavita*, edited by Papineni Sivasankar, Bandla Madhava Rao and M.V. Rami Reddy, Guntur: Muvva Chinnabapi Reddy Memorial Trust, 2004, p. 34)

RACHAPALEM CHANDRASEKHARA REDDY

Rachapalem Chandrasekhara Reddy, born in 1948 in Kuntrapakam, Chittoor, was Professor of Telugu at Sri Krishnadevaraya University, Anantapur, and Yogi Vemana University, Kadapa. His work has focused on literary criticism, and his book *Mana Navalalu–Mana Kathanikalu* won the Sahitya Akademi Award in 2014.

Drought Land

The Seema that feasted on millet rotte, hot chilli, millet gruel
mashed lentil, fermented gruel, and dry pickle once
Drought has turned men into withered trunks
And served up tears for dessert
Flung into a corner of the nation's map
This drought-stricken barren Seema.

Drought
Blooming in Seema's courtyard
A strange tree indeed.
Its tricks are eternal
It forces you to sell a cow, dear as your child
Makes you chop down a tree big as a hill
Turns a gentle soul into a brute
Sending a girl who knows not the sun
water pot in hand for miles and miles

The farmer, once smiling and twirling his moustache
finds a fire raging in his belly
Extinguishing the fire in the home of the coolie
whose sweat watered the land that bloomed
It speeds the new bride swiftly to the graveyard
and turns dustbins and canals into cradles for newborn babes
Turning homes into exits
Emptying whole villages
It converts humans into migratory birds

The rainbow, the eastern breeze
the calf trotting with lifted tail
The rain coming down from the mountains
like a curtain falling on the stage
The laughter of children—this
A rare scene indeed, a year-old dream
for the people of Seema

Dying in a flood is better far than dying of hunger
Instead of dying inch by inch
swinging between consciousness and unconsciousness
It is far better to be carried away by raging floods!

Drought
is the golden tree for the Seema gangs
In the Seema that once played music on its rocks
melting hardened hearts

Drought
has turned men's hearts to stone
Severing all friendship and bonds
Turning men into falling stars
Transforming men into vengeful brutes
Humane men into hunting dogs

The Tree of Drought is laden with schemes that are its branches
and funds its fruit
Guarded and fenced by offices
Yet the fruits will soon vanish
But the drought remains always safe.

Written 1998

Source: 'Karuvugadda' by Rachapalem Chandrasekhara Reddy (*Raitu Kavita*, edited by Papineni Sivasankar, Bandla Madhava Rao and M.V. Rami Reddy, Guntur: Muvva Chinnabapi Reddy Memorial Trust, 2004, p. 118–19)

N. Gopi

N. Gopi, born in 1948 in Bhongir, Nalgonda, is a poet and literary critic from Telangana. He was Professor of Telugu at Osmania University, and was later appointed the youngest Vice Chancellor of Potti Sreeramulu Telugu University (1999–2002). He retired from teaching in 2008. Gopi has been a pathfinder in Telugu literature, having created a new poetic form, 'naaneelu' (four-line poems with a distinctive structure), and published 21 collections of poems. He is also recognised for his important contribution to understanding the work of Vemana.

Border Villages

Who knows who will die when?
They die too after all.
Darkness spreads
like the shadow of the dead.
In the villages on the border
Danger with no borders
Even fear becomes a habit
Like disease.

No small matter
to transport your life
in a moment…
Easier far
to give up life.

You can pack bag and baggage
But what of relationships and memories
To sweep them into a basket
Is so painful!

Gunfire
from the other side.
This side retorts.
The wounded from the last war
Yesteryear's heroes
Unheeded today.

What of the fields ready for harvest?
What of the rivers of sweat
that have poured for months?
What will you do to drive away
the lifelong nightmares of children?

Aiyyo!
Better far to die once and for all
Than die each single moment.
Better a war that is final
than this bursting of firecrackers.

To love one's country must be good
But this forced patriotism is tragic.

War is but news for us
For them it is boundless sorrow.
A border is but a nation's map here
But there
the line dividing life and death.

Written 2017

Source: 'Sarihaddu Gramaalu' by N. Gopi (*Andhra Jyothi*, 2017)

B.S. Ramulu

B.S. Ramulu was born in 1949 in Jagtiyala. Active in the Revolutionary Writers' Association and civil liberties movement, he was underground between 1985 and 1990, during which period he actively organised revolutionary cultural forums. A prolific writer, he has written countless songs, over 150 short stories, as well as political and literary essays. A leading literary figure and political activist in Telangana, B.S. Ramulu was Chairperson of the Telangana State Backward Classes Commission.

The Lessons of Life

'Your name?'

'Erragolla Mallayya, saar…'

'What do you do?'

'We are shepherds… We graze sheep…'

'Why did you come to jail?'

'It seems we killed some fellow. Somebody got us a life sentence…'

'How many children? What happened actually? Tell me the whole story…'

'What do I say? Where do I begin? I paid the old saredar[1] saab of our village five hundred. Within two months, this dora[2] came, dora.[3] The dora who went said he would tell this dora, dora. But this dora said I don't know anything about that. If you pay me six hundred, it's okay. Otherwise, no. So I paid and was grazing, dora.

1 revenue official

2 officer

3 sir (respectful mode of address)

It had not been even two months since I paid it. He shouldn't have asked even a paisa for the next four months, dora.'

'Where is your receipt? Give it to me.'

'What receipt, dora? When I asked for the receipt, he just said, "It is my responsibility to let you graze for a year", dora.'

'All lies, saar.'

'If you say lies, will the money I paid just blow away? Gollarajudu, Kittadu, Yenkadu, we all paid at the same time. Call them and ask them, dora!'

'Arey! Don't tell us all that. You have to pay twelve hundred rupees fine. Otherwise I will challan your sheep. Go get the money.'

'Where will I, your slave, get it today? I will bring it tomorrow morning. Where will you be?'

'I will be in the dora's gadi.[1] You must bring it in the morning. I will eat my food and leave by noon.'

'Ayya! The sheep are not all mine. Half are the dora's. Half of the rest are the village folk's… the rest are mine. I will pay the fine for my thirty sheep. Ask the dora for his, I beg you. I will send the other villagers to you. Ask them to pay for theirs.'

'I don't know about all that.'

'For the villagers, I will ask them or I will pay. But at least you ask the dora.'

'Again the same story? I don't know all that.'

'Then keep the sheep. Do what you will… I will also see.'

'Arey! You are talking a lot. What is it?'

'Then what? You sleep in the dora's house. You eat in the dora's house. And you ask me to pay his fine. You think only you can talk?'

'Eelam… Tie up this bastard and throw him in the jeep…'

'What is this, ayya! The more I keep quiet, the louder you get. Earlier you asked them to tie me to a tree. Now you ask them to tie me up and throw me in the jeep. You call me a whoreson and a bastard. Can't you talk to me properly?'

My cheek went 'Tchal! Tchal!'

---

1 landlord's mansion

'Beat me! Beat me more. Seeing I am alone, four of you set on me. What more can you do? You catch a shepherd and beat him up. Half the flock belongs to the dora. If you have the guts, beat that dora… He doesn't even pay me my wages… Just blows. I am a poor man… I live in this village. Why can't you ask? You can eat in the dora's house, you can sleep in the dora's house, but you can't ask the dora? Educated fellows like you? You are government servants. All you can do is beat a poor, skinny man.'

Tchal! Tchal!… He stopped because his hand was paining. My teeth were bleeding.

'Are you finished? Is your hand paining with hitting? Beat me more, kill me. You eunuchs… bastards who don't have the guts to ask the dora! Eat what he gives you and flap your arms. With stolen wood he built houses in town for his son-in-law and son. Don't say anything to that dora! Just kick us. Tax the sheep that graze in the forest. Where will sheep graze if not in the forest? Shall I graze them in the fields? Thoo! Theri! Sarkar, my…! What sarkar is this!'

'Orey Malliga! Hasn't the drink gone down yet? It seems you were fully drunk yesterday and said something to them?'

'Where did I drink? I'm your slave.'

'Tchat! Why are you talking back again, ra? Do you want to stay in the village or not?'

'It is your mercy. I am your slave. What do I know how to speak? I move between sheep and house.'

'Move around with some fear in your body.'

'Ayya…!'

'Aaa, why have you come?'

'Ayya, all the shepherds insisted that we come.'

'What do they want?'

'Why should we pay the fine? Isn't he charging us for it? Who asked him to graze them in the forest?'

'He will pay, you go… What did you do with the money that you got a couple of days ago from the field below the Pochampadu canal? If they were small fellows from here, I would tell them.

But this checking party came from Warangal. These fellows won't listen if told… Go and bring it…'

'The Warangal men took twelve hundred and gave a receipt for two hundred, dora! It is not even four months. Again they are asking for money.'

'I don't know all that, I am telling you beforehand. Don't say that you gave the chowkidar or saredar money to the officers. Their mamools are different. The fines are to be paid separately. Give me what you agreed to give me. What did you say yesterday? Didn't you say yesterday that you would bring the money today? Again you have gone back to where you started?'

'Okay. Rajugadu has it. I will bring him, wait… Rajugo, Rajugo, Raroo.'

'…'

'Hit the bastard… Isn't the axe sharp?… Kill him… The bastard…'

Saredar: 'Ammo, I am dying…'

'Then did all twenty of you get jail sentences?'

'Only four. They are here.'

'If they release you, will you live happily with your wife and children?'

'My wife died. The boys wash dishes in a hotel in the city. The girl is being looked after by her maternal uncles.'

'Then what will you do?'

'After we kill the dora who turned us out of home and graveyard, we will think about that question…'

'What did the dora say?'

'The dora is the real reason behind everything! When the Pochampadu canal was flowing through the dora's fields, he turned it and it submerged my field. For his sheep, he made me pay fines and put me in debt. Who would know… if he were killed in the jungle, we thought… But making this an excuse, he sold all the wood in the forest and accused us of stealing it… and killing the saredar who caught us. He produced false witnesses and handed us over to the police and got us jailed, dora.'

'Whatever happened is over. We have come to help you. If you change your opinion, we will see that the government releases you. The government will give you some financial aid. You can live your life, isn't it?'

'This sarkar! It didn't let me live my life. And now again it will help me! Lies…'

'We came just for that. We come on behalf of the All India Humanist Association and Kindness to Animals Association. We will get you help. We will see that you are rehabilitated.'

'Then first set right the mistake that the government did… Get me back my acre of land. Bring my wife back to life… Educate my sons like yours. See that our boys are put in good jobs for educated people like you… Then we can discuss the help that the government wants to give.'

'No one can turn the clock back. No god can turn time back. Ask something else.'

'What did I ask that was so great? I asked for my life back! If you can't do that, what can you do for us? What did you expect when you came here? Why did you come?'

'We just thought poor fellow, we would help you. But you are talking too much!… There is no limit to your greed…'

'You are getting mighty angry. What did I ask, ayya?… Why do you say poor fellow?… What crime did we commit?… What are you talking, ayya?… The shepherd caste was not born today… Sheep were not born today… There were shepherds before Sri Krishna was born, and sheep. Even in olden days, people did not graze their sheep in their houses. They grazed them in the forest. They worship Sri Krishna for allowing them to graze in the forest. I did the same thing, and see what plight you have brought me to… When sheep have grazed in the forest from olden times, if you say don't graze them now, where will they graze? So a sarkar that has such goodwill could ban eating sheep meat… and ask us to stop rearing sheep, isn't it? I would have given up sheep and reared buffaloes. Sheep meat is loved, but the shepherd is not wanted? Does the sarkar think about how he will survive?…'

'You are stubborn. That is why you are here… Someone is teaching you all this.'

'Why should anyone teach me? Is it wrong to say I want my own life back?'

'You are not at fault… We are wrong… We took a lot of trouble searching for you and came here. That was our stupidity.'

Written 1979

Source: 'Bathuku Nerpina Paatham' by B.S. Ramulu (*Kalam Tecchina Marpu: Kathala Samputi*, Hyderabad: Visala Sahitya Academy, 2013, pp. 96–101)

Gaddar

Gaddar, born Gummadi Vittal Rao in 1949 in Toopran, Hyderabad State, is known across the country as a revolutionary balladeer. A founder of Jana Natya Mandali, his singular contribution has been to bring song to the centre of Telugu literature. As a member of the CPI-ML, he spent long periods underground and travelled extensively in villages and forests, mobilising people through his songs which told stories of the valour and courage of ordinary people in the face of violence by the state. He played a crucial role in the movement for a separate Telangana.

Lashkar Bonalu

Chorus
It seems
Today and tomorrow
Is the Lashkar Bonalu
When is our Bonalu, O Balamani?
When is our Bonalu, O Balamani?

I do not have a clean sari
Not a change of blouse
Not a smear of kumkum[1] for the bonam pot
No chicken to slaughter for Kali Ma
How can I raise a bonam, O Bavayya?
What do I pray for, O Bavayya?

(Chorus)

The children are young
They gaze longingly at the neighbour's faces
By the next year, who knows
Whether we will be in the house
Or in the flames?
Somehow we manage
Scrounge here, scrounge there
Somehow we will manage
Slaughter a chicken, O Balamani!
Cook a coconut biryani, O Balamani!

A curse on all festivals!
May there be a funeral in the festival house!
Festival follows festival on each other's heels
For each festival the daughter and son-in-law arrive!
The mother-in-law promptly follows to fetch the daughter home
And we must serve toddy and arrack to the in-laws
Or lose our dignity and self-respect
We are hungry people without food, O Bavayya
We will be buried in debt, O Bavayya

You keep saying debt-debt-debt
How much, after all, is this debt you speak of?
I am the one who brings home the food
I am the one who clears the debt
You only have to cook food and serve

---

1 vermilion

And yet you grumble 'Hoon… haan'
Let the young one grow just a little bit more
We can bond him to a farmer for a sum, O Balamani
And clear all our debts, O Balamani!

Last year's debt is still unpaid
I begged and begged the butcher
And brought home a goat head and legs
You can't see any of this, can you?
You won't see that we don't have a crumb
You say, 'Bring it on! Bring it out! Bring more!'
You order, 'Serve! Serve! Serve! Serve!'
I have wiped every pot clean, O Bavayya!
I slept on an empty belly last night, O Bavayya!

(Chorus)

What is in your heart, O Balamani, tell me!
Do not disturb my mind like this, O Balamani!

My younger brother, the one after me, left home, O Bavayya!
He has gone to fight for the rule of the poor, O Bavayya!
If we follow that path and struggle beside him
Perhaps one day we too can cut a goat, O Bavayya!
We can raise a red bonam, O Bavayya!

(Chorus)

Translator's note: Bonalu is a festival in which the goddess Kali is worshipped for protection from disease, pox and poverty. Typically, a goat or chicken is sacrificed to Mother Kali while women carrying decorated pots of water ('bonam') on their heads go dancing to the temple. The chicken is then cooked and eaten with pots of toddy. 'Lashkar' (army) refers to Secunderabad—so called after the army camp set up there by the East India Company after a treaty with the Nizam in 1798.

Source: 'Lashkar Bonalu' by Gaddar (*My Life Is a Song: Gaddar's Anthems for the Revolution*, translated by Vasanth Kannabiran, New Delhi: Speaking Tiger Books, 2021, pp. 92–94)

DEVIPRIYA

Devipriya (1951–2020) was the pen name of Khaja Hussain. He was a widely respected journalist, script writer, lyricist and poet from Tadikonda, Guntur. His books include *Amma Chettu*, *Neeti Putta*, *Chepa Chiluka*, *Tuphanu Tummeda*, *Gareebu Geetaalu*, *Samajananda Svaami* and *Gali Rangu*.

Song of a Season

Seasons come
Seasons pass
Water camps and bonfires
remind us
of changing life
Soldiers marching on the streets of the town
The police
guarding the Secretariat
The security forces
shielding temples and mosques
Are these reminders
that we roam imprisoned
in this great big world that is a cage…
What does the earth that yields ragi know
of the Constitution?
What does rain that falls somewhere far away know
for whom red millet is sowed?
In a land detached from the seasons
What does a grain of sugar trapped by an ant
care about what Kalidasa said in *Rutu Samhara*?

Source: 'Oka Rutugeetam' by Devipriya (*Gandhakuti Kavita Sankalanam*, Secunderabad: Samata Books, 2009, p. 8)

Chilukuri Devaputra

Chilukuri Devaputra (1951–2016), born in Kaluvapalli in Anantapur, was a novelist and short-story writer, and an important dalit voice in Telugu literature from Rayalaseema. His novels *Addamlo Chandamama* (1989), and *Panchamam* (1998) explore dalit lifeworlds. His short stories have been published in three volumes.

Descending Scale

Not just this Sunday. No Sunday seemed like a holiday. Even if there was no office work, there was no escape from cooking…

'Radha! Tea, quickly! My folk are in a hurry to leave', shouted Jeevan from the outer room.

'Aaa, I'm coming!' I yelled back.

In five minutes, I had served everyone tea. Jeevan looked at the four men sitting around and, addressing a man who was thin and dark, said, 'See Mr Jayaraj, my missus, Radha. A typist in the Irrigation Department.' Then, laughing, he turned to me and introduced us: 'He is Jayaraj. My colleague. He was transferred to our office recently.' We greeted each other with namaskarams. I sat on a chair beside Jeevan.

'Mr Jayaraj! Perhaps you don't know. Ours is an "intercaste" marriage. Intercaste! You know my caste, isn't it? She is a mala; your caste only, SC. So you and I are indirectly related', said Jeevan laughing. Jayaraju laughed uncomfortably while the other three laughed heartily.

I was embarrassed sitting there. How do I leave the place? Jeevan was always like that. He never bothered about occasion or context. It was enough if he just got a chance. He would start talking about his intercaste marriage.

'There is no other fellow lucky like Jayaraju, Radha! He joined our department as a junior assistant three years ago! He is already a senior assistant. Tomorrow or day after he will become a deputy tahsildar.' Jayaraju sipped his tea with head bent as Jeevan talked.

Jeevan didn't stop there. 'We should all be proud of the fact that the government is encouraging SCs like this. What do you say, Seshayya!' Jeevan asked the man with thick glasses. Seshayya nodded in agreement, laughing.

'Actually, Ambedkar being born in this country is a great turn in the lives of these dalits, you know! That he included reservation for depressed classes in the constitution is a great good fortune for dalits. We should be happy about this', said Srinivasa Rao.

'Yes, how will people who have been oppressed for generations be capable of brilliance? Their genes will be encrusted with backwardness and inferiority', said Mohan.

Except for Jayaraju, the other three were always here on a holiday, playing either cards or checkers with Jeevan. So I couldn't believe my ears.

Sounds of vessels falling in the kitchen… I rushed into the kitchen. Rohit gadu stood there with a glass in hand. 'Eraa?' I snapped. And he said, 'Water, amma.' His face always looks as innocent as a three-year-old's to me. Jeevan tried very hard to put him in an English convent for LKG and UKG. I had to battle with Jeevan to see that he started school only at six and studied in his mother tongue. As a result of that battle, he had joined a Telugu school just a month ago. Jeevan had admitted him in school recently. Rohit gadu drank water and ran off to play.

In the room outside, Jeevan and his colleagues were discussing dalits. If Jayaraju had not been present, I know how chaotic that discussion would have been.

The sole reason for my losing all faith in human beings was Jeevan! Before we became life partners, we were classmates in BA. Then, he was first among students with modern ideas. He was a leader in the students' union. In those days, I used to sing at all college functions. Jeevan was crazy about my songs! He used to come home and tape my songs. My parents also respected Jeevan. He used to say, 'Your voice has the luxuriance of Lata and the sweetness of Susheela.' I can't describe my joy when I heard those words.

We grew fond of each other. Jeevan used to criticise the youth who took dowries as animals in the market. He used to say very passionately that untouchability was a blot on the race and that the word was obscene. By then Jeevan knew that I was a dalit. Soon after I joined BA, I took the exam for the clerical cadre Group Four. I got a job as a typist under the SC quota in the Irrigation Department and joined without completing my BA. It was the first turn in my life. Jeevan was overjoyed. About a week after, he appeared waiting near my office at closing time.

I said, 'My colleagues might misunderstand if you...', in a low voice.

Without replying, he took me to a hotel nearby. We sat at a table in the corner, sipping the coffee brought to us by a server. Suddenly Jeevan said, 'I am thinking of marrying you.'

I was speechless for a while. Talk of marriage without any talk of love! I couldn't tell if I was dreaming or this was real!

'If my father and mother agree... Besides you are from a higher caste!' I said. I felt that caste was a huge invisible fortress wall between human beings. My father listened to the whole story and said, 'You are capable of thinking clearly. I won't say no to your decision... Maybe Jeevan kept his economic status in view when he was asking you... Would he have asked you to marry him if you didn't have this job? Think it over.' However much of a rationalist, perhaps it was his old age that made him obdurate, I thought. We were married in a month. After our wedding, he finished his BA with a second class and got a job as a teacher in a private convent with my father's recommendation. We lived happily for a year and a half. Rohit was born. He used to worry sometimes because he didn't get a government job. Occasionally he would fall prey to thinking that because of reservations he couldn't get a government job. Luckily, in six months he got a job in the Revenue Department as a junior assistant. There was a new enthusiasm in Jeevan.

I don't know when the spark of hatred towards dalits ignited in Jeevan, but it flared up when dalits were massacred in Chunduru. 'These fellows are not ordinary sons of —, Radha! They must have teased the landlord's women… If lower-caste fellows come and strut around and boast and show off with their sanghams, what will they do but kill them?' he said one morning after reading the paper.

'What is this, Jeevan? Is it you speaking?' I said, not knowing what to say.

'Radha! It is because you belong to that caste that you are not able to shed your pride in that caste and are surprised. As long as they behave, our people will look upon them like human beings. But if they cross limits, that's all.'

Something snapped… I wept, wondering at the hatred this man harboured. We did not speak to each other for a week. Then when there was an agitation against the Mandal Commission recommendations, he exposed himself yet again in support of the agitation. Although I said that reservations were part of the government's vote-hunting drama, and that untouchables would gain nothing from this, that it was just an empty gesture of wiping their tears, he would not listen.

***

The next day I came home to find Rohit sitting on the steps. I had arranged for him to stay at the neighbours till one of us returned home from work. Yet, I often found him sitting on the steps. 'Eraa! How long has it been since you came?' I asked. 'A very long time', he answered. He held onto my sari while I unlocked the door.

He said, 'Amma, they gave me new clothes and books in my school. See!' He pulled the clothes out of his bag as we stepped inside. A crumpled green cotton shirt and khaki shorts… It was a dress that would fit a ten-year-old. So children in Telugu schools got clothes and books! But for some reason I was uneasy. Perhaps the government decided to give clothes with needy children in mind. We can afford to pay. Was it right for us to take it? With both of us in government jobs, I felt we could not waste the resources of the government like this.

After dinner I told Jeevan that they had given free clothes and books to Rohit gadu in school.

'It is okay, it does not matter. The government will not go bankrupt by giving your son clothes. If you don't want them, give them away to a beggar', he said, smoking a cigarette.

I was not at peace. So I sent a letter to my office through Jeevan seeking permission to go an hour late and went to the school.

I went straight to the headmistress and explained the matter. 'Give these clothes to a child who needs them. They have been given to my son by mistake', I said.

'We did not make a mistake, amma. We gave your boy his quota of books and clothes because he is "SC".'

'Who said he is "SC"?'

'His father wrote SC in his application', she said.

My head just swirled.

Written 26 May 1995

Source: 'Vilomam' by Chilukuri Devaputra (*Chilukuri Devaputra Kathalu*, Kadapa: Penneti Publications, 2006, pp. 98–101)

K.N.Y. Patanjali

Born in Alamanda in Vizianagaram, Patanjali (1952–2009) was a journalist at different daily newspapers, finally serving as the editor of *Sakshi*. Immersed in the culture of north Andhra, he used humour and satire as tools of social critique. An acclaimed novelist, he reflected on the lives of journalists (in *Pempudu Jantuvu*), on the ways of the royal lineages of that region, on the lives of the common people, and on the pitiable lives of the police (in *Khakivanam*). *Veera Bobbili* and *Gopatrudu* are among his best-known stories.

Chittema impatiently threw her husband's pancha and lalchi,[1] which she had taken out of the wooden trunk, on the bedpost of the string cot. Bobbili, who had been sleeping under the cot, noticed Chittema and jumped up.

He stood up and, bending, emerged.

'Oh there you are! So you are not ready yet? Hurry up and apply some bath powder and take a bath. Tie your pancha and your turban and get dressed! By then your king will also get ready. It is time you set off on the town, isn't it? Get ready to go! When it's time to eat, hurry back urgently on the dot! It's not good for your health if you don't eat on time, after all', said Chittema.

Bobbili understood the sarcasm in her voice.

'I have fur like gold on my body. My ears are a wheel-like turban… Why do I need a pancha and turban… What do I lack?' Bobbili almost said it loudly but thought better of entering into a dispute with Chittema and walked out of the room quietly.

If he dared to show any haughtiness in his bearing, he knew Chittema would pick up the nearest object and fling it at him. So tucking his tail in, he walked out respectfully.

Of late she had become unbearable… She used to abuse him as if he were an ordinary street dog… 'If things continue like this, I will confront Fakirraju in the courtyard and ask him a few questions that I have. What have I to be afraid of?' And he stalked out to the front yard.

'Fakirbava! Fakirbava!' He heard someone calling from the eastern side.

Bobbili went that side and looked out of the window. He could see a stranger sitting on the stone platform. Bobbili's flagging spirits rose. His tail rose straight up.

Anyway there was no respect at home… If at least strangers were startled and showed some fear and respect, that would be enough. Being a pedigree dog, he should earn at least that much respect…

---

1 *pancha* = dhoti; *lalchi* = kurta

So, walking with dignity, he crossed the path and came to the stone threshold of the eastern door.

He didn't look at the man on the platform. He knew that the man was looking at him without blinking. Pretending to look at the doorstep, he held his breath and blew out his chest. He cocked his ears and arching his back like a bow, the black fur on his shoulder bristling, he looked at a red ant crawling on the stone and growled. He bared his fangs to frighten the ant. Then, casually, he turned towards the platform.

The stranger, who was sitting on the platform elegantly till then with his left leg crossing his right, on seeing Bobbili's proud stance decided it was better to uncross his legs. He tried as far as possible to seem friendly.

As soon as the man's eyes met Bobbili's, the latter growled and bared his fangs, his fur bristling.

He could smell the fear on the man sitting on the platform and his joy bubbled over.

The man pulled his legs up onto the platform for good measure and looked back through the corner of his eyes.

He saw the platform was against a wall that was not too high, from which the paint had flaked off.

'Fakirbava… Bava!' called the stranger, a little anxiously.

'Shabash! After so long, I found one fellow—let me show him my strength.' Bobbili took two more steps towards the platform.

The stranger stood up on the platform. He had a canvas bag near his feet.

'Tchi!… Tchi!… Go! You black cur!… You cur!' he said. Bobbili felt humiliated by that abuse.

'Tchi!… Even in dwellings of clans descended from kings, courtesies are scarce', thought Bobbili.

'Talk with some respect, gentleman. I am not any old dog. My name is Bobbili! Veera Bobbili! You must have heard of me. I belong to a high breed and am a fine dog. I belong to the lineage of Tandra Paparayudu's house. I am not just any common dog. I don't harm those who are scared of me. Sit down. Don't be scared', said Bobbili.

The man on the platform twirled his moustache. 'Pooh! Me? Scared? Who do you think I am? I am from the lineage of

Denkada Pusapati. I have fought a wild pig singlehanded and survived. Eeti Suri is my name. Why would I be scared of you? I would lose respect', said Eeti Suri with pride.

Bobbili was enraged. 'Shall I tear this Karri Suri gadu's thigh? Whom will he complain to…' And he leapt forward so that his front paws landed on the margin of the platform.

But Denkada Raju was a very smart fellow. He had fought a wild pig and survived. By then he had leapt onto the wall.

'Now are you scared or not?' asked Bobbili sarcastically.

'Rubbish! What can you do to me?' said Denkada Raju boldly since he was on the wall.

Bobbili climbed onto the platform and looked at the wall.

'I am a hunting dog! This wall is no obstruction for me. I can climb even huge trees easily. If you want, ask Gopatrudu and find out. I won't harm you. Just admit you are scared and get off', he said.

Denkada Suri Babu sat on the wall and crossed his legs.

'I won't come down… I like this place.'

'If I climb the wall…'

'If you climb the wall, I will climb the roof. How will you compete with me? But don't imagine I am scared of you. What is your status after all? You are a bloody dog. I am a man of high caste. I am a child of the Pusapati house. I find it demeaning to stand on the same level as you. I am standing on the wall so that I can stand at a higher level than you do, you understand?'

'You don't seem to know what my reputation is in this neighbourhood and in this firka. Who do you think sleeps in the easy chair at home when our Fakirrajugaru is not at home? It is me! Just now my Chittema asked me to wear a Glasgow pancha, lalchi and brocade shoulder cloth, wrap a tasselled turban, and go into the big square. They look after me with such respect and affection. What is the comparison between you and me?' asked Bobbili.

Source: Excerpt from *Veera Bobbili* by K.N.Y. Patanjali (Visakhapatnam: Pramila Publications, 2009, pp. 14–17)

Katti Padma Rao

Katti Padma Rao, born in 1953 in Guntur, is a founder of the Dalit Mahasabha, formed after the massacre of dalits in Karamchedu in 1985. A public intellectual and dalit leader, Padma Rao's writing ranges from theoretical work on the status of dalits and women, and Phule-Ambedkarite-Buddhist philosophy, to poetry collections and literary criticism. He has written extensively about Gurram Jashuva's interrogation of the caste order.

Birthing Downpour

The very corners of the house
steeped in darkness of day
The whimper of the child
in my lap
tugs at my heart
Mother!

Wherefore is this unseasonal rain
beating down mercilessly
The skies split asunder
like the heartless black mountains

In the flame of the flickering lamp
My child trembling
with half-closed eyes
Wrings my heart, Mother!

From the gaps in the thatched roof
water streams down

pounding
the breasts of the hut
The floor you lovingly smeared
with fanlike movements
roughening your fingertips
is now but a heap of slush…

Mother! You
have not shed the tattered rag
you wore
these last three days
Since I birthed
your labour is unceasing

Each year one of us
comes to birth here
Scraping
the few grains left in your pot
How then will you thatch your roof, Mother…?
Like the straw simmering away
in the pot of dumplings
you shrink each day

The drop of castor oil
you saved for yourself
you fed my child
The coriander you got
for sifting rice in the komati's house
you used to make a broth
to keep me warm
So wise at pouring life into others
How little you know
To sustain your own, Mother!

In this ceaseless downpour
father has gone to bind sheaves

When he returns drenched
where is the dry pancha?

Mother!
Light me with those bright eyes
Your smiling face
never fading in the face of troubles
Like you, I too will conquer time.

Source: 'Puriti Vaana' by Katti Padma Rao (*Neelikeka Kavita Sankalanam*, Ponnuru: Lokayuta Prachuranalu, 1998, pp. 5–7)

Papineni Sivasankar

Papineni Sivasankar was born in 1953 in Nekkallu (Guntur) and studied at Andhra University. Among his books are *Matti Gunde* (1992, a collection of short stories), *Sahityam—Moulika Bhavanalu* (1996, a book on literary theory), and the verse anthology *Aaku Pacchani Lokamlo* (1998). He was awarded the Sahitya Akademi Award in 2016 for his collection of poems *Rajanigandham* (2013).

Melodious Grief

It is good for the body to grieve now and then
Good to be burnt in the heat of suffering.
We were all taught to enjoy
Our knowledge sought solely to increase man's comfort on earth.
Weeping, anxiety, suffering, bereavement, mourning, grief, were outcast.
Home, body, learning, work, wife—purely for comfort.

Few realise that grief is a truth
To grieve of a broken heart—they know not.
To draw grief close now and then like a pet dog is good.
Like springs flowing forth free in a cleared well
It is good for tears to flow.
The dim hard rock behind your eye
Will dissolve drop by drop when you grieve.
At the end of grief your eyes grow clear
And you become pure inside
Like a sky clear of clouds.
Only the one who has grieved truly understands life
A world without grief is incomplete.
Your two eyes have a precious purpose
One for your own grief
And the second for the other's.

Written 2004

Source: 'Dukhameghamalhari' by Papineni Sivasankar (*Oka Khadgam, Oka Pushpam: Kavita Sankalanam*, Guntur: Papineni Prachuranalu, 2004, p. 60)

GANTEDA GOWRU NAIDU

Ganteda Gowru Naidu was born in 1954 in Dalaipeta, Vizianagaram. He is a popular writer from north Andhra and has helped organise writers from the region. His writings have focused on oppressed peoples, and his anthology of short stories, *Yeti Paata*, is particularly well known.

Wild Jasmines

The sunlight slanted though the window. The sun was rising slowly behind the hill. The morning breeze, wafting the fragrance of the wild flowers mingled with the chirping of countless birds, was humming the morning ragas. Through the window, tall trees… the mountain peak… flying birds, the beauty of nature appeared like an exquisite painting. The sound of the stream rushing over the rocks… the sound of the waves like music in the background… a symphony.

Boodi was picking the fallen buds under the ippa[1] tree. Boodi's four-year-old daughter, naked, was playing, throwing stones… at the baby lizard on the tree.

Poor Boodi.

Boodi was not the kind to talk to anyone. She was innocent. People from our guda[2] went every Thursday to the Kurupam santa, bought things they needed, saw a film, and returned home. That was the only entertainment for our guda people. Boodi never did even that. How did Boodi fall prey to that Sukkadu's gaze? Sukkadu joined as the cook in our school hostel. He lived alone; he was not married. Who knows what spell he cast? Boodi went every evening to the cashew farm behind the hostel to meet Sukkadu. This was known to the school… and to the whole village. I was studying in the tenth class.

Our exams were over.

Boodi is going to be a mother, they said.

The school holidays began.

The Sukkadu who went home for the holidays did not come back.

Boodi and I… were about two years apart. We… used to roam about together. We used to graze goats… and collect ippa buds together. While our elders chopped logs… we tied the small bundles together… and loaded them on some lorry… or jeep.

---

1 mahua tree, cultivated for its flowers and seeds

2 hamlet

When the kandi kottala panduga[1] came… such commotion… We used to dance in a frenzy. Our feet would not stay still if they heard the sound of the tudumu dappu[2] beats.

In our Savara guda of forty huts, there was no one who was educated. Among the girijan[3] communities, our Savara were the most backward.

Earlier, but for a small torn towel there would be nothing on our bodies. We wore nose rings and silver ankle kadas.

In the matter of food, we had no great desire for tastes. We ate the fruit and leaves and tubers in each season. The korralu, samalu, jonnalu[4]… that we harvested through our podu[5] farming, the gruel made from jilugu and tenka[6] flour… This was our food. We never knew about paddy rice. If I compare those days with today, I am filled with wonder. Behind this change… behind this comfort, how much suffering. My father used to relate tale after tale of those struggles… and those sacrifices. As he told us, his eyes would fill with tears. My body would prickle.

When I was old enough to understand, it seems it was meningitis (we came to know later)… The disease spread. It turned the girijan gudas and the whole forest upside down. There was no day without deaths. When my uncle Ejjodu said that he would cure the disease with prayers and potions, the authorities shouted at him and sent people to the hospital. I still remember that. Boodi should have died then. If she had depended on my uncle's methods, she would have died. That was the year that the hostel warden came and talked to my father and admitted me in school. Her father refused to send Boodi to school. 'Does she need schooling to graze goats? I won't send her', he said to the warden. I felt very bad. As I went to school,

---

1 lentil harvest festival

2 *tudumu* and *dappu* are percussion instruments used widely in adivasi performance

3 adivasi (tribal peoples)

4 *korralu* = foxtail millet; *samalu* = little millet; *jonnalu* = sorghum (jowar)

5 shifting cultivation

6 *jilugu* = a variety of perennial palm from which toddy, seeds and sap are extracted; *tenka* = the kernel of the mango seed, which is dried and ground into flour

Boodi was confined to doing podu work... and grazing goats... and picking ippa buds.

I feel sorry when I see Boodi. But Boodi did not seem to mind her condition at all. She became the mother of a child. There was no other change in her.

Boodi kept gathering ippa buds.

Girls from the hostel were going in lines to the stream to bathe. Four or five years ago, I used to go in that line to the lake, telling cinema stories. Now I am a responsible teacher. Everyone said, 'You are very fortunate.' True. To get a job in the same school in which I had studied... was luck after all.

Recently I began to feel... that people were talking about me behind my back. No one said anything to me. But the Telugu saar told me. I understood a little and didn't understand all. After it's all over, now I've understood everything.

I got up lazily and went to the mirror.

My appearance was strange to me. Unconsciously I placed my hand on my heart. Yesterday morning when I saw my reflection in the same mirror at the same time, it was as if a yellow gleaming snake was twined around my neck, resting its head on my heart and flicking its tongue. My body prickled with gooseflesh. A husband had tied a thali[1] it seems. What guts! How he had played his part!

Outside the window, the sound of bangles, as though someone was standing there. Boodi was smiling. In her hands, red flowers, on her head, a basket of ippa buds, her daughter behind her, naked. I looked closely at Boodi's face. Her eyes were sparkling like tangudu[2] flowers.

Boodi gave me the flowers and left.

'There is no difference between Boodi and me. I was educated. She was not. But how am I better than Boodi? If the uneducated Boodi fell into Sukkadu's net, that was one way. And me? What did I do? Are all girls the same... in matters like this?'

'Ammagaru...'

---

1 woman's marriage pendant

2 avaram/tarwar tree

Aruna was standing with the milk pot at the door. She emptied the milk and left saying, 'Haven't you had a bath yet, ammagaru?'

Aruna was a smart girl. She was studying in the tenth class. First in class. She used to sing well. Once I was just like Aruna. Looking at Aruna, I could see myself in those days.

After my tenth exams, I was at home for the holidays. I was waiting for the result. I was pounding korralu in my house. Ayya[1] was talking to the contractor Rangaraju... standing under the drumstick tree in front of the house. There is a stream at the entrance to our village. A bridge was being built on the stream. The bridge contractor Rangaraju came to our house. Ayya and he became good friends.

From taking coolies to get work done on the bridge to arranging meals for the contractor, ayya looked after everything. He forgot about his podu work. His daily routine had changed. How many days had it been since ayya went up to the hut on the hill? Ayya, always in a gochi,[2] learnt to wear lungi and lalchi... No, the contractor taught him. Contractor garu returned to his village once in a fortnight or a month. He would carry yam, tamarind, jackfruit and pumpkin... with him.

Reading a paper, the contractor called out, 'Girl, what is your number? The results have come.'

I told him the number. He looked at the paper and said happily, 'You have passed in first class... You must give me a party', he joked, and turning to ayya he said, 'Let's admit her in Vijayanagaram College... She can stay in the hostel and study...'

'My daughter is after all your daughter... It's your wish... Let's do that', said ayya, agreeing with him. I was elated.

The contractor bought me new clothes. At that moment, I felt he was ayya.

I joined Vijayanagaram College. In the Tribal Welfare Girls' Hostel... new friends... new enthusiasm... studying... days spent happily...

---

1 father

2 waistcloth tied with the front end taken between the legs and tucked at the back

I came home for the Dassera vacation.

Ayya learnt to go to the ITDA office. He learnt to talk to authorities. He learnt to put his thumb impression on the papers written by the contractor and get loans sanctioned. But all his jobs were in the contractor's control.

When I came home, the work on the bridge was going on briskly. But contractor Rangaraju was not there. Some young man was there. Ayya said… that the contractor was unwell, and that boy was his son. The ten days that I was there, he tried to pick up a conversation with me. When I made tea, he would deliberately try to touch my fingers. I found it amusing. Gradually I grew close to him.

One day, it was very late.

Ayya was sitting under the drumstick tree and counting the empty cement bags. Far away, from the hills, one could hear the sound of the flute. In the middle of the street, Sannayigadu was beating the dappu, Sombara was keeping time on his tudumu. Children were jumping around.

Then a jeep came and stopped there.

The police got out and one policeman asked 'Who is Venkanna?' As soon as ayya said, 'It is me', the policeman hit him with the rifle butt.

The beating of the drums on the street stopped abruptly.

The beating with lathis started.

My ayya… and four other old men were beaten badly. I went and hid in a lane. They said that they got news that Naxalites had been fed last night. It was true they were fed. I cooked the food. I didn't know they were Naxalites. Ayya told me to… and I cooked. But how is it a crime to feed people who are hungry, I didn't understand.

I felt like crying when I heard ayya shouting in pain. I was afraid to come out. I remembered the stories of struggle… that ayya had told me.

'Amma… in this stream, only blood flowed… Never water.' I remembered amma weeping as she said this. The police were still beating them… 'Tell us who they were.' Then the contractor's son came and spoke to the SI. It seemed as if they were good friends from the way they talked. The police stopped the beating and went away. My respect for the contractor's son grew.

After the holidays, he said he had work in Vijayanagaram and took me with him on his scooter. I had a strange feeling sitting behind him. Later I rode many times on that scooter. I finished my Intermediate. After my last exam, he took me to Annavaram and said, 'Let us get married.' He told me the story of Shakuntala and Dushyanta and said, 'Ours is a Gandharva marriage.' I listened silently… I agreed, nodding my head. For some reason I did not feel like refusing him. Saying that many educated people did this, he tied the thali round my neck.

Unexpectedly I got called for an interview… Soon I got appointment orders as a second-grade teacher… In the school I had studied in.

Marriage… a job at the same time—I was thrilled at my good fortune. We began our married life in the teacher's quarters I was allotted. My ayya refused to leave the old house and move.

Ayya had lost all his earlier enthusiasm. He would not disclose what was troubling his mind…

One day, ayya was moaning in pain. Just then the postman gave the letters and left. One was from the bank, asking him to pay the loan for the bullocks with the full interest.

When I told ayya… he was astonished and said, 'What? Hasn't the contractor babu paid it?' I understood… The contractor had cheated ayya and told him so… First, he didn't believe it. 'Will the contractor babu do that?'

I told my husband. He looked irritated and said, 'I have nothing to do with it.'

I was angry… I was tearful.

Just then, another letter came. It was from my husband's wife, saying the children were ill, asking him to come quickly. Till then I had not known… my status…

Ayya was sunk to the throat by the contractor's debts… By his son's actions… me…

The fact that my fellow teachers stopped talking sometimes when I entered made sense now.

The bridge work was finished.

After five days, my husband came back. He brought an engineer with him. He arranged food… drink… He made me cook dishes the engineer liked. He told me to dress attractively. After that, I wept bitterly, unable to bear that fellow's words… I was so angry that I felt like stabbing him with a knife right there. But I was so drained that I could not even stand. That night I went back to my father's hut. What could I say to my father who asked me what was wrong?… I lay down without a word. The man who left that day came back a week later. I did not speak to him or look at him. He said, 'I have got your transfer orders. You are coming with me.' I was furious. I took the transfer orders, tore it to bits, and threw it at his face.

'Are you a man… tchi… We didn't realise that wolves in lamb's clothing had come to our hills… and set fire to our green forests. Educated people!… We thought educated people would care for us and make our lives better. We never dreamt they would tear our lives apart and shred us and play with our lives… We thought you would improve our girijan gudas… but did not think you would destroy us in the name of development.

'We were under the illusion that you would build a bridge and bring civilisation… and science… in cars and buses across that bridge. We did not realise that you would loot our hills and load them into baskets and go over that same bridge.

'You used your civilisation… and your wits to loot us. That is enough. Go! If you stand here for another minute, I don't know what I will do.'

He said arrogantly, 'I tied a thali around your neck… Don't forget that…' The fire in my feet rose to my head. My anger rose like the flames from setting fire to dried grass. Like a podu fire. My anger rose wildly.

'What did you say? You tied a thali? You who asked me to go to the bed of a stranger—are you a husband who tied a thali?… Is this your culture? May your civilisation be drowned in the middle of the stream… Here fellow, take your damn thali!' And plucking the thali from my neck, I flung it at him. The yellow thread lay coiled like a dead snake around his feet. When he bent to pick it up, he seemed like a snake charmer. But snake charmers are far better. They remove the fangs and make snakes dance and spread joy. But this fellow himself turns into a snake and bites.

'I will not come with you and become a servant to your wife and children. I won't put myself in the pathetic situation of handing over my salary to you and begging you for money. Your father cheated my father, and the mountains that are our father… and you exploited my youth… my freedom, and ruined my life. As if that were not enough, you wanted to make a business by selling my body…

'You cheated the government by saying you had entered an intercaste marriage… and caused us untold suffering socially and politically… Tchi… Each thought of yours is like a cobra. Get out of here… Carry on with your deceit, get buried in your own deceit and die from it… Go!'

I felt my nerves would get crushed with fury. Everyone gathered around us looking. I banged the door shut.

In the mirror, my neck… like the noose had been lifted off. It was a relief. I stroked my neck. It felt like I was touching the smooth mirror. Far away, the blue mountain ranges, like waves… The sun falling on them a feast to the eyes. I felt like it was a sublime invitation.

Boodi was plaiting her daughter's hair under the drumstick tree in front of our old house. Around her, goat kids were leaping about. Chang! Chang! The hostel children, plates in hand, were lining up for breakfast.

I stepped inside the threshold. In the prayer area in the school, the Telugu teacher was sitting on the platform on which the flag is hoisted and teaching a new song. Aruna and Ganapathi saar were practising it. I stepped to the other side… casually.

In front of my eyes, the girijan gudas spun into view.

In the name of development… under the pretence of civilisation, I could see the destruction of my people and our culture in its undisguised form… My younger brothers and sisters like forest birds… were moving far away from freedom and goodness in the name of education… I thought. They were going away from dhinsa dance, and celebrations like the kandi kottala panduga. I was troubled.

I was concerned about youth who give up studies after primary school and go around the ITDA offices looking for petty jobs.

My brothers and sisters thrashing about on the banks of the sea of civilisation appeared before my eyes. If my people believe that they should only tread the paths laid by these new lessons of deceitful 'civilisation'?… I shuddered at the thought. I felt as if my mother forest was looking piteously at our tattered culture.

I looked out on the road.

A girl who had joined the job with me was sitting on the pillion of a bike. The boy was saying something to her and she was laughing. I felt sorry for her.

The song Aruna and Ganapathi saar were singing wafted melodiously through the hills, echoing and spreading forth…

'Sister, sister, wild jasmine, my sister…
Take care… take care, my sister
Careful with your life… my sister
My sister who knows neither deceit nor stealth
You who are a jasmine… must become a thorn
Hearing the name of the girl of the hills, my sister
His heart should stop beating, my sister…'

The song resounded in my ears. It reminded me of my duty. The lorry of the contractor crossed the bridge towards the village.

The ode to my sister followed me.

Mountains… trees… streams… canals… birds and wild animals… The whole forest seemed ready for another change… In the distance, from afar, faintly the sound of drumbeats…

Written 1994

Source: 'Konda Malle' by Ganteda Gowru Naidu (*Etipata Katha Sankalanam*, Srikakulam: Srikakula Sahiti, 1997, pp. 92–99)

NANDINI SIDDHA REDDY

Nandini Siddha Reddy, born in 1955 in Bandaram in Siddipet, taught Telugu literature in a government college till 2012. A poet and educationist, he has played a central role in bringing writers in Telangana together, by forming writers' groups and popularising Telangana literature. He started the Manjira Rachayitala Sangham and was appointed chair of the Telangana Sahitya Akademi in 2017.

I Have My Dreams

Whatever anyone thinks
I cannot live like a little finger
Wrenching my heart
I cannot lead the procession
of the parading deity

To enjoy
it isn't a single day's darkness
To adjust
not a single day's death

Whatever anyone thinks
I cannot live like a soiled rag

For anyone
the blood boils
For everything the time must come
Even the blade of common grass
Suddenly gets strength

Whoever says I must
I will not wander carrying a drum

Though the river did not caress me
I decked the town in wealth

Though the moon did not feed me morsels
I decked the garden with flowers
When there were hammocks on the trees
I rejoiced
When the sky hummed, I embraced it

I did not see what I ate
I did not see where I lay
The grief that welled up in me
I burnt under the palm leaves

Do only you have dreams?
Are you the only ones who should dream?
You wind rivers round your houses
And plunder the stars
Binding the girth of towns
with gold shops
Thrones and cinema hoardings
bond together in marriage

Whatever anyone thinks
I have a dream
That the earth has risen from slumber
The sacred fire is lit
And scattered shoots
grow into swinging fields

Whatever anyone thinks
My dreams come back to me
That the fistful of mud
turns into a sparrow and flies away

That the bees have moved away
from my eyelashes
That Charminar has come to life
dancing at the crossroads

Written 2013

Source: 'Naaku Naa Kalale' by Nandini Siddha Reddy (*Nalugu Dasabdala Nandini Siddha Reddy Kavitvam*, Siddipet: Manjira Rachiyitala Sangham, 2017, pp. 479–80)

Kondepudi Nirmala

Born in Vijayawada in 1955, Kondepudi Nirmala is a well-known feminist poet and the recipient of several awards for her work. Her book *Sandigdha Sandhya* won her the Free Verse Front Award in 1988. Her other books are *Nadiche Gayalu* and *Badhasapta Nadi*, and a collection of stories *Satru Sparsa*. She is also an essayist and has published socio-political satires.

Synonym for a Heart

Not so suddenly you see
but gradually like
    moisture under a mat
    that twelfth year
    creeps on you unaware
Your body lengthening softening
transparent as a glass jar
centring anguish
fear burrowing mouse-like
an exclamation mark

stopping your downward gaze
like a bloom at the tip of a branch
    beneath the neck
fluidly flanking
    the silken cleft of your bosom
    smooth as a banana leaf
behold that synonym for a heart
Oh!

Now you can seize your heart in your palm
those tiny twin hillocks
tipped crimson
    like a hennaed fingertip
    pointing to the moon
Silent jasmine buds
quivering slightly as you walk
bathing when you bathe
sleeping when you sleep
and shadowing your waking moments
spreading softness for all eyes.
Dissolving all bonds in detachment.

Drenched in the heat of that beauty
tremulous with longing—
obstructing folded palms
    from joining in greeting
mesmerised
like melting sculptures
or frozen waves
now no longer in control
they burst forth like two miraculous globes.
Shrinking from each passing glance
in a movement of revulsion
like prisoners of war
trying to escape
appear to have committed suicide.

Now striving for motherhood
in rigorous penance
onerous with motherly pride
drooping slightly
    like a neck weighted by garlands
asking
is love dark or light.

Now in the summer of the middle years
When the shadow of doubt
    lengthens and haunts you
your heart sinks
to the sound of 'Hush, you know nothing'
and to hide your shrinking heart
your voice grows louder
your words inconsequential
fumbling at your glasses with
your sari edge
you can no longer tell the difference
    between suffering and pleasure
moving like a patchwork guilt
and in the final analysis
if you set aside the ex gratia gifts
the Kanchi silks, the gold-moon necklace
what is left save that
thickening line of darkness
skirting your blouse
circling your waist
coming to rest on your heart
Like timorousness discovered
and buried within.

At sixty
trapped by time
wasted by disease
worn out by bitter reality
as if my guts had been ripped

to garland my neck
the dark veins stain
against my skin
my juices dry
welcoming death and resignation
in the same moment
your breasts lie flat as veined betel leaves
bearing a dried black betel nut
indescribably pensive—
piteous, patient—

Written 1990

Source: 'Hridayaaniki Bahuvachanam' by Kondepudi Nirmala (*Neeli Meghalu: Streevada Kavitvam*, edited by Volga, Secunderabad: Asmita, 1993, pp. 39–41)

V. Pratima

V. Pratima, born in 1956 in Chennai, is a feminist poet and short-fiction writer. Her important works are *Rendu Bhagalu* (a poetry anthology), and two short-story collections, *Pakshi* and *Khandita*.

A Rocky Shrub

We may think
plants will not grow on rocky soil…
But through the cracks that split the old walls of that house
The banyan tree thrusts out its shoots
to greet the sky.
Looking at the trees stunted in pots
She looks proudly with natural dignity

She has yet another pride…
The sun and moon cannot enter the house
without saluting her…

Gazing on that rocky tree
In that moment
a boundless pure joy in her eyes…
Collecting all the undreamt melted dreams
She wants to fling a bunch of dream flowers
into the sky.

The grief that has dripped away drop by drop
Under footprints in the darkness of night
She wants to change into paper flowers
that can be hidden in history.

Gathering letters one by one
From shards of broken glass
Futile she tries to treadle them
Shaping the letters into a pair of wings
to wear on her shoulders.

We may think
plants will not grow on rocky soil
But crossing the thorny fence
Surrounding her… and her house…
She seizes a fistful of hopes
From the rocky tree…

Source: 'Raatimokka' by V. Pratima (*Rendu Bhaagaalu*, Nayudupeta: Sahitya Prachuranalu, 2008, p. 73)

MANDARAPU HYMAVATHI

Mandarapu Hymavathi, born in Vijayawada in 1956, is a feminist poet and the author of the acclaimed poetry anthology *Nishiddhakshari*.

The Serpentine Embrace

It is all quite good till then
What if it is lust?
What if it is passion?
After two bodies are one
After they have reached union
When this world itself is forgotten
in the hour of delight
From the bow of letters
you shoot an arrow
'When will they pay your salary?'
Not even a prostitute will ask that question at that time
Even an animal will behave
differently
All of a sudden
It is as if a thousand giant lizards
crawled over me
In that second, when my heart froze in fear
I wanted to fling you
far, far away from my life
But being a Bharata stree
Buried alive in tradition
Struggling, choking for breath
When I am drowning
in the swamp of marriage

Not just from life
not even from my body
am I able to distance myself even an inch
Every second
I compromise and keep living
Till death comes in your serpentine embrace.

Written 1993

Source: 'Sarpa Parishvangam' by Mandarapu Hymavathi (*Neeli Meghalu: Streevada Kavitvam*, edited by Volga, Secunderabad: Asmita, 1993, pp. 76–77)

ANISETTI RAJITHA

Anisetti Rajitha (1957) is a dalit feminist poet and activist from Warangal in Telangana, and a member of the Telangana Prajaswamika Rachayitrula Vedika (Telangana Democratic Women Writers' Forum).

Avva

The endless tales my grandmother told
Earth, grass, branch and leaf, flowers and fruit
mingle to release their friendly fragrance
Those visions would turn into thoughts
Spreading across the countryside.
Avva's[1] words were always sweet and
wonder-filled as the guavas and berries
She pulled out of the folds of her sari.

---

1 grandmother

For a woman of the earth smeared with slush
Where she had earned such knowledge and learning
was always a wonder to me.
Like the water in the village pond
that turned red at sunset
Her life was a marvel to me.

Setting off for work outside the village
Turning me into a mouth-watering
expectant look she would disappear.
She would return at sunset like a faded sun
Turning into the fruit she had knotted in her sari
wafting its fragrance from far away.

The day she stayed at home
She was like a cat with burnt paws
Sprinkling floors, decorating them
Dusting cobwebs from the sky
And patching the roof.
Avva was like a huge winged bird circling the sky.
Lying on my cot under the tamarind tree
My pockets full of tamarind
My eyes blinking at the sourness
She seemed like a wonder woman
Sprouting countless hands working miracles
Like a vision in my dreams.

At the village temple
I stoned the black jamuns on the tree
to fill my stomach.
But when I went with avva for coolie work
She wore out her muscles
And shed blood and sweat to worship nature
and feed the bellies of her people
Like a hermit in penance
A warrior fighting enemy hunger each day
As if avva was the village

As if she was the living breath of all the produce
Of the village.
She was the cane that taught me
the things no school ever taught me.

My pride that my avva is the Jaganmatha
who feeds the people
would fill my heart with tears.
She is the university for working people
I as a pupil of hers
would wash her muddy feet
with the handful of water I collected
to quench my thirst.

Written 2000

Source: 'Maavva Badi' by Anisetti Rajitha (*Usuru*, Warangal: Self-published, 2002, pp. 26–27)

SIKHAMANI

Sikhamani was born in 1957 in Yanam, an enclave in East Godavari that is part of the union territory of Puducherry. A dalit poet and literary scholar, he was on the faculty of Potti Sreeramulu Telugu University. Sikhamani has eight collections of poetry to his credit—*Muvvalachetikarra* (1987), *Horugali* (1988), *Chilakkoyya* (1993), *Kirrucheppula Bhasha* (2000), *The Black Rainbow* (2000), *Nallagetu Nandivardhanam Chettu* (2005), *Tavvakam* (2009) and *Gijigadu* (2011)—as well as collections of essays. He received the Free Verse Front Award in 1987.

Digging

I asked my parents with wet eyes
They said I was their darling
I asked my wedded wife, shiny-eyed
She said you are my hero, my solid cement wall
So I let it be and asked my children
after Cartoon Network
We love you most daddy, they said
I asked someone, he said friend
I asked another and he said enemy
Some said Andhra
Some said dalit
Others said mala
All spoke of the man they knew
Not one spoke knowing me
This won't do I thought
So I asked my inner self
Do you really want to know?
Smiling easily he disappeared
behind a curtain
Since then I keep digging into myself
Someday will I not find the man!

Source: 'Tavvakam' by Sikhamani (*Tavvakam*, Hyderabad: Nandini Prachuranalu, 2009, pp. 95–96)

Vimala

Vimala Morthala, born in 1958 in Hyderabad, is a feminist poet and social activist with a special interest in child rights. She was Vice President of VIRASAM and General Secretary of the Progressive Organisation of Women (Stree Vimukti). Her well-known works are *Adavi Uppogina Rathri* and *Mrugana*, anthologies of poems in Telugu. Her work has been translated into English and Hindi.

The Procession of the Naked

Why should we bow our heads in shame and disgrace?
Why should we grieve with broken hearts?

Come mothers!
Let us fling our siggu billas[1] at their faces.
Along the pathways of the history of stripping
Let us set ablaze the morals of the civilisation of clothing.
Come!

In some tragic dawn
we lost our mother right.
We lost our voices, our dreams and our weapons
Our history is one of the giving of wombs, and abortion
Our history is one of the alienation of labour.

When have we not been stripped?
Either for love, revenge or profit
When have our bodies and souls not been auctioned on the street?

---

1 chastity amulet strung on a thread and worn around the waist by girls

When have we not shed our blood, shed tears?
A pawn in a game of dice, stripped in open court
Draupadi is our sister

Muttamma! Muttamma!
Amaravati echoes countless tales of nakedness
We are women after all!
But for our bodies, we lack souls and brains
Objects of lust for passion and rape
We bestow rich experience.

We are mothers bearing good sons
Virtuous wives by daylight
and whores who strip at night
We are maids who know not sunlight
Baring naked limbs as wares of beauty.

We are women after all!
We possess two breasts and a vagina!
Drinking our milk, they cut off our breasts
Pouring vitriol on the vaginas that have birthed them.

Eve! Eve!
Let us shout aloud
about the conspiracy of the forbidden fruit!

Why should we wrap the earth around our bodies
veil ourselves with the clouds
and crumble in shame into womanhood?

To clothe and strip us
has become a symbol of manhood.

In Bosnia, El Salvador,
And the streets of Chilakurti, Trilokpuri,
Or Dandakaranya
Does it really matter where?

Stripping us is their entertainment
Sexual violence a declaration of power.

Let us spit revenge
in the face of these arrogant male beasts.

Come my mothers
grieving in shame and disgrace!
Let us confront the savagery of the clothed ones
Demolish the culture of clothing and weapons of nakedness
The march of the 'naked women' has begun.

Source: 'Digambarula Uregimpu' by Vimala (*Neeli Meghalu: Streevada Kavitvam*, edited by Volga, Secunderabad: Asmita, 1993, pp. 223–25)

YAKOOB

Born in 1958 in Rottamaku Revu in Khammam, Yakoob is an award-winning writer and a teacher of Telugu literature. Yakoob published his first anthology of poems, *Pravahinche Gnaapakam*, in 1992, and the next one, *Sarihaddu Rekha*, a collection of over a hundred poems, in 2002. A prolific and popular writer, Yakoob's early work was translated into English in a collection titled *Arc of Unrest* in 2000. In 2009, Yakoob published the anthology *Yedategani Prayaanam*. His work has been translated into Hindi, English, Malayalam, Tamil and Kannada.

Towns Are Afloat on Water

A piece of cloud is absorbed in the sand
An earthworm ploughs the earth sowing seeds
The earth gleams wetly clad in green

The trees mirror brilliantly hued blossoms
The huts covered with stars gleam brightly
The calves under the rafters are startled
The sun and moon hide in the cloudy sky

The bird seeks a new melody
The gap turns into a stream
The night inhales the scent of raindrops!

The forest sees its image in the river
As if the town seeks respite
the roads smiling blackly
control the vehicles

The thrill of the raindrop falling on the earth

Phalguna's chariot loses a nail
Arjuna... Phalguna... Yali...
The lightning mocks the darkness

It is water everywhere
Towns are afloat on water!

Source: 'Jalayatri' by Yakoob (*Sarihaddu Rekha*, Hyderabad: Madhyamam Prachurana, 2002, p. 195)

Yendluri Sudhakar

Yendluri Sudhakar (1959–2022), born in Nizamabad, was a versatile and popular writer, poet, translator, literary scholar and teacher. He has several books to his credit on a range of themes—from writings on the iconic poet Jashuva, to short-story and poetry collections such as *Vartamanam*, *Kotha Gabbilam*, *Nalladrakshapandiri* (a bilingual collection of poetry), and *Mallemoggala Godugu: Madiga Kathalu*. He was an influential voice in Telugu and dalit literary worlds.

A New Dream

Peeling the hide off the five elements
Stretching them from the sky
to the underworld
For you
who soaked that hide in the seven seas
The sun and moon
should become each a shoe!
With bent head
Either out of hunger
or out of shame
You who are sewing shoes
From your own skin, grandfather!
I dream dreams
One day
This world
should turn into a ring

To decorate your big toe
and kiss it.

Written 1996

Source: 'Kotta Kala' by Yendluri Sudhakar (*Nalladrakshapandiri*, Secunderabad: J.J. Prachuranalu, 2002, p. 30)

Vadrevu China Veerabhadrudu

Vadrevu China Veerabhadrudu, born in East Godavari in 1962, is a poet and an officer in the Indian Administrative Service, known for his work among adivasi communities in Andhra Pradesh. Dedicated to the cause of education for adivasi children, he has focused his energies on strengthening school education in remote tribal areas of the state for over thirty years. He has worked with teachers, creative writers and school children from marginalised communities across the state. His poetry collections *Nirvikalpa Sangeetam*, *Aranyam* and *Prasnabhoomi* are well known.

This Too I Realised

I realise this too.

If a sentence is to awaken in you
First you must wake up.

With eyes wide open, with listening ears
You must wait at your doorstep.
You need to wipe out the stains within you
You must wipe off the dust.

This too I realised, or maybe
I realised this was the most important

For a single sentence to emerge from you
You will need to examine your path
You will have to protect it
You must brush aside all the rest.

First you will have to step aside.

Source: 'Idikooda Grahinchannenu' by Vadrevu China Veerabhadrudu (*Kokila Pravesinche Kalam*, Hyderabad: Sree Prachurana, 2009, p. 68)

Tripuraneni Srinivas

Tripuraneni Srinivas (1963–96), born in Tirupati, was a journalist who worked with various Telugu dailies. He was known for his love for literature and his keen interest in foregrounding new voices in the literary world. He published fourteen anthologies of poetry by different poets. A poet himself, his own published works include *Rahasyodhyamam* and *Ho!*

Missing

He was not for death
Nor for life
He disappeared.

Like a blossom
Falling from a branch
Lost in the air
Not reaching the earth.

He was not for home
Nor for the movement
Not in jail
He disappeared.

Like a blossom
Falling from a branch.

Not reaching the earth
He was not for his parents
Nor his wife and children
Not for his enemy
He disappeared.

Like a blossom
Falling from a branch
On the earth.

He was not for crime.
Nor for punishment.
Nor for release.
He disappeared.

Like a blossom
Falling from a branch.

He was not there for the end
Nor to carry on
Disappeared.

From the branch

Disappeared.

Inside, a thin stream of rain.
A swing of wild flowers.

A startling flash of memory.
The pendulum of the past.

When the fallen bloom reaches the earth
The essence of the earth
Spreads through the tree.

Written 1994

Source: 'Missing' by Tripuraneni Srinivas (*Ho!*, Vijayawada: Kavitvam Prachuranalu, 1997, pp. 25–26)

Pydi Theresh Babu

Pydi Theresh Babu (1963–2014), born in Prakasam district, was a poet, writer, music composer, screenwriter and film maker with an active interest in art, culture, cinema, history, Buddhism and dalit literature. He authored three volumes of poetry—*Nishani*, *Hindu Mahasamudram* and *Alpapeedanam*.

Bugle Call for Unheeding Elders

No, we are not grabbing anybody's hard-earned savings by force
Nor are we taking over anyone's inheritance unobstructed
There is no need to trip on your panchas and rush to attack us
We are not ploughing anyone's grandfather's property secretly
We ask
who drew these crooked lines
dividing the same blood into five colours?

Whose devouring greed dragged our lives onto the streets,
We ask

What needs to be asked we ask directly, hot as blazing fire
We are not crowing like cocks that do not know the dawn.
We have been trapped by so many hooks without any bait
Trusting the meditations of storks without demur
we broke our backs
Like little fishes thrown out of the lake
we grasp the waves by the locks and question you
We are not flying on our own to the shores of the lake.
Though we scour the eastern hills, our bellies
are full of hunger.
We demand to know, placing a leg
on the throat of the sky
Where is our rightful share of light?
We are not unjustly squeezing out the light
from others' lamps.
For a people whose life itself is a wound
How will they understand what a wound is?
If you leave the taproot alone
What does it matter how many branches you chop?
Till we find the root we must keep probing the wound then—
We will no longer stitch up our open wounds
with cowardly strings
As in the past.

Source: 'Chaviti Peddamanushulako Shankham' by Pydi Theresh Babu (*Padunekkina Paata: Dalita Kavitvam*, edited by G. Lakshminarasayya, Vijayawada: Dalitasana Prachuranalu, 1996, p. 257)

Joopaka Subadra

Joopaka Subadra, born in 1964 in Damaranchepalle in Warangal, was the first dalit woman to contest the Employees Association elections in the Andhra Pradesh Secretariat, where she works. A poet, short-story writer and dalit rights activist, she has published widely to critical acclaim. Subadra played a key role in establishing the Mattipoolu Women Writers' Forum, bringing dalit, adivasi, bahujan and minority women writers together. Significant among her published works are *Rayakka Manyam* (a collection of short stories), *Aiyyayyo Dhammakka* (a poetry collection), *Nalla Regadi Sallu* (an anthology of madiga women's stories, as co-editor) and *Kaitunakala Dandem* (a collection of madiga poems).

Aiyyayyo Dhammakka

Though a slave to the outside world Mallana
In our wada,[1] he was a hero
Just wearing a basingam[2]
I became a slave to Mallana
Aiyyayyo dhammakka
My stories and tales go awry
At the stone marking our gudem
Aiyyayyo dhammakka

If Mallana rubs a bit of lime and ash
On the face of that heavy mother skin
Transforming her into a drum, a slipper, a medley

---

1 hamlet
2 bridal ornament tied to the forehead

Will she say look at me, look at my beauty!
Will this dark mother skin
Catch the moonlight in ninety ways?

Mallana is a hero outside
At home, he is but a heap of wet dung
A hero to look at, a wastrel at work
Bring the grinding stone… Bring the pestle…
Carry me to the grinding stone…
Yes, that is how Mallana manipulates
Aiyyayyo dhammakka

To stretch a hide
Is not like drinking gudumba[1]
and digging a grave
To wet the hide and the veins
You carry water that wears out a pathway of miles
Protect it from the eye of dog, fox, crow or hawk
Forgetting to eat, you guard it
Worms wriggling, flies buzzing
gusts of stink
Knife-like twisting your guts into strips
Eyes rolling as you fall fainting
This is a fate you cannot escape
Aiyyayyo dhammakka

Handling the lump of hide as if it were the moon
Your body turning into dry sticks
Burning the whole day under the fire
Drinking tamarind seed gruel
While Mother Hide comes fresh for birthing
Stretched on the frame
And hung from the shoulder
Aiyyayyo dhammakka

---

1 liquor

I am finished with the dappu
I have made the dappu
An infant that has not climbed my arm, alas
The sound of sticks, like footsteps
Never reaching my lap, but
Making thunderous sounds that break my head
And famous Mallana with his smart boots
Has become a melodious kinnera![1]
Dhon dhonka dhom
Aiyyayyo dhammakka

Source: 'Aiyyayyo Dhammakka' by Joopaka Subadra (*Aiyyayyo Dhammakka: Kaitala Donti*, Hyderabad: Dandora Prachuranalu, 2009, pp. 50–52)

MADDURI NAGESH BABU

Madduri Nagesh Babu (1964–2005) was born in Guntur district and was a deputy tahsildar in the Andhra Pradesh Services. A well-known poet and a strong dalit voice, he published many volumes of poetry, some of which are *Velivada*, *Raccha Banda*, *Vooru Vaada*, *Loya* and *Meerevutlu*.

Threshing Fields

As I travel to collect taxes
the old women sweeping threshing grounds
looking for scattered grain
grate my eyes like a gust of sand.

---

1 stringed musical instrument

Come summer
my stepmotherly SC hostel
would thrust me out barring and locking doors, but
our Rudraram Malapalli
would throw its welcoming doors wide open.

There on the dora's threshing floors
Like a broom sweeping, a winnowing tray
A field harvested bare
My ammamma
Like a coarse cloth wrapped around a crime
or a deep hunger
Like a lamp flickering without oil
Ammamma.

Leaving for the fields long before dawn
to gather scattered grains from the furrows
Returning long after noon
bearing a sack of grain
Ammamma.
Exchanging a precious measure of grain
for a few candied sesame sweets
would brighten my wearied eyes
dimmed with long waiting.

When ammamma, like a withered leaf
would pound the paddy at that hour
I would tremble like a seed
caught in her pounding stone
Toiling as long as she lived
to barely stay alive
her strength drained
Coughing, coughing, coughing, coughing
she spat out blood
on the face of this wretched earth
Dust unto dust, poor thing.

For those who toil sweating blood
from sowing to reaping,
the castoff grain
For those who have never set eyes on the fields,
granaries filled with golden grain

Amma!
You deftly picked out even the grains buried in the slush
But in this threshing ground of castes
Have you left me these poisonous seeds…

Source: 'Kallam' by Madduri Nagesh Babu (*Meerevutlu*, Narasaraopeta: Sreeja Publications, 1998, pp. 82–83)

Sitaram

Born in Khammam district in 1964, Sitaram has published three collections of poetry: *Rakta Sparsa* (co-authored), *Idigo Ikkadidake* and *S/o Manikyam*.

Yousuf Has Not Come Home Yet

The curfew was lifted
The streets opened up
Dry-throated pumps
were gargling out water
Milk sachets and musty rice
were being handed out
Komarayya wiped traces of
the corpse from his gun
Of thirty bullets there were but three left
He handed in the account to the company

Where all did Komarayya
plant these twenty-seven bullets?
From the corpses being cut
A bullet or half peeped out
Here and there, shops
one door open, another closed
are watching
But Yousuf is not home
Nor is he on the path that leads to his house…

Written 1991

Source: 'Yousuf Inka Intiki Raledu' by Sitaram (*S/o Manikyam*, Hyderabad: Literary Circle Prachurana, 1995, back cover)

Afsar

Afsar (born 1964) is a poet and critic whose doctoral dissertation explored the evolution of modern Telugu poetry. He is the co-author of the poetry collection *Rakta Sparsa*, and the author of the verse anthologies *Ivaala* and *Inti Vaipu*. He has published a book on criticism, *Adhunikata-Atyadhunikata*.

Globalitis

Everything has come to the doorstep
The world like a market
in front of the house.

Everything has turned to rupees
Except for me
Everything ready for sale.

Rules for everything
No space
to breathe.

There is no stir in the air
I never thought the world
would shrink so much.

Only the white man's rule ended
The Company[1]
has learnt a new language.

The streets
wires of electricity
just a touch
and the bloody carcasses of dead birds.

We are being sold
completely
on some strangers' signatures.
We are turning
into a list of objects.

The language of the market
has entered the house.

What else is there
to pledge, it asks.
Moistening us with wet words
Choking us
Beautiful knives
dance around us.

---

1 a reference to the East India Company

Sworn oaths will not work
Lies
the only truth.

Post-mortems on the living.
Then again
If dead
the freshness
will be lost after all.

Everything must be fresh
in the market.

Written 2000

Source: 'Globalitis' by Afsar (*Valasa*, Anantapur: Sweeya Prachuranalu, 2000, pp. 143–45)

Goreti Venkanna

Goreti Venkanna, born in 1965 in Gowraram (then Mahbubnagar), is a poet, lyricist and folk singer with unparalleled popular appeal. A cultural icon of Telangana, he won the Kaloji Narayana Rao Award in 2016 and the Sahitya Akademi Award in 2021.

Black Thumma

Your branches laden with yellow blooms
Without you where is the village?
Where the name?
O black thumma

Thrusting tender shoots through stony rocks
Proudly you grow through stony hills
Ne'er a thought of water or food
The grazing goats' urine your water from the sacred Ganga
Growing unfenced you turn into a fence
shading the tired peasant at rest

Your hard, thorny body
a soft bed nesting countless birds
Your sooty body is black as collyrium
From within you, tender yellow juice springs
Your leaves though tiny, your foliage luxuriant
sways in the fresh breeze like a beautiful end of a sari

Your tender fruit, like milk for weaned goat kids
Like the rhythm of a lullaby
Like anklets on tender feet
When the shepherds pull down your branches
goats flock to feast on the sweet fruit
Bees bustling to bathe
in the pollen you shed

Filtering through your leaves at dawn
The sunlight bathes your threshold with light
Butterflies flock to the patches of light
as if they were flowers
Bees and queen bees all and sundry
buzz around flaunting their beauty
before your youthful elegance

The squirrel eating its fill in the forest
darts in and out every moment
The stork wandering from pond to pond
rests on you the moment the sun sets
Tiny birds that feed on tender sheaves
swing on your branches in the breeze

Birds weary with flying and fluttering
sink into your dipping branches
Your tender thorny finger tips
gently stroke their bodies
as they sleep peacefully in your arms
while your thorns keep the snakes away

You darken the eyelashes of poor children
with the gift of collyrium
When village urchins' books are torn
yours the gum to paste them
Orphaned children use your thorns
to fasten their tattered shirts

Poets and pandits rarely behold you
But the peasant's poetry weaves around you
What matter which king built the tank?
To make his name immortal
he engraves his name and lineage on stone
What happened to his name?
It is you who name the village
Thummalarevu

Your sweet scent wafting in the breeze
Your bent branches the beam of a plough
Your beautiful trunk yielding planks
for doors, tables, cots, axles, pulleys, tops and rattles
and heaps of ploughshares
You are the ornament that adorns the whole village after all

He who boasts that he owns the earth
and does not forsake the six evils
He who prides himself on his beauty
is but a corpse when his breath leaves him
But when you give up your life you attain new beauty
displaying all the wonders a tree contains

A chisel turns you
into a gift for carpenter Balayya
Kites, spinning tops
shining nosepins for tender cheeks
Your shoot is within reach to freshen our mouths
Your leaves turn to manure and mother earth smiles

Source: 'Nalla Thumma' by Goreti Venkanna (Unpublished)

Challapalli Swaroopa Rani

Challapalli Swaroopa Rani, born in 1968 in Guntur district, is Professor of History and Archaeology at the Centre for Mahayana Buddhist Studies, Acharya Nagarjuna University, Guntur. Her work explores the fields of dalit studies, dalit feminism, dalit Buddhist perspectives and Ambedkarite philosophy. She has two poetry collections to her credit, *Mankena Puvvu* (2005) and *Astitvaganam* (2012). She has also edited a collection of poetry, *Padunekkinapata*, and is the editor of the monthly journal *Bahujana Keratalu.*

Mankena Puvvu

I am a bird helplessly trapped
struggling in a thorny fence
Wherever I turn, the thorns prick me—
They are not the thorns of today—
They are the chains of slavery
spread for generations around me

Before me, a deep well
Behind me, a great ditch
Around me always

Danger hissing at me
When has my life been truly mine…?
In the home, male arrogance
sets my cheek stinging
While in the street, caste arrogance
splits the other cheek open
When I go to work in the fields for money
the landlord covered in sweat
tries to trap me as well
I want to bury myself as a seed
deep in the earth
Chasing the faraway distant hope
of an education
Reaching the shore of the hostel
Shrinking from the hungry look
of the warden
I long to gather my body into
a fist and fling it into the distance
As a child they mocked me in school
because I had no bottu
As I grew up, for not having caste
When they all taunted me
Looking at the stinking village in disgust
I would want to close my nostrils tight
Good enough to fulfil lust
but not good enough for a family
I feel like hiding my face
in a stream
Confronting these insults
I learnt a few letters
Became a working woman
and went to the office…
Unable to bear loud whispers of 'Reservation Category'
I wanted to pour molten lead into my ears
When patience dies
even a grass blade becomes a heavy needle piercing
I have no more patience to run

In the flames of this suffering
I will wash away my troubles
Blooming forth crimson like a mankena puvvu[1]
I will stride across fierce forests
And spring forth like a gushing stream.

Source: 'Mankena Puvvu' by Challapalli Swaroopa Rani (*Padunekkina Pata: Dalita Kavitvam*, edited by G. Lakshminarsayya, Vijayawada: Dalitasana Prachuranalu, 1996, pp. 3–4)

JAJULA GOWRI

Jajula Gowri was born in 1969 in Secunderabad and married before she completed school. She went on to obtain a bachelor's degree and study journalism. She writes poetry and stories from a dalit perspective. Her works include *Mannubuvva*, a collection of stories, and *Voyinam*, a novel.

A Meal of Mud

I've been watching from the days I was little—quarrels and squabbles all the time at home. I couldn't understand anything. Why did avva and nayna[2] fight like that, why did they abuse each other? After fighting a while, they would talk to each other.

'Is there any grain in the house? Are there rations? The children's bellies are always burning. I starve and they starve. You see all this, yet you do what you want! I am asking because I can't understand; if you don't drink so much, will there be mud in your mouth? Or will there be dust? Bring your wages straight here and put it in my

---

1 scarlet mallow flower
2 *avva* = mother; *nayna* = father

hands. If you don't, I can't run this home. Mind you. If you bring your entire wages here then it is good, otherwise we will starve like this. Do you understand or not?' said avva, sitting at the fire and looking at nayna.

'You wretch, what is wrong with you? Kicking up such a fuss. I bring my hard-earned wages and pour it in your hands. I work all day long and if I drink a drop at dusk you make such a ruckus! You never think he has toiled hard the whole day, let me give him some food and water. You cannot see my toil. You cannot see to my comfort. All the time it is home, family, children. That's all you think about. I am giving you all the rupees I can. Where can I get more than this? Thoo! — your mother! You are never satisfied; it is never enough, whatever I bring!' And nayna would leave the house.

He would leave at sunset and come back at midnight, staggering and swaying. In that drunken stupor he would shout, 'Orey Lacchmi! What are you doing? — your mother! I'm starving. My belly is on fire. Give me food. Give me food. Can't you hear even when I'm calling you?' He would roll his eyes and glare at avva.

Avva then: 'If you come at any hour of the night, who do you think will sit waiting for you? Don't you know you should come early? You have learnt to drink a lot. Aren't you ashamed? How many times should I tell you not to drink?' And she would start abusing nayna…

'You wretch, the more I keep quiet the more you talk! It is my wish! I will do whatever I like. If I want to spend my wages on getting drunk, that is my wish. Did you bring something from your mother's house to talk back to me like this? Will you talk back?' And he would start beating my mother.

The noise would wake us all up but we would lie quiet because if nayna saw us awake then he would abuse us also.

And so they would fight. Nayna would yell at avva, and avva would yell back. As the fight grew heated, he would go wild and start beating avva. Seeing this we would be filled with grief. Crying, I would lie there looking at my little sister. And crying like this, we never knew when we fell asleep. Whether they fought and fought and made up by the time the cock crowed, we didn't know.

As I grew a little older, I understood a few simple truths. We were all sitting at home and eating. But only nayna was going out to work and bringing money home. And from the wages he got, some money went for his drink. 'If only you brought the entire money home instead of drinking it would be good. You are not willing to do that. How do I suffer you? At least think of the fate of our children!' avva would say to him when he was sober. He would listen to avva quietly, but in the evening he would go back to the toddy shop and it was the same story.

Avva hadn't cooked anything in the morning. My belly was on fire and I went quietly to her and said, 'Avva, I am hungry. Make something for me to eat.' 'Wait child, I have sent your brother to the shop. As soon as he brings the rice, I will cook it and give you some. Bear it a little while longer'. She comforted me.

Today I had been feeling faint from the morning. I waited and got more and more tired. Anna hadn't come back from the shop. My stomach was on fire. I went again to avva and said, 'Give me something. I will buy something to eat! I am so hungry.' And I began to cry loudly.

'Ayyo, bidda![1] Just bear it. If there is food in the morning, there is no food in the night. What am I to do? I gave the money I had to anna. Even nayna went hungry. The sun is blazing. I wonder how he is working in the sun. There has been no work this week. And so we are suffering so much. Nayna gave the money he had and went. Just bear it a little, bidda. There, your brother is coming! I will cook some rice for you'. And she went to light the fire. I was so hungry. Slowly I went to the pot and drank some water. Then I went to the door. The sun was beating down on my head. The shadow was under my feet. I felt giddy standing in the sun. I went to the tree in front of the house and sat under it.

It was cool under the tree but my stomach was afire. I sat there drawing lines in the mud and playing with the mud. The hunger in my belly did not go down. I looked quickly around to see if anyone was looking. I took some mud in my hand and shook it so that all the big stones fell out.

---

1 child

There was only fine mud in my hands. It smelt sweet. I gulped a mouthful. I began to eat the mud quickly. My hunger receded. Then I walked to the hut.

When I got there, avva had cooked the rice and was draining the water. My brother and sister were sitting near my mother and watching her. But I went to the water pot, drank a small pot of water, and lay down. I didn't look at my mother or the pot on the fire. After having asked for rice till then, I just lay down. Avva, my sister, brother and all looked at me curiously. I don't know what happened after that. Perhaps they thought she will get up and eat now. She will eat now. Maybe they are still waiting for me to get up.

Written 2003

Source: 'Mannubuvva' by Jajula Gowri (*Telangana Kathalu*, edited by Kaluva Mallayya, Sadanand Sarada and Chandra, Hyderabad: Visalandhra Publishing House, 2005, pp. 756–58)

Mohammad Khadeer Babu

Mohammad Khadeer Babu was born in 1970 in Kavali in Nellore, and is a journalist by profession. His poems 'Karim Bhai', 'Noore Chashmi' and 'Jawab' have been widely appreciated. His stories portray the lives of Muslim people, drawing out experiences of suffering, vulnerability and exploitation.

It Has Touched Me, the 'Black Beast'

'Re-re-rey... Stop pushing me, ra... Stop pushing... re-re-rey! — your mother! You rascal!' I said with a tearful face.

He laughed kikkikkikkee, showing all his teeth—that fellow Satish Singh—after pushing me on the pig.

This was his regular prank. After school when I walked home on my own, he would come as if to walk beside me and push me on a pig.

Startled, I would jump from side to side shouting and screaming, and that was his tamasha.

But how many times could I escape?

This time, my screaming and his pushing at the same time frightened a passing pig that was going past quietly, and in confusion it came towards us. And when it reached, its belly touched my leg.

Its wet and hairy skin slowly rubbed against my body.

Abba! I was so nauseous. I felt a churning as if my stomach was being dredged, and vomited. I just wanted to jump into a well and cleanse myself.

Without my realising, my eyes filled with tears and I began to cry!

When he saw my tears and my discomfort, the laughter on Satish Singh's face vanished. He came to me and said, 'I am sorry ra! Please ra! Sorry ra! Come ra, you can wash yourself at the tap', and he put his hand on my shoulder.

I was furious at his shameless words.

'It's enough what you have done; let go you rascal. Not now—I will settle with you tomorrow. I will tell Malayadri teacher and have you beaten to pulp, you watch out…', and weeping bitterly, I went home.

All the way, my suffering wasn't just suffering. All kinds of fears filled my heart. 'If a pig touches you, it is a big dosham, sami. Unless you bathe in the waters of seven wells, that dosham will not be cleansed.' I kept recalling the talk of the children on my street. I tried to count the wells on our Kasab Street to see if there were seven.

Then I remembered Shammi's brother Khader Basha. Once when she heard that a pig touched him, his mother Khursheed bi and she scolded him for three days and three nights.

'And will you play at the school again? Will you? Will you?' And she ripped his skin off before she left him alone. (Khursheed bi never called a pig 'pig'. Not just her, many of our people would never allow the word 'pig' to cross their lips. Even saying that word, for us, was prohibited. If they had to refer to it, they would say the 'black beast', 'kala janwar'. That meant pig. There is also another word for pig in our language, 'suvar'.)

When I remembered that kicking, I was very frightened. What if I didn't mention this matter at home?

Then again, a doubt. Why risk dosham? Who knows... If we don't mention things like this at home and fail to perform a ritual cleansing then the gates of heaven may lock us out forever! And so the fear of the afterworld!

Then I decided that come what may I would tell them at home that a pig touched me. But when I reached home I did not step across the threshold.

'Ma! Amma!' I called from outside.

My grandmother heard my shout and came out.

She saw my tearful face and the slush on my legs and in a troubled voice asked, 'What is it, my boy? What have you done?' With a frightened face, like someone who has committed a grave sin, I said, 'A pig touched me, ma!'

'Arey Maula... So it touched you! Stop right there. Don't come in', she said and went into the house in haste.

I could hear the talk inside.

'What is it with him?' asked my mother.

'It seems a pig touched him. You don't say anything. As it is the child is terrified.' And my grandmother brought a big pot full of water.

'I will pour water, step aside.' She made me stand near the side canal.

'Don't take off your clothes. They also have to get wet', she said, and filled a vessel with water.

She would pour one vessel after the other every two minutes and mutter some mantram. Then she would blow the mantram into the vessel with a 'shoo shoo', and then pour the water over my head. This was what she did. (Fortunately, my grandmother was not foolish enough to get water from seven wells. Otherwise I would have been soaked like wet paper with so many baths.)

When the purifying bath was over, she gave me a towel and said, 'Leave your clothes outside and come in.' After I shed my clothes and wore the towel, she picked the clothes up with a stick and threw them near the well.

When I felt that the trouble of being touched by a pig was over, that I had been purified of my sins and the story was over, my mother entered the scene.

'Come, my son, come. I have been waiting for you', she said, raising a stick.

My grandmother came between us.

'Keep quiet, amma. Did he go and touch it purposely? Did he dance on its back? It just came on its own and fell on him.'

And then she laughed as if she was making fun of my mother.

'Come to think of it, why won't a pig touch him? Won't brothers show love for each other? Isn't this all the greatness of your grandmother's blessing?' she said to my mother.

Hearing this, my mother threw the stick away and said, 'Oh, now her taunts have started', and went away sulkily.

My grandmother laughed again.

Hearing that laugh, I knew that there was some pig story here. That night I got into my mother's bed and beseeched her, 'Amma, what was grandma teasing you about in the evening… Won't you tell me that story?'

Then my mother laughed and said, 'It is not a joke, ra… It is really the cool blessing that my grandmother gave to our lineage.

'This is not about today… It is a story from before my mother's birth. My grandfather (mother's father) Ali Saibu came from a prosperous family. But when he was still young, all the property his elders had earned had gone. He was very poor, they say. In these circumstances, my grandmother Mahubi (Ali Saibu's sister), widowed at twenty, came to live with her brother. How old do you think my grandfather was then? Seventeen years. On the one hand his widowed sister, and on the other, his useless brothers. Without any help, my grandfather bore the burden of the family. My grandmother stayed on with him and was more like a mother to him than a sister. My grandfather depended completely on my grandmother's advice. He would do as she said.

'After some time, he learnt the goldsmith's trade… gradually got a few clients… After marriage, he set up a shop and started to save some money. With that money he wanted to buy a house and bargained for one in Varavakatta. He then asked his sister for advice—"Akka! There is a house for sale. But it belongs to an oddodu[1] who rears pigs. We are saibus.[2] Should I buy a house like that in which pigs have wallowed? I am not sure, akka", he said.

'Then after deep thought my grandmother said—"Nayna![3] You say it is an oddodu's house. You say pigs have rolled there. If this is true, you must buy that house immediately. The children born in that house will experience contentment as cool as the pig's belly. You will have children and they will bear children and your lineage will shine forth." She blessed him. My grandfather bought that house. My grandmother's blessing came true. After that, there was no one in our family who was childless. In your father's family, there may be one or two cases. We have no such troubles. My grandfather had four daughters. They had no less than four children each. My mother gave birth to six, and I ended up with your father and bore four. You who I bore will marry tomorrow and bear countless children…' And so my mother finished the story.

(If my mother's story of the pig's benediction and my grandmother's blessing was true, then her soul would suffer greatly today! Because the tradition of each bearing four children ended with my mother. Nowadays it is only cut and cut. My aunt had two girls, cut. My uncle had two daughters, cut. The younger uncle had one son. Even before he could have another, he said cut, cut. My cousin also has two daughters. On my mother's side, everyone says, 'One? Or two?' If ever I say to them in jest, 'Why don't you have another', they say, 'Even before we raise one, God descends on us… Why two and three? To run helter-skelter for food and clothing? You get married and bear children. Then you will get a taste of it.')

Source: 'Nanu Taakesindira' by Mohammad Khadeer Babu (*Dargamitta Kathalu*, Kavali: Kavali Prachuranalu, 1999, pp. 63–67)

---

1 a pig-rearing community in Nellore, classified as a Scheduled Tribe

2 a Muslim caste traditionally associated with the carding and cleaning of cotton

3 father (used here as an affectionate mode of address for a younger man)

Khaja

Born in 1970 in Khammam district, Khaja is well known for his poems. His collection *Fatwa* earned him critical acclaim. Among his popular poems are 'Fatwa', 'Sharat' and 'Jihad'.

The Cotton-Thrashing Caste

If asked what is my caste
What shall I say to people, empty talkers
To scoundrels and to the treacherous
Dudekula Siddhayya

This is my story
The story of how worldly castes isolated and thrashed me

The mosque is divided into four domes
A faith that united all threads of people
This is about the Manu-mullahs
Who tore us into bigger and smaller pieces

Saying all are equal, they flung chilli powder in Allah's eyes
Cutting off the steps of my ladder
Turning me into a dwarf
This is the story of the betrayal of the deceitful maulvis

Finding flaws in my kalma
And faults in my prayers

They described me as a ladaf[1] Latif
This is the story of the deceit of the khandani conspirators

I do not know when the Prophet said it
Or how the conspiracy happened
But the floor under my mat was flooded by the river

As I flicked my collar in my new nawabgiri pride
My foot tripped, throwing me into a bale of cotton like an insect

All my Moghlai glory
Melted like incense on hot coals
A fine smoke-like thinned cotton
Turned into my shroud
In the test of the faith that spoke of a universal caste
I was reborn into the cotton-thrashing caste

I am a Mussalman…
No, I am a saibu…
No! No! A pinjari…
Ahahahaha! I am noor basha!
Tcha… hmm… I am a fellow from the cotton-thrashing caste…

Source: 'Ekekulam' by Khaja (*Alava: Muslim Sanskruti Kavitvam*, edited by Shahjahana and Sky Baba, Hyderabad: Nasal Kitab Ghar, 2006, pp. 70–71)

---

1 another name for the *saibu* caste (also referred to as *pinjari* and *noor basha*) associated with the carding of cotton

M.M. Vinodini

Born in Guntur in 1970, M.M. Vinodini teaches at Yogi Vemana University in Kadapa. A poet, short-story writer and dalit rights activist, she has worked extensively on exploring the trends in feminist creative writing in Telugu and dalit literature. Her poem 'Onti Nittadi Gudise' won her critical acclaim. Her collection of short stories, *Black Ink*, was published in 2015.

Black Ink

The cellar full of children looked like a garden in full bloom. Children's screams, games, songs, shouts—little cycles with children humming on them like butterflies. Sudden brakes—laughter bubbled forth. Faces like flowers in full bloom. Sparkling laughter like showers of pollen. Surr surr! The tea boiled over and put out the stove.

A teacup in one hand and a remote in the other.

'Let us sing together' said Shobhan Babu as he sang with them. Was it *Balipeetam*?

Instead of the calling bell, the sound of rhythmic knocking.

I put the song on mute and opened the door.

A little girl wearing a dress woven of butterfly wings. Eight years maybe? Her eyes were full of laughter bubbling over. There was laughter stuffed into her mouth and some more laughter stuffed in her cheek. She raised her thumb to her lips. She looked like a flower that had come to have some water sprinkled to regain her freshness.

Nodding to her to come in, I walked to the fridge. She followed me. The anklets round her flower-petal feet jingled softly.

'Aunty, will you give me that pot water?'

From her mouth, that was like a basket of flowers, a flower-like smile sprang out.

She drank two glasses one after another.

'Thank you, aunty. I came in the middle of the game.'

Tucking her tiny dove-like feet into the high-heel sandals outside the door, like a dolphin which had grown wings, she flew away.

Beside her glass was my teacup. I bent to pick them up and changed the channel. In black and white, little Padmini, rolling her eyes, sang 'Children and gods are pure indeed; they know no deceit or falsehood.'

My tea was cold. Tea must be drunk hot. I made myself some hot tea, and as I was about to sit—that same sound of knuckles on the door.

Again that full moon, her cheeks full of a smile, like the air in a balloon.

Now she had her little finger raised between her eyes, the fingernail towards me.

So that was what it was this time. I pointed to the bathroom.

'One should pee only in the latrine, never in the bathroom. Mummy told me. I went to the latrine now.'

Eyes that looked like two petals plucked from the moon and touched with honey. Lashes to flutter on them that were like two bees. Her face covered with sweat. I felt like laughing.

Did she laugh all the time? What could be her name? Hasini, Hasya, Hasitha, Smiley?

'Aunty, can I stay with you for a while?'

If the creeper on the palm-leaf bathroom in my village, that bloomed in the evening with yellow gourd blossoms, had come walking all the way here to my concrete home, and offered to spill a few petals and pollen for a while, could I even think of saying no?

'Sit down. What is your name?'

'Shriya, Fourth B.'

'Which flat?'

'We live in Gandhinagar. My grandfather's brother, Mohan Rao garu, lives in 202 on the second floor. My father's small daddy. Today and tomorrow are holidays, so I came here. My daddy dropped me in the morning.'

One cable connection. A hundred channels!

'Do you have a job, aunty?'

I told her. All the details.

'This is the time my school finishes. At four or four-fifteen. As soon as I come home, my mummy gives me Horlicks.'

I made myself some tea and mixed some Horlicks for her.

A chocolaty smile wrapped in some shyness.

Grasping the cup in both hands, she drank it with relish. She left a little bit at the end, and swirling her waist and her cup like the girl in the advertisement she said 'Apang! Japang! Japang!'

Even as I was laughing, she took my cup and hers and put them in the sink.

'Why are you looking at me like that? I don't like to be lazy. I always do some work or the other. Even at home. I help my mummy. So give me some work.'

'Okay. I will. Come and sit first. Do you have friends near your house?'

'Hmm… Tarun, Ashutosh, Lalasa. Are these vegetables to be arranged in the fridge?' She pointed to the bags I had picked up that morning from Reliance. Laughing, I dragged the bags to the fridge.

The child kept talking. No word came out on its own. A laugh before and after each word. A convoy of laughter. She explained how to make ornaments from the vegetables, and with a peeler and knife went at them trying to make birds and animals out of them.

When she failed, she dazzled me with stories that this one broke her wing, or that one's leg remained in its stomach and has to be operated to be removed. I doubled over laughing at her stories and her manner. Helplessly! There wasn't even a short break between one laugh and another.

We finished sorting the vegetables. She stood up and gave me her hand. Her fingers were like they were made of cream—soft, so delicate that even my touch would leave a mark, transparent, beautiful and endearing… I didn't feel like letting go of her hand—I don't know what my touch told her, she raised her head, looked into my face and put her arms around my waist.

A child like a delicate creeper with blossoms of white flowers! I was in a stupor.

This child who barely reached my heart, stood on her toes, smiling and planted a tender, wet kiss on my cheek. My mind and body soared through the clouds and were playing see-saw on the edges of the earth.

We came into the hall. My hand around her shoulder, her arm around my waist.

'What shall we do?'

'Let's do some work. Let's do any work.'

We brought in the washed clothes from the balcony and began to fold them.

She folded the kerchiefs like samosas, placed them on her head, and calling out 'Samosas! Samosas!', she walked around the house. I bought samosas at the rate of two kisses per samosa.

'Okay. Aren't you going to go and play?'

'Unh-hun! I will stay with you', she said.

If you chanted and cast a spell on a smile to give it shape, this face would be the shape of that smile.

'Alright', I said.

'Give me some more work', she said.

'Let us do one thing. Let us eat something.' I brought a steel plate full of shell-shaped crisps.

'Oh! Megastar foods!' she said.

'Why? Does he like them?'

'No, it's my translation of chiru.'[1]

We laughed, and she listed out the 'megastar foods' she loved.

Like flowers of many colours heaped in a marketplace, she filled my home with the colours of laughter. This child's words, clinging like the coloured paper ribbons that decorate the ceiling, walls, doors and windows of my home during Christmas, were swaying in the breeze.

'Aunty, what is that sound?' she asked, raising her eyebrows at the loud slamming of the door in the flat next door.

'The people next door have locked their dog in the flat. It will keep jumping at the door till they return. Nobody will believe it's

---

1 snacks (here, a reference to actor Chiranjeevi, popularly known by the sobriquet 'Megastar')

a dog. It keeps banging the door with its front legs exactly like a human would.'

'Poor thing. Why should animals be treated so badly?'

'...' What could I say?

'I cannot bear it when animals suffer. Do you know what happened to me? I was returning from school in an auto one day. Driver uncle dropped each one at their house. I was the last to be dropped. We were five minutes away from my house. A piglet suddenly ran out of a lane and came under our auto and broke its leg. When I asked him to stop, auto uncle said, "It doesn't matter... Let's go." I fought with him and lifted it into the auto... and tied its leg with my kerchief. I put it on my lap and got its leg dressed in Narayanaguda hospital. Then we brought it back to the same lane and let it go—to where its mother was...' Her face lit up as she told me this in candle-light.

'Didn't your mother worry because you were late?'

'Why? I called her from driver uncle's cell phone and told her.'

'After I came home, I felt sad thinking of the piglet. I sat up till midnight and wrote all this in my diary...'

'What? You write a diary?' I asked, interrupting her.

'Yes, aunty. I write in my diary every day. My Raghava mama taught me this. I have no sisters and brothers. I am alone. So I share my feelings with my diary...'

Darkness fell outside. But my flat lit up with the moonbeams of this standing Chandamama, three feet tall.

As she chattered away, I made some carrot fry, some buttermilk curry and soft dal, knowing she liked these.

'Shall we eat our food then?'

'So soon? One thing. I'll just tell my grandmother that I am eating with you and come back.'

'Come soon!'

Two minutes later, she was at the door, leaving her slippers and wearing that rainbow of smiles. Lifting her tiny finger, she said, 'I am eating with you', and leapt up, hugging me.

Her fragrance enveloped me from the inside—making me hers... I feel that children by nature have bodies that spread warmth.

Lulled, I kissed her forehead. Both of us went into the kitchen. She settled the vessels on the teapoy in the hall.

Like the sliver of light that came through the thatch in my childhood home, a shining circle travelling on the mud floor, this child was spreading her light all over my home, showering my heart with her warmth.

'Tomorrow evening, when I go home, I will write about you in my diary', she said, placing the spoons in the curries. 'I haven't told you an important thing about my diary.'

'What is it?' I asked her, handing her the water bottle from the fridge.

'I write about the things I like in blue ink. The things I dislike, I write in black ink.'

'So you wrote about the piglet in black ink?'

'No, I liked the pig.'

'Once, I went to Mahima's house, and her mother gave me tiffin which I ate, but I wrote it in black ink. What is in this bowl, aunty?'

'That is chicken. Yesterday's. I had some in the fridge, and took it out.'

'What is that? You eat non-veg?' Very surprised. Very doubtful.

I served her some rice, dal and carrot fry.

'Yes. Why?'

I served myself some rice, chilli pickle, and a couple of chicken pieces.

'Aren't you brahmin?' Her ever-smiling eyes now pitch black like a charred pot.

'No.'

'Are you a Chowdary?'

'Are you a Reddy then?'

'No.'

'Then what caste are you?'

'Dalit.'

What to tell the girl or how to tell her, I didn't know.

'So you are separate Hindus?'

'No; Christian.'

'Harijans? Like Mahima and all?'

In my sixth class, when the drill master made me run on the grounds, a thorn as big as my forefinger pricked my foot. Today, that same thorn came back doubled and pierced my heart.

'First eat your food', I said, as I mixed mine.

'Tell me the truth. Are you harijan?'

'Yes; but why all that now? We are friends. Why all this between friends?'

'No; my daddy and mummy have no harijan friends. Neither do I. We don't even like to make friends with them. My friends are all brahmins, Reddys, Chowdarys, and other Hindus.'

The kite that had risen to the heights of the sky snapped and fell.

'You like me, don't you?'

'Yes.' But the child's face was as if she would vomit any moment and was controlling it with difficulty.

'Then sit. Let us eat.'

She refused to sit, and stared at me without blinking. The distaste in her eyes was as if she was looking at worms squirming.

'Grandmother is calling.' She moved quickly, walked hurriedly to the door, put on her shoes, and ran away so fast that I was afraid she would fall.

The brightness of the day vanished, turning pitch dark. I felt like butterflies had turned into caterpillars and were crawling over me.

Source: 'Black Ink' by M.M. Vinodini (*Black Ink Kathalu*, Hyderabad: Likhita Press, 2015, pp. 33–40)

Shahjahana

Shahjahana, born in 1970 in Kamalapuram in Khammam, is among the first poets to focus on the specific issues of Muslim women, and write about the Muslim consciousness. As a Muslim woman from a backward class, Dudekula, her writing brings in the distinctive language spoken by her people that blends Urdu and Telugu, asserting an identity through speech and voice. She has published two volumes of poetry, *Nakhab* and *Dardi*, and one short-story collection, *Laddafni*.

Another Sky

When did I think that misfortune would
pull us apart, flinging us in different directions?
The burden of your sisters' marriages
The problems of the children's schooling
drove you to another shore
at twenty-five
Leaving me alone, bird in an anxious cage…

In the letters you write
I seek the shadows that you roam…
Caught in the embrace of dinars on distant shores.

In what mail can I pack
the bitter feeling of your not coming this way
to you?

How can the currency you send
convey your touch?

Every night your empty half of the bed
mocks me…
Once in two or three years
news of your coming.
My look is like the thirsty earth
gazing skyward after Rohini,
How many of your comings will cool me…

Behind the fulfilled and unfulfilled desires of mind
and body
The swirling grief that you will go again.

You who fly cleaving the skies each time
Just turn back once and look behind the window
At a second sky filled with nothingness.

Written 2000

Source: 'Doosra Aasman' by Shahjahana (*Nakhab: Muslim Stree Kavitvam*, Hyderabad: Nasal Kitab Ghar, 2005, pp. 48–49)